White Weddings

Second Edition

White Weddings

Romancing Heterosexuality in Popular Culture

Second Edition

Chrys Ingraham

Routledge
Taylor & Francis Group

NEW YORK AND LONDON

First edition published 1999
This edition published 2008
by Routledge
270 Madison Ave, New York, NY 10016

Simultaneously published in the UK
by Routledge
2 Park Square, Milton Park, Abingdon, Oxon OX14 4RN

Routledge is an imprint of the Taylor & Francis Group, an informa business

© 1999, 2008 Taylor & Francis

Typeset in Interstate and Nuptial by Florence Production Ltd, Stoodleigh, Devon

Printed and bound in the United States of America on acid-free paper by Edwards Brothers, Inc.

Library of Congress Cataloging in Publication Data
Ingraham, Chrys, 1947–
    White weddings: romancing heterosexuality in popular culture/by Chrys Ingraham. – 2nd ed.
        p. cm.
    Includes bibliographical references and index.
        1. Marriage–United States.   2. Weddings–United States.   3. Weddings in popular culture–United States.   4. Heterosexuality–United States.   I. Title.
    HQ536.I545 2008
    392.50973–dc22   2007033793

ISBN10: 0–415–95194–1 (hbk)
ISBN10: 0–415–95133–X (pbk)
ISBN10: 0–203–93102–5 (ebk)
ISBN13: 978–0–415–95194–4 (hbk)
ISBN13: 978–0–415–95133–3 (pbk)
ISBN13: 978–0–203–93102–8 (ebk)

Visit the companion site for this title at http://www.routledge.com/textbooks/9780415951333

*To my family
and to all those
children and adults
whose labor
and imaginations
are too great a price
for our comfort.*

*And in memory of
Dame Anita Roddick.*

Author's
parents, 1946

Contents

Acknowledgments

This book is the product of the biggest "unwedding" ever assembled! The unwedding reception was enormous and the costs were mostly intellectual, emotional, and spiritual, but the gifts offered by so many were beyond compare. Etched into the pages of this manuscript are the fingerprints, coffee stains, ink, dog hairs, and love of many who helped to bring this to reality. To all who helped put on this critical spectacle, I owe an enormous amount of gratitude.

This book came to fruition in large part because of the enormously caring and collaborative contributions of friends, co-workers, family, and students who have touched, coaxed, coached, and inspired it into existence. My gratitude to all exceeds my ability to find the right words or to thank all who participated in both the first and second editions. I would also like to thank all of the contributors to various television and radio talk shows as well as those who braved the book signings and told me their stories. Over these past years, the stories and perspectives of both interviewers and participants have had an indelible impact on this work.

I owe a special debt of gratitude to a few people who have continued to provide significant encouragement in many important ways.

I can't begin to thank my friend and mentor Steven Seidman who has given me enormous opportunities and who has been a steadfast and loving supporter personally and professionally.

Acknowledgments

And to my family of origin and my extended family, I offer a special thanks for always being there and for celebrating this work just because it was important to me.

I especially want to thank the Russell Sage College faculty and students for lighting the way. This work wouldn't exist without their trusting and enthusiastic contributions.

And, to my partner Eileen Brownell, I am eternally grateful for her loving and consistent support for *all* that this work means and for sharing the commitment to live consciously, compassionately, and critically in a world that is all too eager to define who we are for us.

Most importantly, I want to acknowledge the adults and children around the world who have labored and suffered far too long at the hands of our greed and ignorance. Your day is coming.

Chapter One

Lifting the Veil

*D*riving from Ithaca to Albany one spring night I heard a report on National Public Radio's *All Things Considered* about the fact that thirteen TV shows were ending their season with weddings. Ever the alert sociologist and not usually surprised by such events, I exclaimed out loud to the radio, "Wow! What's that all about?" Since I frequently teach courses on social inequality, marriage and family, and women's studies, I was more than idly curious. In the weeks that followed I watched some of these shows and became conscious of the degree to which weddings—especially *white* weddings—permeate popular culture. White weddings were not only main fare on situation comedies but were also used to sell everything from antacids to Visa credit cards. Even when weddings weren't the central theme they were frequently inserted into the background. Television, however, was not the only medium in which this trend was visible. The movie industry appeared to be capitalizing on the same theme, particularly after the 1991 success of *Father of the Bride,* a remake of the classic 1950s version, by using weddings as the main theme or as a plot device somewhere in the film. Even a visit to the grocery store was enlightening! In every store I visited, checkout lines were stocked with numerous magazines for wedding consumers or people interested in celebrity weddings.

When I turned to research journals for help in understanding what was going on, I was surprised again. While sociologists had produced a significant body of research on marriage, not one U.S. sociologist had ever published a study on weddings. In fact, with the exception of Diana Leonard, a British sociologist, and Dawn Currie, a Canadian sociologist who also wondered why weddings hadn't been studied, they were rarely examined in any academic discipline with the exception of anthropology where they are primarily studied as ritual.[1] This glaring omission seemed particularly stunning considering the popularity of the practice and its presence in popular culture. This discovery left me with several questions: Why were weddings receiving so much attention from the media? How could they be so present in popular culture yet so absent from scrutiny? Do we take them for granted to such an extent that we don't notice that they merit study? Or do we understand them to be of so little importance that we assume there is nothing to be learned from studying them? And, why the pervasiveness of *white* weddings? What exactly is the significance of the white wedding?

The first edition of this cultural study was published in 1999 and was received as a ground-breaking (and somewhat controversial) examination of weddings and the wedding industry in the U.S. The attention it received from the media, students, and scholars was substantial and provided many new insights. One particularly important contribution was that the second edition must have a clearer starting point. To this end, let me say the following. While this study starts with an examination of white weddings, in the end this is *not* a book about weddings. Instead, wedding culture and the wedding industry provide clues as to the larger social interests they serve. They provide a very rich source of data about how we give meaning to heterosexuality and marriage and to what end. White weddings, while important in themselves, are a concentrated site for the operation and reproduction of organized heterosexuality. More so than other prominent heterosexual practices and rituals, e.g. dating, proms, and engagements, weddings are

"It's the only formal party some people are ever invited to. It's the only couture dress many women will ever own. It's the only catered event many people ever attend. There's no mystery to why people love weddings and are thrilled to sit through them again and again. And in today's popular culture, geared to pander and give the people what they want and only what they want, audiences are getting plenty of opportunity to sit through weddings. Again and again."

—Amy M. Spindler, "The Wedding Dress That Ate Hollywood," *New York Times, Sunday Styles,* August 30, 1998: 9.1

Primary wedding
market trinkets

culturally pervasive, symbolically prolific, and are rarely questioned or examined. Yet, they are so taken for granted they seem naturally occurring and function to naturalize a host of heterosexual behaviors that are, in fact, socially produced. In other words, *one is not born a bride or with the desire to become a bride* yet we have an abundance of evidence that shows that many people believe otherwise. But that's putting the bride before the fairy tale! From the moment we enter the world, culture works to install meaning systems about everything from sex to gender to social class to ethnicity to sexual identity. Heterosexuality, whether naturally occurring or chosen, is organized by those meanings.

This second edition of *White Weddings: Romancing Heterosexuality in Popular Culture* invites you to learn about the institution of heterosexuality using the lens of white weddings.

Eight years after the publication of the first edition much of the wedding culture landscape remains the same with a few notable exceptions. The ground has shifted to accommodate changes in popular culture, globalization, same sex marriage, new technologies, and the aftermath of 9/11. In those years wedding industry revenues have increased dramatically and the price of the average wedding has soared. Wedding research, once scarce, has also grown significantly, uncovering a wedding party of insights, history, patterns, and interests. And we've become smarter about the issues related to weddings, marriage, and heterosexuality. We now know, for example, that we can't talk about weddings without talking about marriage. Given that weddings and marriage have been historically central to the institutionalization of heterosexuality, to overlook the significance of that institution to these practices is to miss the point entirely. Furthermore, we have learned that we must make the terms of the investigation and the debates clear. In this historical moment when the American public grapples with who should be allowed to marry, we are not talking about who should be allowed to have a wedding. Weddings are rituals. They have the capacity to organize larger social arrangements and to reflect dominant and non-dominant beliefs, but let's be clear here. The late great marriage debates are about state-sanctioned and legalized marriage or who should receive federal and state marriage entitlements. This is not the same discussion we will find on Dr. Phil or Oprah or talked about extensively in bridal magazines and popular culture since few people are even familiar with the laws surrounding marriage or with the consequences to those who don't participate, regardless of their sexual identity.

While new research covers various aspects of wedding culture, this text focuses primarily on the institutionalization of heterosexuality through the operation of the traditional white wedding: the dominant wedding form in the U.S. This practice permeates both U.S. culture and the wedding industry and has come to symbolize what it means to marry in the western world. The stereotypical white wedding is a spectacle featuring a bride in a formal white wedding gown, combined with some combination of attendants and witnesses, religious ceremony, wedding reception, and a honeymoon. Historically, the white wedding has served as a symbolic rite of passage for heterosexual men and women entering (state- and

"Marriage is a relation between a man and a woman and the state regards with a jealous eye any attempt to intervene in this relation."

"Marriage is the cornerstone of organized society."

—Excerpts from *New York State Domestic Relations Laws*

**Woman with
wedding cake hat**

religion-sanctioned) marriage. Given that they are integrally linked to marriage, weddings provide an important cultural site for understanding the organization of heterosexuality in contemporary society. To this end, it is necessary to examine current trends regarding marriage and remarriage particularly in relation to wedding culture and the wedding industry. The social, economic, and cultural patterns these trends reveal provide fertile ground for determining how and to what end heterosexuality is *institutionalized*.

Typically studied as a form of sexuality, heterosexuality is, in reality, a highly regulated, ritualized, and organized practice. Sociologically, then, heterosexuality as an "established order made up of rule-bound and standardized behavior patterns" qualifies as an institution.[2] Moreover, heterosexuality as an "arrangement involving large numbers of people whose behavior is guided by norms and rules" is also a *social* institution.[3] In other words, heterosexuality is much more than a biological given or the fact that someone is or is not attracted to someone of the other sex. Our sexual orientation or sexual identity is defined by the symbolic order of that world through the use of verbal as well as non-verbal language. How we come to understand what it means to be heterosexual is a product of ruling interests, a culture's symbolic order, and its organizing practices.

"Naturally" occurring or not, heterosexuality is highly organized by society and by culture. While you may argue that "heterosexuality is natural" or that you were "just born this way," it is important to understand the difference between naturally occurring phenomena and the symbols we create to give order to that natural world. Women didn't enter this world knowing they would want to wear a prom dress, practice something called "dating," buy a white wedding gown, or play with a "My Size Bride Barbie." These desires have nothing to do with biology—they are products of culture. Likewise, men did not exit the womb knowing they would one day have to buy a date a corsage or spend two months' income to buy an engagement ring. Rules on everything, from who pays for the date or the rehearsal dinner to who leads while dancing, drives the car, cooks dinner, or initiates sex, all serve to regulate heterosexual practice. What circulates as a given in American society—heterosexuality—is, in reality, a highly organized social institution that varies across culture, history, region, religion, ethnicity, nationality, race, lifespan, social class, and ability. As is the case with most institutions, people who participate in these practices must be *socialized* to do so. Historically, w*eddings have served as one of the major events that signal readiness and prepare heterosexuals for membership in marriage as an organizing structure for the institution of heterosexuality.* How this is achieved is the focus of the wedding industry. A close examination of this industry and its relationship to marriage provides a rich medium for understanding both heterosexuality and the relations of ruling it secures.

The Wedding Industry

Weddings are big money, and everyone wants to get in on the act. Bridal gown stores are mainstays in most cities and towns regardless of size; giant bridal shows

"William Signs" [owner of Swedish Auto Inc. in Farmers Branch, Texas] is offering a free marriage ceremony with any 30,000 mile inspection on Hondas, Volvos, and BMW's. For the $290 price of the inspection, he will throw in the cost of being married by the local justice of the peace, a $25 value . . . Mr. Signs says he got the idea during a trip to Las Vegas, where he noticed a helicopter operator offering a free marriage ceremony with the purchase of a deluxe helicopter ride. He decided to borrow the concept and bring some joy to the unhappy business of auto repair. 'Normally people don't get good news, at auto shops,' he adds. The mechanic isn't concerned about his offer hastening the nuptials of mismatched partners or cheapening the institution of marriage. 'After all, inspections aren't inexpensive. They're going to have to spend almost $300,' he says."

—Andrea Gerlin, "Your Wheels Need Realignment, and You May Now Kiss the Bride," *Wall Street Journal*, May 17, 1994, B1

Leaving the wedding

are held several times a year in most cities; wedding consultants and internet sites abound; popular magazines feature special wedding issues; paparazzi go to extremes to get photos of celebrity weddings; television commercials and popular films incorporate weddings; soap operas, romance novels, reality TV shows, Hollywood films and video producers depend upon them; home video and bloopers shows feature wedding gaffs; thrift stores showcase bridal gowns; discount stores offer bride and groom cake tops; and toy stores sell everything from bridal dolls to wedding toys. Just look around and you'll see how pervasively weddings appear in American culture.

Bride and Groom
oven mitts

The wedding industry, where the average American couple currently spends $27,852 per wedding, thrives in large part because it serves approximately 2.3 million couples per year, down from 2.45 million in 1994.[4] According to recent studies, the price tag for the average wedding has increased by 38 percent in the past 15 years. While the bridal gown industry experienced a mild recession in the late 1990s largely due to changes in marketing and dress manufacturing, its customers now pay *twice* as much, spending an average of $1553 on a wedding gown and alterations and an additional $258 on headpiece and veil ($1811 total).[5] With most textile manufacturing occurring outside the U.S., the labor costs to

Museum of the City of New York

Invites you to attend

a special exhibition

New York Gets Married

Dressing for a Special Day, 1765–1997

May 21, 1997 through September 21, 1997

Museum of the City of New York

1220 Fifth Avenue at 103rd Street

(212) 534-1672

Sponsored by Tiffany & Co.

Reprint of New York Museum invitation

produce wedding apparel have decreased dramatically at the same time that the price of the average wedding gown has doubled. Coupled with a decrease in the number of weddings performed annually, these conditions have contributed to an increase in costs for the consumer. Considered in relation to income levels across various groups, it becomes evident that the wedding market is increasingly targeting upper-level income groups or encouraging a significant level of wedding debt for what has become a compulsory ritual.[6] Held up as the dominant and taken-for-granted rite of passage for people wishing to enter into marriage, the white wedding is becoming increasingly expensive and, to some extent, unaffordable, raising alarming concerns as to the long-range consequences of these trends.

As the wedding industry changes to accommodate a decrease in the number of weddings, one strategy they are using to secure their consumer base is market diversification. To this end, weddings are no longer confined to the so-called "Bride" pages of local and national newspapers as they once were. Instead, they have become a mainstay of American popular and consumer culture. In everything from wedding toys to bride and groom oven mitts, the wedding market now reaches into nearly every facet of American culture. Television seasons frequently end with weddings tying up the romance that has been building all season and they sometimes open with them as well. For example, shows such as *Baywatch, Dharma and Greg, Dr. Quinn, Everybody Loves Raymond, For Your Love, Friends, Frasier, Gilmore Girls, Jag, King of Queens, NYPD Blue, Spin City, Suddenly Susan,* and *The Nanny* are just a sampling of the TV series that have used this plot device.[7] Typical headlines announcing upcoming shows in publications such as *TV Guide, Entertainment Weekly,* and *Premiere* include titles such as "*Friends* Wedding Scandal Revealed!" as *Friends* opened with the conclusion of the wedding that ended the previous season.[8] Sitcoms *To Have & To Hold* and *Will & Grace* both began a season with weddings while made-for-television movies *Forever Love, The Marriage Fool, A Marriage of Convenience,* and *I Married a Monster* all feature a wedding. Even *The Sopranos,* the HBO hit about the mafia, and *C.S.I.,* the top-rated CBS crime drama, have featured a wedding plot.

Prior to the advent of reality TV shows in 2003, sitcom seasons regularly included a romance, an engagement, and a wedding. *Frasier,* which ended its 11-year run in May of 2004, included an aborted wedding and a completed wedding along with the promise of another for viewers to take away with them following the ending of this popular series. *Friends,* long considered among the most popular of all TV sitcoms, included several weddings as well as an episode totally focused on the "feel-good" experience of wearing a wedding gown. Reality TV brought us a so-called real-world version wedding plot in shows such as *Joe Millionaire, Temptation Island: The Wedding,* and *Who Wants to Marry My Dad?*, a show where female contestants practiced proposing to the father of a family while wearing a wedding gown.

Weddings are regularly featured on "bloopers" shows and frequently appear in television commercials for everything from Aleve to Metropolitan Life Insurance to Tums and Visa; ads for antacids, chain saws, credit cards, real estate, and cars. As for soap operas, long a source of romance drama, *General Hospital* continues to claim the most viewers of daytime television for the wedding episode of Luke and Laura. Daytime television programs, from *Live! With Regis and Kelly* to *Good Morning America, Oprah,* and *The Today Show,* regularly devote valuable blocks of time, entire shows, and entire weeks of shows to celebrity weddings, wedding products, or to the presentation of—and sometimes participation in—actual weddings.

Given the growth of technologies that increasingly allow television viewers to eliminate commercials, marketers in all industries have come to rely on embedded advertising—placing their products within television shows and popular films. The *Today Show* is one major example of this development. In recent years, this top-ranked morning show has raised the curtain on embedded advertising, placing the marketing of everything from toys to cars to films to food to wedding essentials center stage. Of all the products they cover, those that focus on heterosexual romance and family receive the most air time, frequently filling up to ten minutes per segment. One major topic they regularly devote time to is their *Today Show Wedding.* This feature directly engages the television viewer/ consumer in the entire production of a television wedding. Using online voting options, viewers select the couple they deem worthy of this opportunity and act as surrogates for the couple in choosing everything from the wedding apparel to the wedding cake and the honeymoon. As embedded advertising becomes a mainstay in all forms of media, the television wedding serves as a major site for wedding industry marketing.

Network television stations are closing their 2007 season with three new wedding shows: *Wedding Belles, The Real Wedding Crashers,* and *For Better or For Worse,* and cable television networks have also seized a significant share of the wedding market with *Battle of the Wedding Singers, Engaged and Underage, Get Married, I Do Over, Married Away, Perfect Proposal, Platinum Weddings, Whose Wedding is it Anyway?, Wild Weddings, Bridezilla,* and *Wedding Stories.* Even the Food Channel has wedding cake contests for professional chefs; Bravo has fashion designers compete over the creation of a wedding gown, and Martha Stewart shows potential brides how to assemble a wedding bouquet (although she says such things are better left to a professional). The Lifetime Channel and E! frequently feature celebrity weddings, and the Learning Channel sponsors "Wedding Stories," an hour-long show on real weddings every weekday afternoon opposite soap operas on other channels. Toy manufacturers have also seized a share of the current wedding market along with the opportunity to develop future consumers by producing a whole variety of wedding toys that feature prominently on Saturday-morning children's television shows.

Today, it is practically impossible to walk through any grocery store or by any checkout counter without being inundated with romance novels, magazines, and tabloids on various celebrity or soap opera weddings, or wedding how-to and fashion magazines. In July 1993, *People* magazine, considered by many to be one of the most successful magazines in recent history, added a yearly celebrity-wedding issue to its lineup. It immediately became "the magazine's best-selling special issue with over four million copies sold."[9] Currently, they devote an entire section of their online magazine to celebrity weddings, complete with photos and timelines, and incorporate celebrity weddings into all of their publications.[10]

Martha Stewart, domestic diva and entrepreneurial genius who has built a food and design empire in the U.S., achieved a niche in the wedding magazine market first with her wedding issues of *Living* and most recently with *Martha Stewart Weddings.* This weddings venture, published four times per year and with a circulation of 250,000 to 500,000, won the 2005 National Magazine Award for General Excellence (The "Ellie"). Following her enormous success and effect on the quality and aesthetics of homemaking in America, Stewart has set her sites on establishing a profound impact on both the wedding industry and on white weddings in general.

In addition to the wedding magazine market, mail-order catalogs regularly devote pages to wedding products, and bookstores offer numerous volumes for planning the "perfect" wedding. Even computer shareware and software programs as well as online wedding sites feature wedding planners for the bride-and groom-to-be.[11]

Not surprisingly and perhaps the most significant development since the publication of the first edition of *White Weddings* has been the virtual explosion of web pages devoted to weddings. The internet, a major global marketplace and communications medium, now hosts thousands of websites covering everything from wedding products and services to wedding toys, wedding productions, wedding videography and video streams, to providing space for newlyweds to mount their wedding photos or to provide guests with registry lists and directions to the wedding reception. This development is so enormous that listing all the sites would take up a volume in itself. Provided in the Appendix is a sampling of some of the larger, more well-established sites.

Perhaps the most powerful and far-reaching effect in relation to the wedding industry has been the proliferation of feature-length wedding films—where weddings appear as the main plot. In the past fifteen years we have witnessed the huge success of movies such as *American Wedding II, Bride and Prejudice, Father of the Bride, Four Weddings and a Funeral* (nominated for an Oscar for best picture), *In & Out, Muriel's Wedding, My Best Friend's Wedding, My Big Fat Greek Wedding, Polish Wedding, Runaway Bride, The Birdcage, The Groomsmen, The Other Sister, The Wedding Banquet, The Wedding Date, Wedding Crashers, Wedding Planner,* and *The Wedding Singer.* Capitalizing on the enormous success and popularity of these wedding films, the industry has also increased its market share by including a wedding in films even when the story line is unrelated, e.g., *Lord of the Rings, Mission Impossible II, Pirates of the Caribbean, Wayne's World,* and *Armageddon* which saves the world for *two* white weddings. Considering the magnitude of wedding culture and the wedding industry it is both shocking and mystifying that so few have studied weddings. White weddings appear to be the

Wedding sign in
parking lot

most watched yet "unnoticed" heterosexual phenomenon in American society and popular culture.

As I mentioned earlier, this is not a study of weddings but an inquiry into the operation of heterosexuality in the U.S. and in relation to globalization and the global economy. The social, political, and economic investment in heterosexuality as it is currently organized holds great benefit for relations of ruling and significant consequence for much of what we've come to hold sacred and personal—the personal is political. How we come to understand what counts as sacred and personal in relation to heterosexuality is a product of a culture's symbolic order and its organizing practices. What we think of when we talk about heterosexuality or refer to ourselves as heterosexual is a product of a society's meaning-making processes.

How we've come to view heterosexuality through the meaning-making processes of the white wedding is the subject of this book.

Setting the Context

Besides the already-stated scarcity of weddings research, there has also been a lack of scholarly attention paid to the operation of *heterosexuality as an institution*. It can be argued that the vast amount of research that has been conducted on marriage and family and on sexuality serves as a substantial contribution to the study of heterosexuality. However, most of this research either treats heterosexuality as the default category—assuming everyone is heterosexual—or as a (naturally-occurring) sexual identity operating outside or independent of meaning systems.

Relatively few scholars have approached the topic of heterosexuality from a critical standpoint—(not to be confused with "critical of" but instead as) applying an analytic capable of revealing its organization, meaning, operation, and structure, separate from debates about its biological foundation.

Why have researchers overlooked the study of heterosexuality *as an institution* and its installation through practices such as weddings? One possible explanation may be the risk involved in pursuing such an examination. Efforts to critically examine sacred or valued practices, rituals, and institutions are frequently resisted and suppressed. Readers often apply suppressionary strategies by reacting to such discussions as personal attacks on themselves or on heterosexuals as a group rather than seeing them as institutional analyses or inventories. Such practices are commonplace in analytical discussions of high stakes issues as racism, classism, capitalism, or politics.

As activists in the nineteenth century discovered, to critically examine heterosexuality's rules and norms was to encounter either legal or social sanction. "Heterosexuality" as a term or concept was not coined until 1868 and, at that time, defined heterosexuality as sexual perversion.[12] Without an adequate term for their campaign, these reformers focused on marriage. For example, marriage reform advocates were often censored and jailed under the Comstock Act of

1872. As part of the free thinker movement, activists dedicated themselves to the elimination of church and state control over marriage, arguing that under these rules marriage was a form of "sexual slavery."[13] When they attempted to distribute their ideas, they were frequently arrested, indicted, and convicted for mailing "obscene" materials through the U.S. Postal Service. To mail writings on "sex education, birth control, or abortion" was deemed by U.S. Postal Code 1461—the Comstock Act—as the dissemination of obscenity and a federal offense. The following three cases (out of nearly 3700) are some of the most prominent examples of the censorship of marriage critique and reform.

First and most famous was the censorship of Ezra Heywood's published treatise, *Cupid's Yokes*, in 1876.[14] In it Heywood critiqued marriage as a form of legalized prostitution, arguing that women, as the property of men, were forced to provide sexual and reproductive services in exchange for economic support and security. This powerful tract was widely distributed and censored twice. Nevertheless, Heywood persisted in trying to pressure the inequities of marriage.

In another notable instance, Moses Harman, publisher of a free thinker newspaper, printed a letter from a reader documenting the death of a woman who had been raped by her husband immediately following childbirth.[15] Because she was the man's wife, no legal action was taken against him. The husband escaped punishment, but Harman's newspaper was impounded and he was sentenced to prison for publishing the letter.

Marital rape was a problem being addressed by several individuals during this period. One of the best-kept secrets among white, middle-class families was the shock experienced by women on their wedding night. Uneducated about sexual intercourse, many young brides were traumatized by the experience. With the rise of the medical profession, social reformers sought to remedy this situation by publishing books and articles addressed to young women, educating them about sex. One such person was Ida Craddock, who published and distributed through the mail a small book called *The Wedding Night*. Craddock's case was particularly tragic. Having already served one sentence under horrendous prison conditions, Craddock chose death as less traumatic than prison when she was prosecuted the second time. Her last effort at public protest was the publication of her suicide letter in a local newspaper, in which she claimed the last word in her fight against Anthony Comstock and the injustice of the law he zealously enforced. The chilling effect these acts of censorship had on the marriage reform movement were significant enough to silence these debates for decades. Even today, few people are aware of either this social movement or its martyrs. Not until the 1960s did similar discussions reemerge.

Late-twentieth-century feminists such as the Furies Collective, Purple September Staff, Redstockings (1975), Rita Mae Brown (1976), and Charlotte Bunch (1975) challenged dominant notions of heterosexuality as naturally occurring and argued that it is instead a highly organized social institution rife with multiple forms of domination and ideological control. In this excerpt from Charlotte Bunch, the link between heterosexuality and systems of oppression is elaborated:

> Heterosexuality—as an ideology and as an institution—upholds all those aspects of female oppression . . . For example, heterosexuality is basic to our oppression in the workplace. When we look at how women are defined and exploited as secondary, marginal workers, we recognize that this definition assumes that all women are tied to men . . . It is obvious that heterosexuality upholds the home, housework, the family as both a personal and economic unit.[16]

While many of these arguments were made by heterosexually-identified feminists, some of the more famous works were produced by lesbian feminists, making a link to the interests of both feminism and lesbian and gay rights. Adrienne Rich's frequently reprinted essay "Compulsory Heterosexuality and Lesbian Existence" (1980) confronts the institution of heterosexuality head on, asserting that heterosexuality is neither natural nor inevitable but is instead a "compulsory," contrived, constructed, and taken-for-granted institution that serves the interests of male dominance:

> Historians need to ask at every point how heterosexuality as an
> institution has been organized and maintained through the female

wage scale, the enforcement of middle-class women's "leisure,"
the glamorization of so-called sexual liberation, the withholding of
education from women, the imagery of "high art" and popular culture,
the mystification of the "personal" sphere, and much else. We need an
economics which comprehends the institution of heterosexuality, with
its doubled workload for women and its sexual divisions of labor, as
the most idealized of economic relations.[17]

Understanding heterosexuality as an institution with processes and effects is one of Rich's greatest contributions.

Monique Wittig's "The Category of Sex" (1992) takes the argument to a different level, declaring heterosexuality a political regime:

The category of sex is the political category that founds society as
heterosexual. As such it does not concern being but relationships . . .
The category of sex is the one that rules as "natural" the relation
that is at the base of (heterosexual) society and through which half
of the population, women, are "heterosexualized" . . . and submitted
to a heterosexual economy . . . The category of sex is the product of
a heterosexual society in which men appropriate for themselves the
reproduction and production of women and also their physical persons
by means of a contract called the marriage contract.[18]

This political regime depends upon the belief that women are "sexual beings," unable to escape or live outside of male rule.

All these essays provide the foundation for a sustained and critical evaluation of institutionalized heterosexuality, one that allows for a level of awareness that is both liberating and transformative. Twenty-five years later, these works have for the most part disappeared (out of sight, out of mind), as the backlash against such challenges has intensified. References to "femi-nazis" and political correctness and gay-baiting tactics have been used as powerful suppressionary strategies to once again create a climate hostile to most attempts to constructively critique the ways gender and institutionalized heterosexuality operate and oppress. Similar to the red baiting strategies of the Cold War period, where any attempt to inquire into the operation of capitalism was met with anticommunist backlash, suppressionary tactics are frequently used to thwart and discredit any critical discussion of heterosexuality, leaving heterosexuality largely unexamined and invisible.

Because of its central role in society, heterosexuality is in a continual state of crisis and contradiction as pressures from a range of historical and material conditions shift and change. For example, pressures from feminism, from the lesbian/gay/bisexual/transgendered rights movement, efforts to pass laws allowing same sex couples to marry, same sex marriage in Massachusetts, Canada, the Netherlands, and Spain, the sexual revolution of the 1960s and 1970s, and the prevalence of AIDS as a life-threatening sexually transmitted disease, research on the prevalence of marital infidelity, disproportionate use of female workers in developing countries, and loosening gender and sexuality norms in the West have altered the taken-for-granted beliefs/ideologies about sexuality, gender, and marriage. A significant divorce rate (4.3 out of 10 marriages end in divorce; in the case of African Americans the number is 6 out of 10), high rates of domestic and sexual violence (1 out of 4 women will be a victim of domestic violence in their lifetime; 33 percent of women murdered in the United States are killed by their male partner or ex-partner),[19] the proliferation of single parenthood, the absence of jobs, women's employment and career opportunities, day care, and job training all have worked to destabilize institutionalized heterosexuality. Of all these, women's increasing economic independence may be the single most important reason for marriage's increasing irrelevance. Middle to upper middle-class income distribution for both men and women has changed enough in recent decades to necessitate that both partners work outside the home. Marriage among the privileged classes—formerly thought of as a structure that guarantees a male breadwinner whose primary role is to support a wife and children—no longer holds the same historical necessity. Now, both incomes support the household.

Definitions of heterosexuality are shifting significantly in areas targeted specifically at teenagers and young adults. Music video networks MTV and VH1 have had enormous impact in this area since they frequently provide gender-bending programming and advertising as well as alternative views of heterosexuality and positive images of gays, lesbians, bisexuals, and transgendered persons. Rock megastars Melissa Etheridge and Elton John and cross-over groups such as Green Day have had a major impact on youth culture and legitimize same sex relations and cultural contributions. Hit series on HBO—*Sex and the City* and *Six Feet Under*—and Showtime—*Queer as Folk* and *The 'L' Word*—experience major popularity, especially among people in their late teens and early twenties. Each of these extraordinarily successful series offers strong representations of same sex relations and challenges to the boundaries of mainstream heterosexual culture.

Targeted at older viewers, primetime network television has also provided programming that pressures dominant heterosexual culture. The first show to challenge sexual norms may have been the long-running and very popular sitcom, *Friends*. In the 1990–91 television season, viewers learn that Ross is married to a woman who is having an affair with another woman. Eventually the marriage ends and this sitcom provides the first on-air lesbian wedding in primetime complete with the congenial cast as participants.

The 1997–98 television season offered the first openly gay sitcom star and character in *Ellen*, portrayed by Ellen DeGeneres. This show was later canceled due to both declining ratings and controversy over (frequently political) gay content. DeGeneres now headlines her own wildly popular and Emmy award-winning daytime talk/variety show where the issue of her sexual identity is positively regarded and taken-for-granted.

The Emmy award-winning series *Mad about You* closed out its 1997–98 season with an episode in which Paul's sister and her lesbian partner professed their love and commitment to each other and decided to wed. They sealed their "engagement" with a kiss on primetime television. *Will & Grace* entered the sitcom world in 1998 bringing openly gay characters Will Truman and Jack MacFarland to primetime television. The female characters in this sitcom—Grace and Karen, heterosexual women whose primary friendships were with these two gay men—frequently engaged in outrageous behaviors that violated mainstream heterosexual norms. The show achieved high ratings for six of its eight years and concluded its run in the spring of 2006.

In an article in the New York Times, *it was reported that Christian conservatives will pressure the Republican Party to "put issues like abortion, sexual morality and family values in the forefront of every campaign ..." In reference to this new push, one conservative leader commented, "No more engagement. We want a wedding ring, we want a ceremony, we want a consummation of the marriage."*

—*New York Times*, March 23, 1998

Other popular television shows, also with large audiences of young people, *The O.C.*, *Laguna Beach*, and *The Real World* all feature openly gay characters and romance. While it can be argued that these representations fail to reach normative status, they also break ground by being present at all. In the past several years, mainstream television has integrated gay and lesbian characters and same sex relationships into its offerings, e.g., *E.R.*, *It's All Relative, Coupling*. Also it has expanded images of alternative lifestyles and has offered more expansive and less traditional depictions of heterosexual relations, including a variety of shows that have normalized cohabitation. The latest show to break ground was the short-lived situation comedy entitled *Out of Practice* about a family of doctors (except for one son) that included a daughter who was a lesbian-identified emergency room physician. This show broke new ground by offering a lesbian character who banters with her male siblings about their shared interest in women. They would even compete for a woman's attention, displacing the notion that sexual identity is something that is fixed and permanent in one's life.

As if this weren't enough, critically acclaimed box office hits—movies such as *Four Weddings and a Funeral, The Crying Game, In & Out, The Birdcage, The Wedding Banquet, Transamerica*—have all pressured dominant notions of heterosexuality through the insertion of either transgendered or lesbian/gay normalizing themes.

In opposition to these growing trends, several powerful groups—the New Right, the Christian Coalition, right-to-lifers, conservative Republicans, President George W. Bush and his administration, the Fox Network, Southern Baptists, the Anglican and Episcopal Churches, and Promise Keepers—have actively campaigned to secure patriarchal heterosexuality (male-dominated as opposed to egalitarian) as dominant. Through moves designed to discredit any practices that do not privilege this arrangement while reclaiming and rewarding those that honor it, these interests have launched a full-scale national attack on any group—whether it be lesbians, gays, single mothers, domestic partners, or transgendered people—which does not subscribe to the dominant heterosexual norm. Their strategy focuses on two fronts: the legal (as evidenced by pervasive national attacks on gay rights and gay marriage legislation) and the ideological (propaganda campaigns against gays and lesbians). Significant examples of these include the "homosexual conversion" ad campaign, funded by religious and political conservatives, which purports to "change" homosexuals to heterosexuals through devotion to Jesus, the crusade to pass a constitutional amendment codifying marriage as "a union between a man and a woman," and the renewed anti-homosexual campaign by the Catholic Church. This initiative came in the wake of a massive pedophilia scandal where priests were found sexually abusing boys and high level clergy were participating in a cover-up. In an effort to recuperate their authority and reputation, the Vatican issued several decrees purging all U.S. seminaries of anyone with a "homosexual" past and condemning same sex marriage.

In various sites within popular culture, the reassertion of dominance is most evident in the proliferation of one of heterosexuality's key organizing rituals, *the wedding*. This romance with wedding culture works ideologically to naturalize the regulation of sexuality through the institution of marriage, providing images or representations of reality that mask the historical and material conditions of life. Consider, for example, how weddings in popular culture are being used to manage the current crisis in capitalism and patriarchy. In 1997, as the U.S. Congress grappled with the Republican Contract with America, arguments over welfare reform escalated. Politicians and conservative interest groups launched a full-scale campaign against the "unmarried welfare mother." The "welfare queen," a stereotype made famous by Ronald Reagan, has been newly revived in a variety of images throughout popular culture. It is the image of the welfare mother as African-American, unmarried, urban, probably under eighteen, caught in a life-long cycle of poverty, and single parent to many small children born "out of *wed***lock**." This stereotype prevails despite the fact that the average welfare recipient is white, has been on welfare for less than two years, has fewer than two children, and collects benefits for less than two years. Incorporated within this stereotype is the view that women and children who have become dependent upon welfare have never done the responsible thing—get married.

To correct what has been identified as a drain on federal and state budgets and the future health of the American economy, federal and state politicians have advanced policy proposals recommending *marriage* as the primary vehicle for both recovery from welfare dependency and from a federal deficit. When welfare spending amounted to only 1.2 percent of the gross domestic product in 1992 and federal welfare spending amounted to about 5 percent of the federal budget, politicians believed that a focus on the marital responsibility of the poor would correct the trillion-dollar national debt.[20] While it wasn't marital responsibility—in fact the marriage rate has declined significantly—that created the budget surplus in the 1990s, it was during those years that welfare became redefined and the plight of the poor and of single mothers was eased through federal policies. By 2000, the U.S. had entered another recession and with the events of September 11, 2001, and the War in Iraq, this downturn deepened. The Bush administration inaugurated tax cuts as a means to correct a rapidly escalating national deficit that has now reached $8 trillion dollars and is increasing at an average of $1.68 billion per day.[21] To ease the national debt by removing more people from the federal rolls, President Bush allotted $1.5 billion to promote marriage among the nation's poor. Since there are significant amounts of research that demonstrate that marriage predicts higher income levels, providing the nation's poor with the interpersonal skills necessary for a "healthy marriage," as the Bush policy states, seems plausible especially given the popularity of lavish white weddings. Unfortunately, this data only correlates income with heterosexual marriage, assumes all people are marriageable, and heterosexual, and doesn't account for the realities the poor actually encounter. Again, the only real means for increasing the lot of the nation's poor is to provide the structural supports that will enable them to improve their work skills, e.g., child care and education.

Since the Enron scandal, 9/11, and the War in Iraq, debates over budgets and record-breaking deficits have intensified. In this context the downsizing of the 1990s has given way to "shrink-and-grow" and outsourcing corporate strategies in the 2000s. Government and corporate policies affecting millions of workers throughout the U.S. and the global economy have had a substantial and sometimes catastrophic impact. The class divide between the rich and the poor is the widest in decades, welfare reform and workfare have become law, CEOs are earning record levels of income and wealth, labor is being compromised locally and globally, the environment has been seriously damaged, natural resources are declining, and multinational corporations and sweatshops (inside and outside the U.S.) are proliferating. Along with many other industries operating in this climate, the wedding industry, made up of hundreds of companies directly and indirectly engaged, is thriving and benefiting from these social and economic conditions. Most wedding products are produced outside the U.S. where companies can secure the cheapest labor—Mexico, Guatemala, China, Bangladesh, Taiwan, and Malaysia—and the least expensive natural resources. Meanwhile, white weddings in American popular culture are increasingly opulent, constructing an image of heterosexuality as holding the promise of accumulation and wealth—the new American Dream, linking heterosexuality to social mobility.

As stated earlier, few studies have taken on the challenge of examining the operation of heterosexuality as an institution. Certainly, an investigation into white weddings and marriage raises a host of issues related to an inquiry of this kind. But how to study heterosexuality and to what end? The following section provides a conceptual and theoretical foundation for this undertaking and for the investigation into the interests at stake in how we have organized heterosexuality and practices such as white weddings.

The Heterosexual Imaginary: What Are the Conditions That Allow Us to Imagine Possibilities?

Culture installs meaning in our lives from the very first moment we enter the social world. All aspects of our social world—natural or otherwise—are given meaning. Our sexual orientation or sexual identity—or even the notion that there is such a thing—is defined by the symbolic order of that world through the use of verbal as well as non-verbal language and images. In America and elsewhere, the wedding ritual represents a major site for the installation and maintenance of the institution of heterosexuality.

But how did this contrived and constructed social practice become naturalized? The task of examining this taken for granted social arrangement requires a conceptual framework capable of revealing how heterosexuality has become institutionalized, naturalized, and normalized. Any attempt to examine the institution of heterosexuality requires a theory—a way of explaining— capable of understanding how this institution with all its social customs such as dating, proms, online dating services, and weddings is often viewed by many of us as natural.

French psychoanalyst Jacques Lacan's concept of the "imaginary" is especially useful for this purpose. According to Lacan, the imaginary is the unmediated contact an infant has to its own image and its connection with its mother. Instead of facing a complicated, conflictual, and contradictory world, the infant experiences the illusion of tranquility, plenitude, and fullness. In other words, infants experience a sense of oneness with their primary caretaker. Louis Althusser, the French philosopher, borrowed Lacan's notion of the imaginary for his theory of ideology, defining ideology as "the imaginary relationship of individuals to their real conditions of existence."[22] The "imaginary" here does not mean "false" or "pretend" but, rather, an imagined or illusory relationship between an individual and their social world. Applied to a social theory of heterosexuality, the *heterosexual imaginary is that way of thinking that relies on romantic and sacred notions of heterosexuality in order to create and maintain the illusion of well-being and oneness.* This romantic view prevents us from seeing how we have organized institutionalized heterosexuality and for what purpose. We don't see how it works to secure power, the social production of material life, and to organize gender while preserving racial, class, and sexual hierarchies. The effect of this illusory depiction of reality is that heterosexuality is taken for granted and unquestioned while gender is understood as something people are socialized into or learn. The heterosexual imaginary naturalizes male-to-female social relations, rituals, and organized practices and conceals the operation of heterosexuality in structuring gender across race, class, and sexuality. This way of seeing closes off any critical analysis of heterosexuality as an organizing institution and for the ends it serves.[23] By leaving heterosexuality unexamined as an institution we do not explore how it is learned—one is not born a bride—what it keeps in place, and the interests it serves in the way it is currently practiced. And, perhaps more importantly, by treating it as taken-for-granted and as natural we lose our ability to make conscious choices—a crucial ingredient for democratic life. Through the use of the heterosexual imaginary, we hold up the institution of heterosexuality as timeless, independent of relations of ruling, devoid of historical variation, and as "just the way it is" while creating social practices that reinforce the illusion that as long as one complies with this prevailing and naturalized structure—"it's just the way it is"— all will be right in the world. This illusion is commonly known as romance. *Romancing heterosexuality is creating an illusory sexual identity category that defines perceived female-to-male socio-sexual relations.*

The lived reality of institutionalized heterosexuality is, however, not typically tranquil or safe. The consequences the heterosexual imaginary produces include, for example, marital rape, domestic and sexual violence, pay inequities, racism, gay bashing, femicide, and sexual harassment. Institutionalized heterosexuality and its organizing ideology—the heterosexual imaginary—establish those behaviors we ascribe to men and women—gender—while keeping in place or producing a history of contradictory and unequal social relations. The production of a division of labor that results in unpaid domestic work, inequalities of pay and opportunity, exploitation of women as sweatshop workers in poor countries, or the privileging of married couples in the dissemination of insurance benefits are examples of this.

Above all, the heterosexual imaginary naturalizes the regulation of gender and sexuality through the institution of marriage, state domestic relations laws, and federal controls on who qualifies for marriage and benefits. These laws, among others, set the terms for taxation, health care, and housing benefits on the basis of marital status and render us subjects of the dominant order. Rarely challenged—except by nineteenth-century marriage reformers, early second-wave feminists, and the gay marriage movement—laws and public-and-private-sector policies use marriage as the primary requirement for social and economic benefits and access rather than distributing resources on some other basis such as citizenship or ability to breathe, for example.

A related concept useful for the study of the heterosexual imaginary and of institutionalized heterosexuality is *heteronormativity. This is the view that institutionalized heterosexuality constitutes the standard for legitimate and expected social and sexual relations.* Heteronormativity represents one of the main premises underlying the heterosexual imaginary, again ensuring that the organization of

Scriptural reading from a wedding ceremony held June 20, 1998:.

Wives, submit yourselves unto your husbands, as unto the Lord.

For the husband is head of the wife, even as Christ is the head of the church: and he is the savior of the body.

Therefore as the church is subject unto Christ, so let the wives be to their own husbands in every thing.

Husbands, love your wives, even as Christ also loved the church, and gave himself for it;

That he might present it to himself a glorious church, not having spot, or wrinkle, or any such thing; but that it should be holy and without blemish.

So ought men to love their wives as their own bodies. He that loveth his wife loveth himself.

For no man ever yet hated his own flesh; but nourisheth and cherisheth it, even as the Lord the church:

For we are members of his body, of his flesh, and of his bones.

For this cause shall a man leave his father and mother, and shall be joined unto his wife, and they two shall be one flesh.

This is the great mystery: but I speak concerning Christ and the church.

Nevertheless let every one of you in particular so love his wife even as himself: and the wife see that she reverence her husband.

—Ephesians 5:22–33

heterosexuality in everything from gender to weddings to marital status is held up as both a model and as "normal." Consider, for instance, the ways many surveys or intake questionnaires ask respondents to check off their marital status as either married, divorced, separated, widowed, single, or, in some cases, never married. Not only are these categories presented as significant indices of social identity, they are offered as the only options, implying that the organization of identity in relation to marriage is universal and not in need of explanation. Questions concerning marital status appear on most surveys regardless of relevance. The heteronormative assumption of this practice is rarely, if ever, called into question, and when it is, the response is generally dismissive. (Try putting down "not applicable" the next time you fill out one of these forms in a doctor's office!) Heteronormativity works in this instance to naturalize the institution of heterosexuality.

For those who view questions concerning marital status as benign, one need only consider the social, economic, and psychological consequences for those respondents who do not participate in these arrangements or the cross-cultural variations that are at odds with some of the Anglocentric or Eurocentric assumptions regarding marriage. All respondents are invited to situate themselves in relation to marriage or heterosexuality, including those who *regardless of sexual (or asexual) affiliation* do not consider themselves "single" or heterosexual, or who think of themselves as the unimaginable: not participating in these arrangements. Issues of social and personal choice and privacy become delegitimized through this process.

To study weddings using this theory of heterosexuality is to investigate the ways various practices, arrangements, relations, and rituals work to conceal the operation of this institution. It means to ask how practices such as weddings prevent us from seeing what is at stake, what is kept in place, and what consequences are produced. To employ this approach is to seek out those instances when the illusion of tranquility is created and at what cost. Weddings, like many other rituals of heterosexual celebration such as engagements, anniversaries, showers, and Valentine's Day, provide images of reality that conceal the operation of heterosexuality both historically and materially. When used in professional settings, for example, weddings work as a form of ideological control to signal membership in relations of ruling as well as to signify that the couple "fits"—is normal, moral, productive, family-centered, upstanding, and, most importantly, appropriately gendered. Consider the ways weddings are used by co-workers in line for promotions or to marginalize and exceptionalize single or nonmarried employees. For example, two employees are competing for a promotion. One is single, the other engaged to marry. The engaged worker invites all members of the office, including the hiring committee, to the wedding. Because of the heterosexual imaginary, weddings are viewed as innocuous, fun-loving, and as signaling membership in dominant culture. As such, they give people significant cultural capital and an advantage in the workplace. Under these conditions, beliefs about weddings work to give one worker an unspoken advantage over the other. Our prejudices regarding people who hold the status of "single"—that is, unmarried (by law)—have critical consequences socially and economically. Weddings are anything but benign.

To undertake a study of marriage is to interrupt the ways the heterosexual imaginary naturalizes heterosexuality and prevents us from seeing how its organization depends on the production of the belief or ideology that heterosexuality is the same for everyone—that the fairy tale romance is universal. This type of study requires a form of systemic analysis—affecting the entire social body—of the ways both the institution of heterosexuality and the heterosexual imaginary, particularly in relation to weddings, are historically bound up in the distribution of economic resources, cultural power, and social and political control. To this end I will make use of a materialist feminist mode of inquiry since it provides a problematic that addresses all of these areas.

Materialist Feminism

Materialist feminism as an approach to social change and as a mode of inquiry provides a global analytic capable of revealing the social, economic, political, and ideological conditions upon which taken-for-granted social arrangements depend, e.g., heterosexuality and weddings. This problematic understands materialism as the economic context framing people's lives and work, specifically the division of labor and the distribution of wealth (private property) in any particular historical moment. Additionally, this methodology considers these conditions in the context of prevailing national and state interests and cultural struggles over meaning and value.

Materialist feminism argues that the nexus of social arrangements and institutions that form the social totalities of patriarchy and capitalism regulate our everyday lives by distributing cultural power and economic resources unevenly according to gender, race, class, and sexuality. Within this framework, rape and domestic violence, for example, can be seen as the effect of social structures and processes that situate men hierarchically in relation to women and to each other. Historically, this has been accomplished using forms of social differentiation such as heterosexuality, with its historically specific *heterogendered—that is, the asymmetrical stratification of the sexes in relation to the historically varying institutions of patriarchal heterosexuality*—and racial components.

Applying a materialist feminist analytic to capitalism means examining it as a regime for (1) the production of surplus value (profit); (2) the securing of private property (accumulation); (3) the exploitation and alienation of life and labor; (4) the division and distribution of labor and wealth; (5) global and state interests; and (6) those meaning-making systems that reproduce capitalism and patriarchy. A materialist feminist approach also understands that capitalism operates under varying historical, regional, and global conditions of existence. For instance, capitalism in Japan is not the same as capitalism in the United States, even though the systems are interrelated and reciprocal and produce similar effects. They emerge from different historical and material relations of production[24] and therefore defy reductive generalization. To study institutionalized heterosexuality and white weddings in the U.S. using a materialist feminist analytic, then, would not necessarily be generalizable to other cultures.

Patriarchy is also historically variable, producing a hierarchy of heterogender divisions that privilege men as a group and exploit women as a group. Patriarchy structures social practices that it represents as natural and universal and that are reinforced by its organizing institutions and rituals (e.g., marriage and weddings). As a totality, patriarchy organizes difference by positioning men in hierarchical opposition to women and differentially in relation to other structures, such as race or class. Its continued success depends on the maintenance of regimes of difference as well as on a range of material forces. It is a totality that not only varies cross-nationally, but also manifests differently across ethnic, racial, and class boundaries within nations. For instance, patriarchy in African-American culture differs significantly from patriarchy in other groups in U.S. society. Even though each group shares certain understandings of hierarchical relations between men and women, the historical relation of African-American men to African-American women is dramatically different from that among Anglo-European Americans. Among African-Americans, a group that has suffered extensively from white supremacist policies and practices, solidarity as a "racial" group has frequently superseded asymmetrical divisions based on heterogender. This is not to say that patriarchal relations do not exist among African-Americans, but that they have manifested differently among racial-ethnic groups as a result of historical necessity. Interestingly, racism has sometimes emerged in relation to criticisms of African-American men for not being patriarchal enough by Euro-American standards. As a totality, patriarchy produces structural effects that situate men differently in relation to women and to each other according to history.

Applying a materialist feminist mode of inquiry to the study of white weddings in popular culture means examining various texts such as the *New York Times* wedding pages, bridal magazines, television sitcoms, weddings web pages, films, and children's toys for their foundational assumptions. It means determining what is concealed or excluded in relation to what is presumed or presented. This mode of inquiry, then, makes visible the "permitted" meanings—what the culture allows us to say—in constructions of weddings, marriage, and ultimately, heterosexuality. What is required, then, is a process of analysis that reveals the power relations organizing the allowed as well as the disallowed meanings and beliefs about white weddings and institutionalized heterosexuality.

Ideologies—or belief systems—are essentially statements or images that legitimize a society's dominant behaviors. The beliefs are disseminated through the dominant institutions of a culture and work to naturalize a host of social arrangements, e.g., femininity or racial difference. While gender or racial difference seems obvious, it is a society's dominant ideologies that shape our view of the world. For example, there is no such thing as race—it is a social construction—yet we believe there is simply because this message has been authorized and legitimized by sources we have learned to accept.

Materialist feminist ideology critique seeks to demystify the ways in which dominant or ruling-class beliefs are authorized and inscribed in subjectivities (what it means to be a woman, a wife, a bride, or a mother), institutional arrangements (marriage), and various cultural narratives (films, magazines, television, and ads). Like those taken-for-granted beliefs, values, and assumptions encoded as power relations within social texts and practices, ideology is central to the reproduction of a social order. Because it produces what is allowed to count as reality, ideology constitutes a material force and at the same time is shaped by other economic and political forces. This theory of ideology addresses the meaning-making processes embedded within any social practice, including the production of wedding and marriage culture.

Inherently contradictory, capitalist and patriarchal social arrangements are in a continual state of crisis management. The work of dominant ideologies, such as romantic love, is to conceal these contradictions in order to maintain the social order. At the same time, however, these breaks in the seamless logic of capitalism and patriarchy allow oppositional social practices, counterideologies, and social movements to emerge.

Central to a materialist feminist analytic is its critical focus on ideology. Critique, as it is called, is a "decoding" practice that exposes textual boundaries and the ideologies that manage them, revealing the taken-for-granted order they perpetuate and opening up possibilities for change. Materialist feminism, then, situates these ideologies historically and materially and offers both a critical understanding of the object of inquiry as well as insights into how to effect emancipatory social change. In the chapters that follow, this form of analysis will be applied to a wide variety of sites organizing what we have come to think of as the white wedding. What this critique will reveal is the terms upon which we have secured the dominance of institutionalized heterosexuality and the interests it serves.

Conclusion

The theoretical starting point for this study is the heterosexual imaginary—the way our beliefs and practices conceal the operation of heterosexuality as an organizing institution. In the following chapters, the wedding industry and white wedding culture will be examined in relation to the heterosexual imaginary. Chapter 2, "The Wedding-Industrial Complex," illustrates the connections among major institutions involved or invested in the production of weddings and wedding ideology and discusses the significance of this complex. This chapter provides an examination of the wedding industry by making visible the commodification, accumulation, and labor issues underlying the consumption of the American white wedding. In addition to the primary wedding market, this chapter also identifies and discusses the secondary and tertiary markets in the wedding-industrial complex. Special attention is given to wedding gown marketing and production, wedding gifts, diamond rings, bridal magazines, honeymoons and destination weddings, children's toys and films, the internet, and the business of popular culture in relation to the wedding industry. This explanation of market forces is set in the context of "who marries" and explicates the material conditions upon which the wedding-industrial complex depends.

Chapter 3, "Romancing the Clone: The *White* Wedding," provides a close-up look at the bridal market, including an examination of bridal magazines, wedding websites, children's toys, celebrity wedding magazines, and the "Sunday Styles" section and wedding pages in the *Sunday New York Times*. This chapter explores the ways in which the heterosexual imaginary and its ideology of romantic love secure gender, race, class, and sexuality hierarchies; consent to the institution of heterosexuality; reproduce the division of labor; and control the accumulation of property.

Chapter 4, "McBride Meets McDreamy: Television Weddings, the Internet, and Popular Film," provides a critical reading of feature-length motion pictures, television weddings, and internet websites such as YouTube. These are analyzed for the ways they participate in the production of the heterosexual imaginary through the patterns they reveal, the interests and consequences they obscure, and the ways they regulate gender, sexuality, race, and class.

The final chapter "And They Lived Happily Ever After . . ." summarizes the findings of this study and offers recommendations for further research. The conclusion of this study, concerning the ways institutionalized heterosexuality has worked historically as a central form of capitalist and patriarchal social control, is elaborated. In particular, the ways the heterosexual imaginary underlies the romance with American weddings are highly consequential for gender, race, class, and sexuality and provide a model for whiteness in cultures that have been heavily influenced by globalization and global economics. Particular attention is paid in this chapter to a discussion of the same sex marriage debates, social policy, and to the new field of critical heterosexual studies.

Whenever a study seeks to intervene in taken-for-granted social arrangements and relations of ruling, it creates significant discomfort for those who benefit from or are privileged by these arrangements. *Allow yourself to be conscious of your reactions to this study.* Keep track of the moments when you experience the greatest resistance. These will provide you with evidence concerning the interests weddings serve in people's lives and in popular culture and the ways each of us participates in the heterosexual imaginary.

The first edition of this study was one of the first in-depth examinations of weddings in American culture. Today, I'm happy to report, there are a significant number of wedding studies from across the disciplines. A listing of these is provided in Chapter 5.

At East High Elementary School in Mrs. Dolan's afternoon kindergarten class, Matthew and Melinda portrayed the letters Q and U during a wedding ceremony to teach kindergarteners that the letters are meant to be together. The wedding was complete with programs that read "Today I will marry my friend," the wedding march, and white wedding cake. The bride and groom exchanged candy rings. A disc jockey played the Carpenters' song "We've Only Just Begun." It was a lesson to show that the letters Q and U are always together in words.

— "East High Kindergarteners Celebrate Special 'Wedding': Mr. Q and Miss U joined in Ceremony," *Elizabethtown Chronicle*, 129(1), October 23–29, 1997

Statues displayed in an office
Photo by
Kristen Constantino

As I've shared this project with numerous people over the past several years, I've heard more wedding stories than it is possible to record. The heterosexual imaginary is sizable, and the consequences of romanticizing seemingly benign and "fun-loving" practices are significant. What the white wedding keeps in place is nothing short of a racist, classist, and heterosexist social order. Is that what you planned for your wedding day?

Chapter Two

The Wedding-Industrial Complex

Referred to by Wall Street analysts as "recession-proof," the wedding industry has reached such proportions that it can be more accurately described as a wedding-industrial complex. This structure reflects the close association among weddings, the transnational wedding industry, labor, global economics, marriage, the state, finance, religion, media, the World Wide Web, and popular culture (see Figure 2.1). To understand the significance of white weddings, it is crucial to attain a sense of the operation of the wedding industry particularly in relation to the workings of the wedding-industrial complex. The scope of this chapter is to provide an overview of the various components of this complex in order to make visible the historical and material foundation upon which the operation of the heterosexual imaginary depends. The role of mass media and popular culture and other aspects of the industry's accompanying wedding-*ideological* complex will be covered in subsequent chapters.

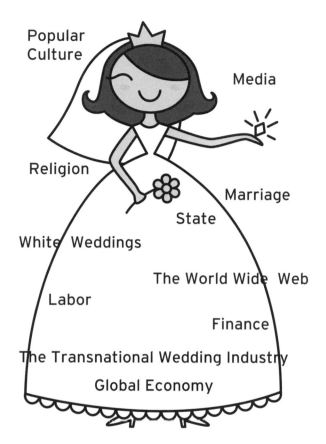

Popular Culture

Media

Religion

Marriage

State

White Weddings

The World Wide Web

Labor

Finance

The Transnational Wedding Industry

Global Economy

Figure 2.1 The $80 billion wedding-industrial complex

"Adds Sharma, 'It's the only recession-proof industry and the only industry where there is investment without looking at returns.' She quotes an Economist study in 2000 that estimated the size of the Indian wedding industry at $11 billion, with an estimated growth of 25 per cent annually . . . Events like 'Vivaha 2003', 'Bridal Asia', 'Bride & Groom' and the 'Marwar Mega Wedding Show' are growing in popularity."

—Deccan Herald, Bangladore, India, Saturday, August 30, 2003

"Marriage is a personal milestone and a consumer turning point. By age 35, the vast majority of Americans have been married at least once. Beyond the boost to industries related to the ceremony and honeymoon, marriage has a significant effect on the housing market, durable goods and financial services, to name a few."

—Bryant Robey, "Wedding-Bell Blues Chime as Marriage Markets Shift," *Adweek's Marketing Week,* June 25, 1990

The Transnational Wedding Industry

Several significant shifts have occurred in the wedding industry over the past fifteen years, inflating the average price of a white wedding by approximately 38 percent. Perhaps the most significant development has been the increased globalization of the wedding industry. Globalization is a complex and highly debated concept that refers to a relatively recent development in advanced capitalism. Capitalism, by definition, requires expanding markets and cheaper production costs in order to increase profits. To this end, producers must locate new consumers either by creating new desires and wants or by expanding into previously untapped regions or markets. Globalization describes the processes by which production, distribution, and markets have made use of global relationships and resources to this end. For example, products formerly made in the U.S. (local) at a higher cost are now being manufactured at a lower cost outside of the U.S. (global), e.g., U.S. wedding gown production in China. These lower costs frequently include paying workers substandard wages, child labor, sexual abuse and slavery, as well as exposure to toxins and excessive work hours. In addition to the role of the global economy in providing cheap labor and materials for the wedding industry, globalization has provided a variety of expanded markets for what can now be considered the transnational wedding-industrial complex.

Globalization also involves cultural, social, economic, and political changes. Examples of these aspects include everything from the desire for white weddings by people in Japan to the westernization of non-western cultures. Governments and business work together to implement world trade policies that affect how business is conducted within and between countries. These policies significantly influence national and international migratory patterns resulting from poverty and production changes and increase struggles over immigration and immigration laws. For the wedding industry, the proliferation of satellite media, the growth of the World Wide Web, increased marketing of weddings around the world, the increasing trend toward destination weddings, and the vast use of outsourcing by the textile industry have combined to link global economics with the development of global culture(s).

As of 2005, industry estimates of the total annual revenues of the *primary* wedding market in the United States range from a conservative $50 billion per year to a more generous assessment of $125 billion.[1] While this latter figure seems excessive, it is not unrealistic given that the wedding industry has, in recent years, benefited from the increased availability of cheap labor and has expanded to include destination weddings and a variety of global markets including Japan, India, Kenya, parts of South Asia, and South Africa. The availability of data regarding the size of the wedding industry is problematic in that most of their facts and figures are collected by the industry itself and not by more neutral data-gathering sources. However, by comparing each of the industry

The Tire Ring
by Deirdre Woollard

If your male partner grouses about wearing jewelry because it's "too girly," we've got the answer. Tire Rings are heavy rings in silver, gold or platinum with the look of car, truck, mountain bike or motorcycle tire treads. Suitable also for female gearheads and cyclists. Prices range from under $100 to over $5,000 depending on size and metal.

—http://www.luxist. com/2006/08/24/the- tire-ring

London store display
of wedding cake

So it has come to this: a flying wedding cake.

In the upward pursuit of the perfect wedding, finicky brides are having their cakes delivered by airplane. "We fly ours with Continental," said Sylvia Weinstock, a Manhattan baker, who has cakes in the air nearly every weekend in May and June. Mmmm: there's the three-tier yellow cake adorned with bunches of sugar grapes for a wedding in Napa Valley and a six-layer Lady Baltimore cake for a bride in Lake Geneva, Wis.

Mrs. Weinstock, who flies her buttercream-frosted layers in cargo, sees this extravagance in relative terms. One of her fancy, many-tiered cakes—enough to feed 300 guests—can cost $5,000, plus another $500 for shipping and more if it is accompanied by a handler.

"When you're spending $200,000 for a wedding, a cake that costs $5,000 is not all that expensive," she said.

—Cathy Horyn, *New York Times*, June 6, 2004

estimates against census data and marketing surveys, the most concise assessment establishes the current size of the U.S. based wedding industry at closer to $80 billion in revenues per year. If this assessment is accurate and the white wedding industry were one company, it would be placed among the top 15 *Fortune* 500 U.S. corporations. Compared to the $32 billion in revenues reported in the first edition of this study, all of these estimates confirm that there has been substantial growth in the white wedding industry.

This multibillion-dollar wedding industry includes the sale of a diverse range of products, most of which are produced outside of the U.S.—wedding gowns and apparel, diamonds, honeymoon travel and apparel, destination weddings, and household equipment. Also included in this market are invitations and paper products, flowers, receptions, photos, video, gifts, home furnishings, wedding cakes, catering and food supplies, alcohol, calligraphy, jewelry, party supplies, hair styling, makeup, manicures, music, books, and wedding accessories, e.g., ring pillows, silver, chauffeurs, and limousines[2] (see Table 2.1). Although newlyweds make up only 2.6 percent of all American households, "they account for 75% of all the fine china, 29% of the tableware, and 21% of the jewelry and watches sold in this country every year."[3] Newlyweds and potential newlyweds are among the nation's largest consumers of major appliances, furniture, and consumer electronics, as well as tableware, linens, small appliances, and cookware, often obtaining these items as wedding presents selected through a registry. Household goods represent up to 90 percent of the registry business, and nearly 93 percent of engaged couples register their wedding gift choices. With nearly 10,000 weddings cancelled each year, even insurers have entered the primary wedding market by offering to cover the cost of any monies spent on the wedding preparation "if wedding bells don't ring." Fireman's Fund Insurance Company offers "Weddingsurance" for wedding catastrophes such as flood or fire but not for "change

Table 2.1		1999	2006
Annual Revenues of $80 billion wedding industry, 1999 and 2006	Wedding apparel, invitations, flowers, reception, photos, gifts (51.3%)	$ 16.4 billion	$41.0 billion
	Engagement/wedding rings (10.3%)	$ 3.3 billion	$ 8.2 billion
Source: McMurray 2006; Fairchild Bridal Group 2006	Honeymoon travel and apparel (14.1%)	$ 4.5 billion	$ 11.2 billion
	Home furnishing, household equipment (24.3%)	$ 7.8 billion	$ 19.4 billion
	Total	$32.0 billion	$80.0 billion

of heart."[4] WedSafe "Weddings without Worries" Insurance offers to "protect your investment . . . because this day is like no other, you want it to be perfect."

> You want to look back on the day the two of you became one and smile at the memory of each flawless detail: the chapel, the flowers, the kiss, the first dance. This is the dream we all have for our wedding day.[5]

In fact, attach the words wedding or bridal to nearly any item and its price goes up. To increase market share in an ever-shrinking marriage market, the wedding industry has expanded the wedding season to include what they are now calling the "engagement season." With the vast majority of engagements occurring in November and December, customers are now the targets of wedding marketers from the engagement period through the leading wedding months of June, August, May and July.

Figure 2.2 Average annual expenditure for the average white wedding
Source: McMurray, 2006; Fairchild Bridal Group, 2006; Fie[...] 2005

Marriage is an occasion
at which questions of rank
come to the surface in the
"house" based societies of
Eastern Indonesia and it
is also an occasion when
notions of family and
alliance flirt with notions of
commerce and commodity.
Brides are transferred
against gold and livestock,
and their "prices" are the
subject of protracted debates.
The transfer of slave girls
at weddings and funerals
mimes the gestures of a
wedding, but is culturally
understood as a quite
different sort of "gift".

—Janet Hoskins, August
2004 *Gay and Lesbian
Consumer Index*, http://
communitymarketinginc.
com/mkt_int_gld.htm
2007

Fact

If American retailers
paid only 25 cents more
per garment, the total in
Bangladesh would be $898
million–more than eight
times current US aid.

—National Labor
Committee, 2007 http://
www.nlcnet.org

According to industry estimates, the average wedding in the United States costs $27,852, with some regional variations (see Figure 2.2). For instance, in the New York metro area the average wedding increases to $38,852 with numerous examples of weddings costing more than $100,000. In the South, the cost drops to $18,624 and on the West Coast, to $24,918.[6] Considered in relation to what Americans earn, the cost of the average wedding represents 62.3 percent of the median earnings of a white family and 92 percent for black and hispanic families.[7] The fact that 40 percent of Americans earn less than $25,000 per year[8] means the average cost of a wedding approximates a year's earnings for many Americans.

To put these costs into perspective consider the following comparisons. The price tag for the average white wedding in the U.S. is equivalent to one year of education at a private four-year college or nearly four years of school at a public college or university;[9] about the same to purchase a new fully-equipped Honda Accord, Ford Mustang GT Shelby, or Toyota Tundra truck;[10] or the down payment on a house. Given the extent to which the wedding industry has become globalized, and that nearly one half of the world lives on $2 per day, consider what else the average cost of a white wedding in the U.S. would buy in those locations where many wedding products are made[11] (Table 2.2).

Table 2.2 What $27,852 will buy where wedding products are produced

---

- Food for 3000 people in South Asia.
- Cost to build 12 wells for people in Southeast Asia, Africa, and Latin America.
- Medicine for 10,000 children for one year in Africa.
- At wages of 12 cents per hour to sew wedding gowns, the cost to pay 111 workers for one year.
- At wages of $28 per week for mining diamonds in South Africa, the cost to pay 19 workers for one year.

"It Won't be a Stylish Marriage . . . I Can't Afford a Carriage . . ."

Following the publication of the first edition of *White Weddings* and other recent wedding studies, a variety of media outlets became interested in exploring the issue of wedding debt. Most notable among these was an article published on the front page of the *Sunday New York Times*[12] and titled "For Richer or Poorer, to Our Visa Card Limit" by Jennifer Bayot.

Wedding bills are weighing down couples and their parents long after the "I do's," and many have been forced to seek financial counseling as a result, according to credit counseling agencies. Young couples with modest incomes are having the most trouble repaying. Whether they celebrate lavishly or modestly, they are more likely than ever to pay for their weddings without help from their parents. And even when parents pay, what more and more people expect of nice weddings is increasingly more elaborate for both the richer and the poorer. And so, with debt do they start.[13]

In this article, Bayot interviewed couples about their wedding choices and discovered that most were spending far beyond their ability to pay. Pundits, experts, and research studies since this article indicate that financial pressures for newlyweds are playing a prominent role in divorce among newly married couples.[14] While the level of debt incurred by newlyweds receives plenty of media attention, this coverage has had little effect on wedding consumption patterns. Not only has the size of the industry tripled in the past 15 years, the number of marriages has actually decreased indicating that couples are spending more to marry than ever before. Another trend contributing to the wedding debt experience is that 32 percent of wedding expenses are paid for by the couple themselves. Only 30 percent of parents are paying the whole cost of weddings and 15 percent of the costs are shared.[15]

In an interview for an article in the *Boston Globe,* one couple referred to the newlywed experience with the wedding industry as "wedding hell."[16] The article described a fairly typical encounter with the wedding industry. Working against classic arguments such as "It's the happiest day of your life" and "It's a once-in-a-lifetime thing," the newlyweds in this article struggled to plan a wedding that would not exceed $5,000.

Joan couldn't afford her college tuition and is now saddled with a $15,000 student loan. They borrowed $21,000 to help finance an elaborate wedding. When they need money for travel or other expenses, out comes the Visa card, which currently carries a $4,000 balance.

"Unfortunately, sometimes the debt lasts longer than the marriage," he says.

—Howard Dvorkin,
Consolidated Credit
Counseling, Ft. Lauderdale

What they found shocked them. After weeks of bartering with reception halls and caterers who were either unwilling to negotiate or were priced out of reach, the bride said, "I was exhausted. Planning a wedding is a full-time job, a second one for me[17]—and not even as rewarding. My fiancé and I were feeling like the victims of highway robbers with sanctioned routines."[18] The final blow was attending a crowded bridal show where they had to "register" for numerous mailing lists and the bride was given a "silly sticker," which proclaimed her "a very important bride," and told her to fill out fifty-eight coupons for special prizes. "These people must think *bride* is synonymous with *stupid*," she thought. In the end, this couple decided not to get married yet and instead to put their $5,000 toward the purchase of a house, where, in the end, they could hold their own wedding and reception.

Having witnessed similar actions by members of the wedding industry, Denise and Alan Fields decided to become consumer advocates for brides and began publishing a variety of books and a website devoted to the consumer. Beginning with *Bridal Bargains* (1997, 2004), *Bridal Gown Guide* (1998), and the *Bridal Passport Wedding Planner* (2004), the Fields have single-handedly taken on the massive unregulated wedding industry. With statements such as "too many wedding businesses have the morals of an average slug" (1998a), the Fieldses have turned the negative experience with planning their own wedding into consumer advocacy for newlyweds. In so doing, they have encountered the wrath of some wedding businesses attempting to preserve their questionable, and in some cases illegal, practices. We'll return to this later in this chapter.

Who Are the Targets of the Wedding Industry?

Who marries, and who are the consumers of this enormous industry? On average, newlyweds are getting older. According to the 2000 U.S. Census Bureau, the average age for brides had risen from 20 in 1960 to 25; for grooms from 23 to 26.8 years. By 2006, the average age increased further to 27 for brides and 29 for grooms. The age of first marriage has been rising steadily at a rate slightly greater than one year every decade for first marriages. One of the primary factors delaying the age of first marriages is the social acceptance of couples living together

All couples want their wedding day to be special. But you can have a memorable wedding without running up huge debts. Consolidated Credit offers a wedding calculator on its Internet site, www.debtfree.org.

"The Wedding-Industrial Complex. That's how one groom we interviewed described dress shops (and the whole wedding business, for that matter). He told us he and his bride felt pressured to have the wedding the industry wanted, not the one they envisioned. That giant sucking sound you hear is the money extracted from engaged couples who walk down the aisle, he said."

—*Bridal Gown Guide,* 1998: 29

prior to marriage, from 500,000 in 1970 to 5.5 million in 2005 or 9 percent of all heterosexual couples.[19] While this has made marriage less necessary, other couples are delaying wedding to finish college, graduate school, or to pursue career opportunities. For the privileged classes, the economic necessity of marriage has steadily decreased, something that causes the wedding industry great concern.

As the total number of marriages and remarriages declined from 2,342,000 in 1996, to 2,253,750 by 2006[20] and the marriage rate has decreased from 8.8 to 7.8 per 1000 persons, the wedding industry has sought new opportunities for growth. Currently, the industry is encouraged by the projections for "echo boomers"—the children of "baby boomers"—that indicate that the annual number of marriages will once again increase. Considering how much growth has occurred in the wedding industry, it is clear that weddings are still a sizable niche market!

Contributing to the health of the wedding industry, the large and complex remarriage market "includes some married people who want to reaffirm their vows in second ceremonies,"[21] people who are divorced, as well as a growing population of widowed seniors who are remarrying. The current divorce rate of 4.3 per 1000 persons is a per capita rate and is based on the total population of persons of marriageable age. Since not all people are "marriageable," this figure is probably higher than 4.3 and increases the size of the wedding market. As of 2005, 4 out of every 5 people who have been divorced remarry and 50 percent of all marriages are remarriages for at least one of the participants.[22] The average age for divorced women who remarry is 35, and the average for divorced men is 39, with 75 percent of divorced women remarrying within ten years.[23] Even though remarriage weddings tend to be smaller, the wedding industry estimates that they total up to 40 percent of their revenues, evidence that at least one sector in American society actually benefits from divorce. In fact, without remarriages, the wedding industry would be substantially smaller.

Since 65 percent of remarriages include children from a prior relationship, the remarried market also incorporates revenues (and practices) affiliated with family. For example, this market now includes "familymoons"—post-wedding vacations that include family members and children. Additionally, people who are remarrying increasingly take advantage of another recent trend—destination weddings. Destination weddings—where the couple invite family and friends to travel to a distant location for

Author Interview, July 2003:
I was interviewed on WOR Talk Radio for their early morning commuter show. One caller responded to questions about the size of the wedding industry with this commentary:

"I don't care how excessive it is [the cost of weddings], I spent $40,000 on each of my three daughters' weddings and I'd do it all again. Today, they are all still married and I have beautiful grandchildren."

It's Official: To Be Married Means to Be Outnumbered
By Sam Roberts
Married couples, whose numbers have been declining for decades as a proportion of American households, have finally slipped into a minority, according to an analysis of new census figures by The New York Times.

The American Community Survey, released this month by the Census Bureau, found that 49.7 percent, or 55.2 million, of the nation's 111.1 million households in 2005 were made up of married couples—with and without children—just shy of a majority and down from more than 52 percent five years earlier.

—New York Times, October 15, 2006

a combined wedding/vacation—have emerged as the fastest growing segment of the wedding industry, growing from 3 percent to 16 percent of the total wedding market. As Lisa Light explains in her book *Destination Bride,*

> Why the surge in popularity? One reason is the Internet, which has improved global communications, put international resources at our fingertips, and made other cultures more accessible. At the same time, the global economy is making the world an increasingly smaller place, allowing us to explore and exchange ideas well beyond our backyard. Another reason is that today's brides and grooms are willing to push the boundaries of a traditional wedding in order to have a truly fun, unique, and memorable celebration.[24]

She goes on to say that it is the "magic" that exotic destinations provide that makes this an appealing option.

According to the wedding industry, today's newlyweds are also more likely to be dual-earner couples, with 83 percent of brides and 89 percent of grooms working; they earn a combined income currently one-third greater than the median household income, at $65,076.[25] Factoring in the age and financial standing of many of those remarrying, the probability of higher incomes increases, as does the focus of the wedding market on the consumption patterns of these newlyweds. Additionally, many young couples own houses and many of the home furnishings they need before they marry. The effect of all these factors is a dramatic change in the wedding market and its strategies. Today, it is commonplace to see ads for wedding gifts that include everything from tools to lawnmowers to sports equipment and travel.

Fascinating, right? But there's something missing from this picture of the white wedding market. In researching data on the wedding industry, a striking pattern emerges. Almost without exception, most state and industry analysts have overlooked the effects of race and class on consumption. In other words, they have focused mainly on the *white* wedding market—those patterns attributable primarily to middle-to-upper-middle-class whites. When recalculated to account for differences along racial, ethnic, and class lines, industry market data reveal significantly greater buying

Only at Viva Las Vegas Wedding chapel can you ride your Harleys up to the altar!

The Harley Wedding celebrates your love of the open road in spectacular style. Make a grand entrance on his-n-hers bikes, or share that ride down the aisle with the bride in the backseat. Fog, lights, and rock-n-roll accompany the festivities. Your wedding is the starting point for the adventure of a lifetime. Get your motors runnin' and ride into the sunset together as husband and wife!

—http://www. vivalasvegasweddings. com, August 2007

power and a very different relationship to marriage among middle-to-upper-class whites than for any other group. The following paragraphs offer a race and class comparison of people who are of marriageable age in the U.S. as a way to illustrate the scope and target of the wedding industry.

The 78 percent marriage rate for Americans cited in wedding industry and census materials is primarily applicable to whites and Asians and is significantly lower for hispanics (67 percent) and even lower yet for blacks (42 percent). While blacks used to marry much younger, they now marry considerably later than the national average, if they marry at all. Twenty-five percent of black women and less than 12 percent of black men have married by their early twenties, and more than 43.3 percent of black men and 41.9 percent of black women have never married, compared to 27.4 percent for white men and 20.7 percent for white women[26] (see Table 2.3).

The typical black couple spends an average of $12,152 on a wedding, much less than the national average of $27,852. Blacks and hispanics spend less on weddings and marry less often than whites and Asians. Is this the result of wedding market targeting? Or does the meaning of marriage change depending on one's racial and ethnic affiliation? And, on what assumptions are these data based?

Comparing marriage rates to socioeconomic status—income, educational attainment, housing, mobility, and social characteristics—provides a more complete picture of the wedding market. Consider the average combined income for marrieds from black and hispanic groups. As of 2004, married couples from within these groups had significantly lower levels of income than whites, earning 79 percent of what whites earn. While this might explain the lower levels of expenditure on a wedding, it does not explain the lower marriage rate.

Never married	Black	White
Women	43.4	22.8
Men	46.8	30.2

Table 2.3
Percentage of Americans who have never married
Source: U.S. Bureau of the Census, 2006

Another important difference between these groups is their degree of poverty. For example, for their numbers, blacks and hispanics are disproportionately poor compared with whites and Asians. For instance, poverty rates for blacks and hispanics greatly exceed the national average of 12.7 percent; 24.7 percent of blacks and 21.9 percent of hispanics had earnings below the national poverty threshold[27] as compared with 8.6 percent of whites and 9.8 percent of Asians.[28]

A key influence on earning potential is education and here again we find significant differences between groups. While black and hispanic high school graduation rates approach parity with whites, only 42 percent complete four or more years of college as compared with whites who graduate at a rate of 62 percent.[29] The result, of course, is that whites and Asians have greater earning potential than do blacks and hispanics. Again, while this explains why wedding expenditure is lower for these groups, it does not explain why they marry in significantly lower numbers (Table 2.4).[30]

As Americans we assume not only that most people desire marriage but that most people do, eventually, marry. Yet, except for some regional variations, the national rate of marriage in the U.S. has declined by about 30 percent in the past 20 years to 52 percent of the nation's estimated 106 million households.[31] Considered in relation to differences in marriage patterns across race and social class, a cursory examination of these data leads one to question if marriage is the universal practice we assume it is and to question what its frequency has to do with one's race and social class standing. Additionally, the data on marriage comes from a variety of

Table 2.4
Socioeconomic factors
Source: U.S. Bureau of the Census, 2006.

	Median earnings	Poverty rates %	College degree %
Black	$30,134	24.7	17.6
Hispanic	$34,241	21.9	12.1
White	$48,977	8.6	30.6
Asian	$57,518	9.8	49.4

legitimate sources that omit data on the complexities of racial and ethnic categories as well as the rising numbers of mixed marriages.

To understand the complexities influencing marriage patterns, researchers have uncovered a variety of factors. Of particular importance is what some researchers call the "marriage penalty."[32] This is not the same as the marriage penalty tax that Congress has been working to eliminate but is, instead, a concept created to explain the contradictory relationship the (working) poor have to marriage. Among those earning the minimum wage or living near or below the poverty line, marriage disqualifies many for the complex array of benefits they need to survive. For single mothers—blacks, 48 percent; hispanics, 25 percent; and whites, 14 percent—who are disproportionately poor and at risk, this is of critical importance in their relationship to marriage. For those living below the federally established poverty threshold, they are eligible for food stamps, Temporary Assistance to Needy Families (TANF), child tax credits, and Earned Income Tax Credit (EITC). While nearly 60 percent of single mothers live with a partner, marital status actually disqualifies some of them for assistance. Take, for example, what the Economic Policy Institute wrote about the Earned Income Tax Credit (EITC), a measure intended to provide income tax relief for the poor.

> The EITC also creates a substantial marriage penalty since combined incomes determine eligibility and benefits. If a householder with two dependent children and an income of $10,000, marries a partner with an income of $20,000, their combined disposable income would be reduced by more than $3,000. The penalty is even more severe if both partners had dependent children.[33]

In addition to this assessment, others have offered similar conclusions concerning the effect of marriage on poor families.[34] In their view, the average poor family of four living at or near the poverty threshold risks the loss of—by some estimates—as much as $6000. In other words, a working husband's earnings (the majority of the poor work) may not be enough to qualify for tax relief and "too much" to qualify for a host of social programs including food stamps, school meals, and child care. Due

Wedding March on Madison
Billed as three days of bridal planning luxury featuring the "Who's Who in I Do", the Wedding March on Madison in New York City October 15–17 is one of the most exciting events of the year for those of us "in the biz." This incredible event is presented by BRIDE'S, MODERN BRIDE and ELEGANT BRIDE Magazines.

—Poster on street lights in New York City, 2003

in part to the inadequacies of tax laws, poverty assistance policies, and the lack of child care programs, not to mention poverty threshold calculations that have not been updated since 1964, marriage among the poor, whether young or elderly, places them at a significant disadvantage. As the latest census data indicate, an increasing number of couples are choosing to live together (cohabitation) without "benefit" of marriage in order to avoid losing valuable assistance, Social Security income, and important tax breaks.

Put simply, marriage frequency drops dramatically as its economic and material benefits decrease. While middle-class women no longer "need" to marry for financial security, poor women do not participate in part because it puts them at greater risk economically. Either way, just considering the economic value of marriage, it comes as no surprise that the number of annual marriages is declining. Contrasted against the rising expenditures on weddings, it is possible to conclude that the primary target of the wedding industry is people who are placed higher up on the socioeconomic scale. The lower one's socioeconomic level, the less likely they are to marry and the less they will pay for a wedding. Considering weddings from an economic standpoint, it is possible to conclude that the white wedding industry targets privileged whites more prominently than any other group. Comparing whites and Asians for earnings and earning potential, the deciding factor in focusing on whites is population size. Asians are still a minority group within the American population.

Given the focus of the wedding industry, wedding advertisers, and the pervasive images of white weddings in popular culture, the comments of a 12-year-old African-American boy recently interviewed for an article in *The Washington Post* are particularly insightful:

> "Marriage is for white people."
> That's what one of my students told me some years back when I
> taught a career exploration class for sixth-graders . . . in southeast
> Washington. I was pleasantly surprised when the boys in the class
> stated that being a good father was a very important goal to them,
> more meaningful than making money or having a fancy title.

"That's wonderful!" I told my class. "I think I'll invite some couples in to talk about being married and rearing children." "Oh, no," objected one student. "We're not interested in the part about marriage. Only about how to be good fathers." That's when the other boy chimed in, speaking as if the words left a nasty taste in his mouth: "Marriage is for white people."[35]

As if to echo the sentiments of the industry, this child's perception is consistent with what the marketers themselves believe. They are aware that the combined earnings of black or hispanic newlyweds are usually significantly lower than those of whites and are likely to remain lower throughout the course of the marriage (which is also shorter). Wedding marketers know that white middle-class women are more likely to consume wedding products than any other group. They target their marketing campaigns to white women who have the means to consume their products. Even within the advertising industry there is considerable evidence of racial segregation and of institutional racism affecting who is hired and what images and strategies are used in wedding advertising.[36] Throughout the wedding industry, images of white women and couples are pervasive and set both a race and class standard for who marries and who has a white wedding. To attract a broader range of consumers, the wedding industry must appeal to non-material needs such as romance, kinship, beauty, morality, consumerism, affection, and sexual identity. While these aspects will be covered later in this book, they play a central role in the massive revenues the industry earns (see Chapter 3 on bridal magazines and honeymoons).

The reality regarding marriage is that it primarily privileges the privileged, those who are able to secure and maintain goods, property, and credit. Marriages among those in the middle class or above generally increase the earning potential of the couple. Certainly, for middle- to upper-class white women, marriage signals financial security with married women earning 37 percent more than single women. The rewards and benefits afforded these couples and their families—from health insurance to health club discounts to lavish weddings—are substantial.

An examination of the wedding industry and its marketing efforts offers considerable evidence regarding the interests at stake in marriage in American

Advertising: An Industry Still So White, but Few Will Discuss It, Ad-World Culture and Pay Scale Hurt Minority Recruitment By Lisa Sanders

NEW YORK—Want to know why there are so few black employees in the ad business? Look to its roots, culture and compensation practices. The New York City Commission on Human Rights investigation into Madison Avenue's hiring practices has stirred a maelstrom of emotional discussion around that one big question – and this time around, industry leaders hope that the discussion might just last long enough to yield some solutions.

Comfort levels

"Curiously, while we operate in an industry that prides itself on participating in the cultural zeitgeist, if you will, we are not an industry that is tremendously comfortable with differences," said Renetta McCann, CEO, Starcom MediaVest Group. Ms. McCann, one of the top-ranked black women in the business, notes that historically, the industry has not had a huge appetite for this issue. "In my 28 years, I've had about five substantial conversations on the issue of racial diversity in advertising. That's about one every five years."

—Advertising Age (http:// www.AdAge.com), June 19, 2006

society. Throughout the 1980s and 1990s, politicians used lower marriage rates among the nation's lower classes to justify welfare policies and cuts in social services. They claimed that the lack of marriage in these communities was an indicator of poor family values. As we enter the twenty-first century, more political "solutions" have been devised to "encourage" heterosexual marriage as a way to reduce dependency on government assistance. The most recent of these was a $1.5 billion grant to poor communities in the hope that increasing the number of marriages among the poor would allow public officials to claim they had reduced public assistance claims.[37] The reality is that marriage itself does not lift the poor out of poverty; it just reduces the number of eligible recipients. It is clear from a brief examination of the material landscape for poor families that opportunities for employment that pay a living wage, safe neighborhoods, inexpensive housing, access to affordable child care and education are the path to prosperity. A close examination of the seemingly benign wedding market offers evidence regarding the economics of marriage and the interests at stake in preserving its power.

A major tension regarding the future of marriage has emerged in the struggle between social conservatives seeking to preserve the status quo regarding marriage and recent efforts on the part of legal and social advocates for same sex marriage. Studying the various facets of the wedding industry quickly reveals the massive market forces invested in the outcome of this battle. The transnational wedding industry, already expanding its global market share, stands to make substantial gains if same sex marriage becomes legal in the U.S. Massachusetts, where same sex marriage has been legal since May 2004, has allowed 8000 same sex marriages and the wedding industry there has been in full bloom.[38] With same sex civil unions legal in Vermont, and same sex marriage initiatives erupting throughout the U.S., the American wedding industry is already building markets and reaping the benefits. Same sex wedding expos have emerged all over the country as have honeymoon marketing, wedding consulting, and advertising to same sex couples. Major newspapers such as the *New York Times* have changed their wedding pages to "weddings and celebrations," regularly including same sex couples, and *Modern Bride* magazine has featured a spread on same sex weddings. Combined with the legalization of same sex marriage in Canada, the Netherlands, England, and Spain, the transnational wedding industry is experiencing rapid and unprecedented growth. All of this is occurring at the same time that federal and state governments in the U.S. are seeking permanent bans on same sex marriage. The conflict between the interests of the wedding industry, consumerism, transnational capitalism, and those who seek to consolidate heterosexual power and privilege *vis-à-vis* marriage is clearly visible. The important question—and one that we will revisit throughout this book—is, which forces will carry the most weight in the outcome of this struggle—market or social?

The Future Market

In addition to the rise of the same sex wedding industry, a variety of developments have emerged since the publication of the first edition of *White Weddings*. In the U.S., one set of market factors of particular import for the future of the wedding industry has to do with recent trends in black, hispanic, and Asian consumption patterns. In an updated version of his 1998 study, economist Jeffrey Humphreys of the Selig Center for Economic Growth reports that black spending power is growing faster than the national average. The study forecasts that black consumers will "account for 8.4 percent of total buying power in 2005 and will reach 8.6 percent by 2010."[39] The other factor that may affect wedding marketers is the increase in the black population, which is also growing faster than the U.S. population as a whole, at 14 percent versus 9 percent. Humphreys credited these gains to economic expansion and educational progress made by blacks in recent years.

One of the key problems with Humphreys's study is that these numbers reflect the gains made in education and economics in the past and do not show the effects of recent rollbacks in affirmative action, tax relief, and financial aid for college, all of which are decreasing black enrollment in higher education. While gains have been made, black men still earn only 72 cents for every dollar white men make, and black women earn 85 cents for every dollar white women are paid. If these disparities continue, "white" weddings will persist as sites to exemplify and perpetuate racial hierarchies.

New to Humphreys's research is his assessment of Native American, Asian, and hispanic buying power. He estimates that Native American buying power will increase to 0.6 percent of whites by 2010; hispanic buying power will rise from 5 to 8.1 percent by 2005;

and Asian buying power will increase from 2.7 percent in 1990 to 4.4 percent in 2005. While these groups marry in smaller numbers, as they achieve greater buying power, they will also become increasingly the targets of the wedding industry.

Wedding marketers are aware of these facts as well. They know that income patterns among middle-class whites promise greater return on their investment. As we will see in the next chapter, bridal magazines are notorious for overlooking women of color in their advertisements and marketing of weddings. The overriding effect of these patterns is that in terms of affordability and necessity, the wedding in American culture is primarily a ritual by, for, and about the white middle to upper classes. Truly, the *white* wedding.

The most powerful new market contributing to the dramatic growth in the wedding industry is the internet. According to *Bride's* magazine, nearly 88 percent of today's brides use the internet to plan their wedding.[40] Growth in this area has literally skyrocketed, providing a vast number of retail and consulting sites for prospective newlyweds both inside the U.S. as well as in the global marketplace. While there is no official source collecting and measuring data on the total revenues from these sites, they literally cover every imaginable (and unimaginable) aspect of the wedding, reception, and honeymoon. The development of new online markets is occurring daily, including global marketing and transnational consumption and production.

One of the most popular sites, TheKnot.com, now boasts 2.3 million visitors per month and includes an online blog for potential consumers. The power of this medium can best be reflected in comments made by vendors' reactions to this blog:

> Many wedding vendors say the website has transformed their businesses. All it takes is one happy newlywed to spread the word, and the customers flood in . . . Business was creeping along at Jupiter's Garden in St. Charles before a single bride gushed about the florist on the Knot's St. Louis message board. "All of the sudden, phone calls started coming like crazy. We went from one wedding a month to 12 to 14 weddings a month."[41] But not all vendors are pleased with "knotties." Some report losing business because of one complaining bride, and others even claim that a few complaints can "ruin" them.

The no. 1 wedding city in the world is Istanbul, Turkey, where 166,000 "I Dos" were said in 2002. Runner-up? Las Vegas, where 114,000 weddings were conducted by Elvis and others. Dollywood honeymoons must be big in Gatlinburg, Tenn., ranked third with 42,000 unions, while veils prevailed in voodoo capital New Orleans, which hosted 36,545 weddings.

—Association for Wedding Professionals International, 2005.

The power of the internet for wedding planning and postings cannot be overestimated. Every aspect of the wedding can be purchased, marketed, and talked about in some location on the web. Maps for guests, suggested gift lists, honeymoon information, and even R.S.V.P. sites are available. Given the global reach of the internet, international communication for newlyweds as well as the industry itself is extensive. When the wedding is complete, there are websites specifically for newlyweds to post their photographs, videos, and commentary. The online wedding industry alone is estimated as worth upwards of $50 billion.[42] And this doesn't take into consideration the proliferating mail-order bride websites.

The popularity of the white wedding has reached beyond the West into a variety of global markets at an ever-increasing rate. Japan, for example, has become an important customer for the U.S. white wedding industry. The white wedding complete with white male clergy has become popularized among Japan's youth. Since 1996, according to the Japan's Ministry of Economy, Trade and Industry, the number of Christian [white] weddings has nearly doubled while the number of Shinto weddings has plunged by two-thirds. Actors are hired to portray Western priests while Japanese brides dress in white wedding gowns to mimic the white wedding so popular in the West.

> Only 1.4 percent of Japan's 127 million people are Christians, but Christian-style ceremonies now account for three-quarters of Japanese weddings. To meet market demand, bridal companies in recent years have largely dispensed with the niceties of providing a pastor with a seminary education, keeping the requirements simple: a man from an English-speaking country who will show up on time, remember his lines, not mix up names and perform the ceremony in 20 minutes.[43]

In Japan, 800,000 couples marry annually and spend an average of $62,000 per wedding, yielding the wedding industry nearly $50 billion in revenues. Since a significant portion of these revenues are spent on white weddings, there is substantial benefit for the American wedding industry as well as for the Japanese.[44]

An *Economist* study released in 2000 assessing the Asian wedding market echoed American analysts by claiming that weddings in these regions are also recession-proof

One San Francisco-based research firm, Community Marketing, estimates that gay spending on marriage could top $1 billion in three years, adding to the estimated $55 billion spent on travel by gays and lesbians annually. While there are no precise numbers, a recent survey by Witeck-Combs Communications, a Washington, D.C.-based firm that specializes in researching the gay and lesbian consumer market for big companies like American Airlines, pegged overall gay buying power at $485 billion for 2003.

"Gay marriage is hot as a marketing category," says Amy Errett, chief executive officer of Olivia, "and will be for a long while."

—K. Swisher, *Wall Street Journal*, March 11, 2004

and "the only industry where there is investment without looking at returns." With events such as Vivaha 2003, Bridal Asia, Bride & Groom and the Marwar Mega Wedding Show gaining in popularity, it appears that this assessment is accurate. This same study estimated the size of the Indian wedding industry at $11 billion, with a projected growth of 25 percent annually, on track with growth rates in the West.[45]

Among the many changes in the white wedding market that are also expected to continue is the proliferation of destination weddings, primarily on the part of Westerners.[46] The estimated market share for destination weddings is currently 16 percent and they are poised for rapid and dramatic growth provided the travel industry does not experience another setback as it did after the terrorist attacks in the U.S. on September 11, 2001.

The primary wedding market depends on numerous production and labor relations issues that underlie the consumption and accumulation involved in weddings. The central purpose of including them here is to make visible the historical and material conditions that set the conditions for the production of the white wedding. While gown marketing is probably the most insidious, other wedding products and services warrant coverage here. To examine each area of the primary wedding market is beyond the scope of this book. However, the following section offers highlights of the primary wedding market in the form of case studies.

Godey's Lady's Book

1850

1857

1856

Primary Wedding Market

Probably the most important wedding purchase is the bride's gown. Industry analysts have noted that most brides would do without many things to plan a wedding and stay within budget, but they would not scrimp when it comes to the purchase of the wedding gown. With the national average expenditure at $922 for the gown and $265 for the veil, the bride's apparel becomes the centerpiece of the white wedding. Most of us have heard the various phrases associated with the bride and her gown, the symbolic significance attached to how she looks and how beautiful her gown is. In coverage of Barbra Streisand's wedding in *People* magazine, the bulk of the photos are of her in a white "shimmering crystal-beaded Donna Karan gown with a 15-foot diaphanous veil."[47] This reference, as well as those of many other celebrities, imitates

19th century miscellaneous American wedding photos

the standard-bearers of fame, privilege, style, and perfection: Queen Victoria, Queen Elizabeth, Princess Grace, and Princess Diana.

Prior to Queen Victoria's wedding in 1840, white wedding gowns were not the norm. Brides occasionally wore white but more frequently were wed in black or gray dresses.[48] If the bride's family had the money and the means, she would wear a dress made from brocades of gold and silver, yellow and blue. Puritan women, for example, wore gray. When Queen Victoria was wed in a white gown, she captured the imaginations of many when this powerful presider over the British Empire, whom many thought of as "plain," married a handsome Prince. She became a real-life Cinderella and

"As a young woman in Anne Tyler's latest novel, Ladder of Years, *asks her father in all seriousness on the eve of her wedding, 'Which is more trouble: calling off the wedding or suing for divorce?'"*

—Bernard 1995

she did so in an opulent ceremony where she wore a luxurious and beautiful (by nineteenth-century standards) *white* wedding gown. Following this grand event, many white Western middle-class brides, already captivated by a growing consumer culture and romance novels, imitated Victoria and adopted the white wedding gown. In an excellent new history of the white wedding, Cele Otnes and Elizabeth Pleck reveal that white had a particular resonance in that it was the color young women were expected to wear at court. But it was also a sign of privilege:

> It was hard to keep clean, and cleanliness was becoming more valued as a sign of privilege . . . The queen herself, and the era she lived in, valued the ideal of female sexual purity and associated this trait with the color white. In Western culture, there were only two kinds of women, good ones (mothers or virgins) and evil ones (whores) . . . At her wedding, the pure woman wore a white veil and gown to signify her virginity.[49]

By the turn of the century, white had not only become the standard but had also become laden with symbolism—it stood for purity, virginity, innocence, and promise, as well as power and privilege.

Queen Elizabeth II's wedding to Prince Philip in 1947 once again seized the attention of people around the world. This post–World War II extravaganza was not only a wedding of royalty and affluence, but it came at a time following the devastation and gloom of the war when many Westerners were desperately seeking images of hope, prosperity, and order. The romances and lives of celebrities had become mainstream popular culture fare and royal weddings gave the public images to which they could aspire. Even though advertisers had been using images of beautiful white brides to sell products since the early 1900s, these celebrity weddings renewed the linking of romance with consumerism at a time when weddings and the U.S. economy were both booming. For years to come, these two royal spectacles secured the promise of, and romance with, the white wedding so prevalent today.

Continuing this powerful tradition in recent years were the weddings of two preeminent princess brides: Princess Grace and Princess Diana. These blond-haired, blue-eyed, real-life princess Barbies married during the mass media era. The former Grace Kelly was a beautiful, famous, internationally acclaimed film star who met

Fit for a Princess: Grace Kelly's Wedding Dress on display at the Philadelphia Museum of Art in Pennsylvania from April to May 21, 2006. The museum exhibited Grace Kelly's wedding gown to celebrate the 50th anniversary of her marriage to Prince Rainier of Monaco on April 19, 1956. The dress was designed by Metro-Goldwyn-Mayer's studio designer Helen Rose. The dress consisted of a bodice with an attached underbodice, skirt support and slip, a ruffled petticoat and an attached foundation petticoat.

—Daniela Gilber, *Women's Wear Daily*, April 4, 2006, p. 13

Princess Grace
of Monaco (Grace
Kelly), 1956

a handsome prince, Prince Rainier of Monaco, married in a wedding extravaganza filmed by MGM in April 1956, and went off to live "happily ever after" as Princess Grace of Monaco.[50] For many Americans, Grace Kelly, born in Philadelphia to Irish immigrant parents, represented the merging of the Hollywood fairy-tale happy ending and the American dream of possibility and wealth. The headlines proclaimed that even a little girl from Philadelphia could become a princess.

Lady Diana Spencer, previously unknown to the public, married one of the most affluent, famous, and eligible bachelors of the late twentieth century, Prince Charles. Also blond, blue-eyed, and beautiful, the nineteen-year-old Lady Diana became the wife of the future king of England. Their wedding was a globally televised public spectacle watched by 750 million people from all parts of the world.[51] In both weddings the brides wore extraordinarily elaborate and expensive white wedding gowns and were married in ceremonies befitting a queen—extravagant, luxurious, and opulent. Here's how *People* magazine described Diana's wedding:

> The euphoria was overwhelming, the images unforgettable. "Perfect!" proclaimed London's *Daily Mail* in the banner headline over its frontpage photo of the kissing newlyweds. "The Very Picture of Fairy-Tale Sweethearts," echoed the *Sun*. It was July 29, 1981, the wedding of His Royal Highness, the Prince of Wales and Lady Diana Spencer, seemingly destined to become King and Queen of England ... It was all spectacle and wonderment and celebration, not a day of doubt.[52]

These modern-day Cinderellas captured the imagination of people from all over the world, regardless of gender, race, social class, nation, and sexual identity. Their lives symbolized possibility: "Fairy tales can come true, it can happen to you." Neither woman came from royalty—Grace was a movie star and Diana was a kindergarten teacher born of nobility who never attended college—yet both found "a handsome prince," leading many to believe that fairy tales could come true. Both women became fetishized by fans, who followed and studied their every move.

Princess Diana, 1981

Both women became tragic figures to their adoring public when they each died at young ages in spectacular car crashes.

Of course, the fantasy marriage this fairy tale wedding promised was shattered when revelations of Diana's and Prince Charles's extramarital affairs were made public and their marriage ended in divorce. Still, Diana's funeral was one of the most watched events in television history. Her death, her failed happily-ever-after life, is considered by many to be one of the greatest tragedies in modern times. During the televising of the events surrounding her death, all networks replayed scenes from her wedding to Charles. Newscasters repeatedly referred to her wedding, replaying images of Diana and Charles on the balcony of Buckingham Palace, their ride through the streets of London in the royal, horsedrawn carriage, the view of her entering Westminster Abbey in her extraordinary white wedding gown:

> London, July 29—For her long walk up the aisle that transformed her into a princess, Lady Diana Spencer, in the most romantic storybook tradition, wore a sequin-and-pearl-incrusted dress with a 25-foot train. Made of ivory silk taffeta produced by Britain's only silk farm the dress was hand-embroidered with old lace panels on the front and back of the tightly fitting boned bodice. A wide frill edged the scooped neckline, and the loose, full sleeves were caught at the elbow with taffeta bows. A multi-layered tulle crinoline propped up the diaphanous skirt.
>
> A diamond tiara belonging to Earl Spencer, Lady Diana's father, anchored her ivory tulle veil, aglitter with thousands of hand-sewn sequins. Also borrowed was a pair of diamond drop earrings from Lady Diana's mother . . . For the final tradition-bound item—something blue—a blue bow was sewn into the waistband of the dress. A fiercely and successfully kept secret, the dress had been guarded day and night by a security organization at the workrooms of the designers, David and Elizabeth Emanuel.[53]

Diana's wedding and gown have had a profound influence on the wedding industry. Nearly every aspect of her wedding has been detailed time and again on television and in bridal and news magazines. The wedding of Diana and Charles became the exemplar of the ultimate fantasy of what a wedding should be:

> The union of Lady Diana Spencer and Charles, Prince of Wales, transformed the way we think about weddings. The images of that event are so thoroughly implanted in our memories, it's hard to separate the idea of a bride from the picture of Diana emerging, Cinderella-like, from her glass coach. That early morning . . . we started dreaming about the day when we, too, would promise to love, honor, and cherish.[54]

Wedding advertising reflects these images in varying forms over and over again. Consider this quote from *Bride's* magazine:

> What makes a woman obsess about her wedding gown? Is it because she's been thinking about it since she was four, because it's the one item of clothing that can instantly turn her into a princess, or because 167 pairs of eyes will be staring at her as she marches down the aisle? Write The Great White Hope, *Bride's* Magazine, 140 E. 45th Street, New York, NY 10017.[55]

Not only does this paragraph invite the reader (bride) to imagine herself as bride, princess, and spectacle, but it naturalizes this desire by suggesting she's had this dream since she was four. In fact, this fantasy is the work of both the wedding-industrial and the wedding-ideological complexes. The play on words characterized by the phrase "the great white hope," a slogan emanating from a battle between a white boxer and a black boxer, offers a troubling association between the desire for the white wedding and racism. (As you will see in the following discussion of the wedding industry and in Chapter 3, this "great white hope" goes far beyond the white wedding gown.)

Another major factor contributing to the escalation of the U.S. wedding industry was the Reagan/Bush era (1980–92) or Reagan "revolution" as some have called it. Ronald Reagan, a former Hollywood actor and Governor of California, "rode" into office promising a return to American prosperity, traditional values, and happy endings. His message to Americans was to celebrate and display consumption, luxury, pleasure, and excess. These messages combined with public policy to create a period in American economic history characterized by a massive realignment of the federal budget. Branding government waste with campaigns that blamed economic downturns on social services spending and so-called "welfare queens," Reagan policies and ideologies created a seedbed for white wedding extravaganzas. Wedding magazines and wedding marketing exploded in consumer culture. The number of weddings increased as did the amount of money people were willing to pay (or go into debt). Stories about happy endings and a return to so-called "family values" escalated and pervaded popular culture along with myths about how long marriages last and what constitutes a family. The marketing of everything from weddings to gowns to children's toys to popular wedding films to Disney was laced with messages about fairy tales and princesses. Even couture fashion shows of world-class designers traditionally featured (and continue to feature) wedding gowns in their grand finale.

As Otnes and Pleck assert in their history of the lavish wedding:

> In the second half of the twentieth century, the belief that every bride could be Cinderella became a girlhood fantasy, a democratic right, and *the* central preoccupation of the wedding. People were able to buy the pursuit of happiness. Having the money to buy the dream bought a form of equality, even in a society of vastly unequal wealth . . . [and] the opulent wedding is no longer only for wealthy white people or heterosexuals.[56]

As I will show in the following chapters, it is the intersection of these forces that creates the foundation for the romance with the white wedding spectacle, the white wedding gown, and the fantasy bride. And it is the illusion upon which this romance is built and that conceals the workings of the heterosexual imaginary. The marriage of conspicuous consumption with the promise of love and romance combines to create a highly lucrative but virtually invisible transnational wedding industry that is interdependent with the historical needs of capitalism. In this context, the wedding gown becomes fetishized, creating a "recession-proof" market where social relations become alienated in favor of the pursuit of the ultimate commodity— the couture or couture-like wedding gown that promises eternal love and romance for all regardless of race, class, nationality, or sexual identity.

Purchasing the Wedding Gown

With elaborate white gowns symbolizing both the wedding and the bride's importance, the mainstay of the gown industry is the specialized bridal stores. These shops or salons cater to the bride with all sorts of distinctive treatment. Elitist phrases such as "bridal salon" are deliberately used to convey to the consumer that she is, in fact, special and, more than that, wealthy or potentially upper-class "royalty," befitting treatment as a princess. To this end, shops will create an ambience to match the meaning of the gown, providing everything from living room settings and circular staircases to chandeliers, flowers, gold fixtures, limousine service, and free gourmet coffee. All of this is intended to justify the exorbitant costs and high markups she will encounter in purchasing her "once-in-a-lifetime" gown and accessories. In addition to the cost of the gown and veil, brides spend hundreds of dollars accessorizing with lingerie, shoes, and jewelry.

A major ripple in this well-established wedding gown business was created by the entry of David's Bridal, formerly David's Bridal Warehouse, a chain of 250 off-the-rack superstores operating in 45 states. David's was recently purchased by Federated Stores, Inc., the nation's largest department store chain and owner of May's Department Stores, Macy's, Marshall Fields, Lord & Taylor, and Bloomingdales. The only other major chain threatening the small-scale specialty wedding shops was Maryland-based Discount Bridal Service (DBS) which went out of business in 2005, leaving hundreds of brides up the aisle without a dress. J.C. Penney, following closely behind Federated Stores, recently decided to become a bridal gown retailer, making it possible for brides to find additional discount options.

What had formerly been a secure and expensive bridal gown market has become pressured by discount stores offering up to two thousand dresses in sizes 4 to 26 with prices ranging from $299 to $1,000, with no special orders and no waiting. The bridal gown industry, threatened by the discount gown stores, is generally hostile toward the discount market, primarily because, as the Fieldses claim in *Bridal Gown Guide*, the "Discount Bridal Service is the bride's secret weapon in the war on high prices."[57] With brides as a "captive" audience, the wedding industry has—and wants to have and to hold on to—their marketing edge. Even the publisher of *Vows* was reluctant to share his industry trade journal with anyone outside the industry for fear it would provide customers with too much inside information.

Wedding gowns in bridal stores

Filene's, a Boston-based national department store and famous for their Bargain Basement sales, opens their doors twice a year for "the running of the brides!" Several hundred would-be brides seeking to purchase couture dresses for a mere $249 begin lining up at 5:30 a.m. and rush the racks when the store opens at 8. They come in teams with a game plan, sometimes wearing team t-shirts or baseball caps. Within minutes, all the dresses are off the racks and women are trying them on in the aisles. When someone finds the gown she wants the crowd applauds and rushes her remaining gowns. Clearly, these sales combined with the increasing presence of discount bridal stores represent an interruption in business-as-usual for gown retailers.

 But specialty gown stores are not all they appear to be. One practice gown stores use is telling the bride they don't have her size or that she is larger than she thought (always fun to hear!); this results in a special order or the purchase of a dress that is too large and requires alterations. Of course, those alterations are done in the store for costs of $80 to $250 by seamstresses frequently working for substandard or minimum wages.

Bridal gown store out of business

Another practice widely engaged in by gown-sellers is the removal of designer labels and prices from dresses. In many surveys, from *Modern Bride* to Dawn Currie's interview study, brides indicate that they rely upon bridal magazines to give them ideas about what type of gown to choose.[58] They take the ad for the gown they like best to area stores and attempt to try on and purchase that particular dress. What they encounter is a system of deception widely practiced by many bridal shops. First, sellers remove the labels. Brides ask for a Vera Wang or an Alfred Angelo or a Jessica McClintock and are told to get the number off the gown so the clerk can check their book and see which designer it is. The bride has no way of knowing if she actually has the brand she seeks. As I toured various shops and saw how widespread this practice was, I asked store owners why they removed the labels from the dresses. Without exception they told me that it was to maintain the integrity of their business and to prevent women from comparison shopping. I also surveyed 43 women who had recently purchased a wedding gown regarding the content on their dress label. Not one person had a gown with a label intact. The truth is, this practice is *illegal* and provides shop owners with a great deal of flexibility in preserving their customer base and profit margin. Alan and Denise Fields have documented many of these practices in their *Bridal Gown Guide,* providing brides with important consumer information:

> By our estimates, three out of four shops intentionally remove tags out of their dresses. Why? They want to keep you dumb. If you knew who made which dress, you could go down the street to that evil Debbie Does Discount Bridal Gown Shoppe and get it at a 25% discount. All this would be fine if it weren't illegal. Yes, there is a federal law that outlaws this practice. The Federal Textile Products Identification Act, Title 15, Sec 70 . . . says all apparel sold in this country must include a label with the manufacturer's name, the fiber content and the country of origin . . . The law was enacted in 1958.[59]

In addition to this federal consumer protection law, many states provide similar protections. But bridal gown stores have little to fear: this law is not enforced.

And, perhaps more importantly, the romance with the white wedding gown distracts the soon-to-be brides from becoming suspicious of store practices.

Wedding Gown Production

With world trade agreements such as the North American Free Trade Agreement (NAFTA), and the World Trade Organization (WTO), textile production has become largely an offshore industry. That is, the vast majority of wedding gowns are no longer made in the U.S. Instead, the vast majority of bridal gowns are produced by women workers in China who are 15 to 30 years old and earn an average of $12 per day. As designers and manufacturers pursue cheaper labor in their quest for profits, the "race to the bottom"—locating the lowest possible cost for production—frequently takes them to countries intent on competing for their business even if it means lowering already low wage rates. The result is that most textile and shoe production occurs in China with significant competition coming from Guatemala, Mexico, Taiwan, the Commonwealth of Northern Mariana Islands (a U.S. protectorate), Saipan, and Bangladesh. Currently, Latin American production is high at $19 per day and Bangladesh has the lowest rate at $9 per day, making them the most attractive to a wide variety of companies.

While bridal gown manufacturers remove labels from their dresses, bridesmaid gowns frequently still have them. A look at the portion of tags bridesmaid gown-sellers leave in the dresses reveals that most are sewn in Mexico and China. Estimates by consumer advocates and industry specialists suggest that somewhere in the vicinity of 80–90 percent of all wedding gowns are produced outside the U.S. in subcontracted factories where labor standards are nowhere near what they are in the U.S. and no unions or regulators keep watch. Elson and Pearson quote from an investment brochure that uses racism and sexism to attract multinational corporations:

> The manual dexterity of the oriental female is famous the world over. Her hands are small and she works fast with extreme care. Who, therefore, could be better qualified by *nature and inheritance* to contribute to the efficiency of a bench-assembly production line than the oriental girl?[60]

"After several weeks of gown shopping, I have learned that this experience is not for the faint of heart or the uninformed. I was not about to plunk down 60 percent deposit only to find out that the dress was made by a noname company in a sweatshop in China."

—From *Bridal Gown Guide* e-mail, 1998, p. 6

$399

STYLE NO. _106_

SIZE _18_

COLOR _Eggplant_

CONTENTS
SHELL - 100% POLYESTER
LINING - 100% POLYESTER

DO NOT WASH OR SPOT CLEAN.
DRY CLEAN ONLY, BY USING
THE ZURCION METHOD.
WE RECOMMEND
CONTINENTAL DRY CLEANERS.
1-800-242-GOWN.
FREE PICK-UP NATIONWIDE.
GUARANTEED PROCESSING.

STEAM ON
REVERSE SIDE ONLY

RN# 85449
MADE IN MEXICO

Bridesmaid gown's tag

In July 1998, United Steelworkers of America, AFL-CIO-CLC, et al. filed a federal lawsuit questioning the constitutionality of NAFTA. "The so-called free trade system that NAFTA established has given predatory corporations a license to hunt for the cheapest labor and the lowest environmental and safety standards on the continent."

—George Becker,
Coalition for Justice
in the Maquiladoras,
530 Bandera Road, San
Antonio, Texas 78228

The recruitment of U.S. companies to contract offshore labor benefits manufacturers on many levels: cheap labor, low overhead, fewer regulations, and higher profits. And with the proliferation of free trade agreements, labor and environmental abuses abound. Particularly in locations such as the free trade zone in Mexico where proximity to the U.S. and economic relations between the U.S. government and Mexico make this a largely unregulated location, occupational hazards, toxic exposure and dumping, sexual harassment, and labor abuses produce immeasurable negative costs to the people and lands in these areas.

Maquiladora housing in
Matamoras, Mexico

NAFTA Center in Ciudad
Juarez, Mexico

With the exception of Jessica McClintock's dresses, most wedding gowns are made offshore. But even McClintock's labor practices in the U.S. have come under scrutiny. While her firm joined the 1996 Fashion Trendsetters List of the U.S. Department of Labor pledging to "help eradicate sweatshops in America,"[61] McClintock's own textile workers in the U.S. went unpaid when her subcontractor filed bankruptcy.[62]

In 1996, then Secretary of Labor Robert Reich (under President Clinton) gathered industry leaders together to head off a labor and offshore manufacturing crisis precipitated by the National Labor Committee's (NLC) exposure of sweatshop use by The Gap and by Wal-Mart's Kathie Lee Gifford clothing line. In a press release that coincided with the holiday season and the anniversary of the Triangle Shirtwaist Factory fire in New York City in 1909 in which 145 women died as a result of sweatshop working conditions, Reich released a "no sweat" initiative in the form of a Trendsetter's List. This directory of garment manufacturers and retailers provided consumers with a list of companies committed to taking "additional steps to ensure their goods are not made in sweatshop conditions."[63] While the list was extensive, the only wedding gown manufacturer in evidence was designer Jessica McClintock.

The Asian Immigrant Women's Association (AIWA) launched a full-scale campaign to force McClintock to pay her workers $10,000 in back wages. When they saw McClintock's name on the Trendsetters List they contacted the Labor Department and threatened to expose the company for labor abuses. Rather than risk media exposure, McClintock settled with the workers over the back pay they were owed.[64]

Each of these events happened prior to the publication of the first edition of this book. At that time, with the exception of an investigation into labor abuses on the part of one leading dress manufacturer by the Union of Needletrades, Industrial and Textile Employees (UNITE), little was being done by designers or governments to ensure legal and humane treatment of wedding apparel textile workers. Compared to major corporations such as Nike, Mattel, and Wal-Mart, most of these smaller textile operations were overlooked and unexamined.

Lifting the Veil: A Special Report, a white paper distributed by UNITE, documented the sweatshop practices of the Alfred Angelo Company.[65] Alfred Angelo, a Philadelphia-based gown manufacturer founded by the Piccione family in 1940, has had a long-standing reputation in the design and production of wedding and prom gowns and bridesmaid and mother-of-the-bride dresses. Under labels such as Christian Dior, Michele Piccione Couture, Tina Michele, Dance-Allure, Flirtations, Bridallure, and Alfred Angelo Bridals, the company sells gowns and dresses through a variety of retail outlets.

In a survey conducted by UNITE of three factories in Guatemala, it was discovered that Alfred Angelo gowns were being made by 13-year-olds in factories with widespread violations of their country's child labor, wage, and hour laws and under life-threatening safety conditions. At two of the firms, 14- and 15-year-olds worked as long as ten hours a day earning $20.80 a week.

Even though sales volumes had risen steadily, according to UNITE, Alfred Angelo had planned to eliminate jobs in the United States and move all of its work to Guatemala. With annual sales at $59 million in 1996, the company still sought to use Chinese subcontractors to assemble dresses. UNITE reported that there was "no way of knowing the conditions under which the clothes are made" and that Alfred Angelo's primary motivation was "greed." Angelo laborers in the U.S. "allied themselves with the exploited workers in Guatemala and China" in an effort to convince the Piccione family to put corporate responsibility ahead of corporate greed.

In June 1997, the Alfred Angelo Company apologized for late deliveries and cited union trouble as the reason. They blamed the problems on "militant and negative responses from UNITE apparel union, which has directly contributed to the delay of shipments to our customers."[66] At the time, a sagging bridal retail market had contributed to sales declines, and companies like Alfred Angelo were pressured by discount bridal retailers who "undercut their prices on gowns," as well as by "rising couture stars like Amsale."[67] In the Spring 1998 bridal fashion review in New York, Alfred Angelo was conspicuously absent, leaving many with the impression that the company was having difficulty recovering from these setbacks.

Today, a world-wide social movement to stop a host of abuses by multinational corporations in the name of free trade has raised significant levels of awareness regarding these issues. Protests on everything from labor and human rights violations to environmental degradation have occurred at each meeting of the World Trade Organization and at the G8, an annual political summit meeting of the heads of government where trade issues are a priority. A number of organizations including

---

The most expensive wedding gown on record was created by Renee Strauss in collaboration with jeweler Martin Katz. It is white and laced with 150 carats of diamonds. It is valued at $12,000,000 and, to date, no one has purchased it.

—Guinness Book of World Records

The longest wedding gown train measured 3,949.8 feet and was worn in Caudry, France on August 5, 2006.

—*People Extra*, July 13, 2007, p. 7

"Every bride sees her wedding day as the culmination of her dreams, and every wedding is a celebration of that," believes [Michele] Piccione. *"Sure, styles change, but the sense of fantasy is always there. And as the largest bridalwear manufacturer in the country, we try to meet every fantasy that's out there."*

Quote by the chief designer and daughter of founder of the Piccione-owned-and-operated gown manufacturer, Alfred Angelo.

—Friedman 1997

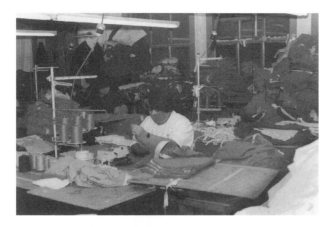

Sweatshop workers

UNITE workers
protest against
wedding dress
manufacturer
Alfred Angelo
at a rally in
Philadelphia.[68]
Photos courtesy of
UNITE

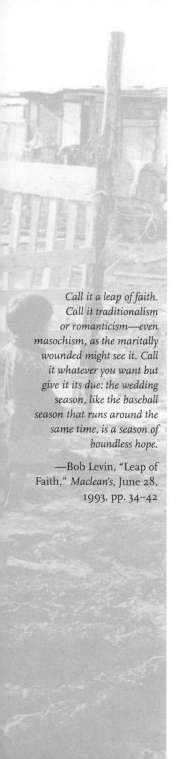

Call it a leap of faith. Call it traditionalism or romanticism—even masochism, as the maritally wounded might see it. Call it whatever you want but give it its due: the wedding season, like the baseball season that runs around the same time, is a season of boundless hope.

—Bob Levin, "Leap of Faith," *Maclean's*, June 28, 1993, pp. 34–42

the National Labor Committee, the New York State Labor/Religion Coalition, and Global Exchange[69] as well as several media outlets including *Dateline NBC, 20/20,* and *60 Minutes* have made it their mission to expose and confront the massive abuses companies have committed in the textile industry. For example, these organizations have made it well known that Mexican and Asian workers are frequently young, female, live in cramped dormitory settings, experience significant levels of sexual abuse, and are paid extremely low wages under very poor working conditions. Yet, despite dramatic efforts to raise public awareness regarding these practices, the current Bush administration has abandoned any effort to address sweatshop conditions, human rights and environmental abuses under a host of free trade agreements. Emblematic of their position (or lack thereof) was the high-profile Abramoff lobbying and political finance scandal that emerged during the Bush years. Federal investigations into Abramoff's dealings revealed that he had traded favors with Republican Congressman Tom DeLay, a leading representative of the Bush administration, to stop legislation banning sex shops and sweatshops that forced employees to have abortions in the U.S. Commonwealth of the Northern Mariana Islands.

While most free trade debates and protests have occurred in the West, the most powerful player to emerge in the globalization of the textile industry is China. The Chinese government has declared textiles and apparel to be a major industrial sector in their economy. As such, they have spent tens of billions of dollars to create a highly competitive textile industry that has become the leading player in this drama. They have provided loan forgiveness to businesses, subsidized utility, land, and shipping costs, export tax rebates, and created some of the lowest wages for textile workers anywhere in the world. These practices have created highly competitive incentives and low costs for the textile and apparel industry, luring the vast majority of wedding gown designers to produce their products in China. Additionally, the Chinese government has established a significant block to any outside scrutiny or standards of accountability on the level of human rights and labor practices, making doing business with the Chinese even more attractive to companies that desire low costs and less public accountability. The Chinese have under-priced their textile production and have outpaced countries such as Bangladesh and India which have lower wage rates. According to the United Nations, China exports apparel at prices 58 percent lower than other countries. Currently, China controls between 60 and 85 percent of the global apparel market and with it the vast majority of wedding apparel production.[70]

Wedding Gifts

More than $18 billion a year is spent on gifts for the bride and groom.[71] Advice abounds in the wedding literature on how much to spend, where to buy, and, most importantly, what to buy for newlyweds. One recent article in *Ladies' Home Journal* advised wedding-goers that "the price of the gift should at least cover the cost of your place at the reception and should reflect your relationship with the couple."[72]

Bridal magazines feature an enormous range of possibilities for newlyweds to consider. Bridal registries in most businesses from china to hardware are now available, so the bride and groom can accumulate a variety of goods for their life together. Department stores are devoting extra time to their registry services in the knowledge that bridal registry purchases can account for 50 percent of sales. In fact, registries have become so successful that some retailers are calling them "gift" registries instead of "bridal" ones, thereby capitalizing on the nonwedding market as well. Crate and Barrel, which sells everything from bathmats to sofas, shifted from the name "bridal" to "gift" to make themselves more accessible to a broader range of consumers. "We now list people as registrant and co-registrant instead of bride and groom, which makes everyone comfortable, including gay couples."[73]

Most retailers acknowledge that the bridal industry is a growing business for them. Not only are the number of weddings considerable, but the persistent trend is toward large up-scale weddings. The average wedding now includes about 184 people.[74] To meet the needs of this growing market, retailers are now increasing staff to service guests who need assistance in choosing the right wedding gift. As a result they are noticing greater returns on their investment. With the age of the couple increasing, buying power also increases, as does the range of gift possibilities. The effect is that stores are expanding their registry listings to accommodate the couple's every whim (though of all the gifts couples are interested in, studies have shown the number one preference for 88 percent of those surveyed is cash).[75]

Reviewing the articles and magazines by, for, and about the wedding industry, it becomes evident that the level of expenditure expected of newlyweds and wedding-

It was the handfasting, not the marriage ceremony, which produced the exchange of vows which are now part of the Anglican wedding service. And, it was the handfasting which produced the word "wed." This originally meant the pledge, the sum of money handed over to the girl's father. Later it also came to mean the ring which was given at the same time, and which was worn on the bride-to-be's right hand until the marriage. During the wedding ceremony, the groom transferred the "wed" to the bride's left hand, holding it in turn over the tips of the thumb and the first two fingers and saying "in the name of the Father," for the thumb; "in the name of the Son" for the index finger; "in the name of the Holy Ghost," for the middle finger; and, finally, "Amen," as he slipped it into place on the third finger. [H]aving been handed one of the bride's slippers by her father (to signify the transfer of authority), he bopped the bride smartly on the head with it (to signify that he was now her master). The weapon was later placed over the bed—on the husband's side.

—Monsarrat 1973

goers is primarily in the interest of creating a spectacle of luxury and status. In these periodicals, two themes resonate throughout but particularly in relation to gift purchases: that marriage increases the potential for consumption and accumulation.

In a recent article, "Wedlock Has Its Benefits" by Larry Strauss, the author advises Generation Xers of the many pluses of getting married: no more singles bars, no more "weird dates from hell," and someone to love you even when you're fat, ugly, and poorly behaved. But, Strauss says:

> [W]ho can forget quite possibly the coolest part: getting of gifts . . . proper planning on your part and a little creativity, your list-making can go a long way to aid wedded bliss . . . [T]oday's young people generally wait much longer than their parents did to get married. Hence they've accumulated a lot of stuff . . . [I]t pays to make your unique needs known to potential gift-givers . . . In noting gifts you'd like, be sure to consider your hobbies and lifestyle . . . [Y]ou have to be mindful of two basic tenets of tactful gift-requesting . . . varying price ranges to suit all budgets . . . [and] don't forget those thank-you cards.[76]

What stands out in this piece is the emphasis on attaining goods from wedding-goers. For this author, anyway, the message is get somebody to marry you and you can be badly behaved and get what really counts: gifts! This advice is very conscious of the changing demographics and the benefits of getting married later—you can be more precise in what gifts you want, what interests these gifts will serve, and how to make sure gift-givers know what to buy.

Diamond Wedding Jewelry

As part of the fantasy of the ever-romantic marriage proposal, the diamond ring takes center stage. In fact, for 83 percent of all U.S. brides the first purchase for the impending wedding is the diamond engagement ring.[77] Long considered a pre-wedding tradition, the diamond engagement ring is nothing of the sort. The pervasiveness of its use in engagement and wedding rituals is largely the result of a very effective marketing campaign launched in the early twentieth century when Sir

Diamond Miners: 23 May 2007, Koidu, Sierra Leone
Image by © Tugela Ridley/epa/Corbis

Ernest Oppenheimer of the De Beers Corporation hired the New York advertising agency N.W. Ayer & Son to create a desire for engagement rings.[78] Using the assumption that men would be the breadwinners, the agency designed a variety of campaigns to get men to equate diamonds with love and eternity. Considered one of the most successful ad campaigns of all time, Frances Gerety of N.W. Ayer created the slogan "a diamond is forever," in 1946. Once you accept this slogan, you also believe that you're making a life-long investment, not just purchasing a bauble for your bride! In fact, De Beers spends about $200 million each year on this advertising campaign and has "committed to spending a large part of [their] budget . . . on the promotion of diamond jewelry around the world."[79] To this day, this slogan has achieved the level of the taken-for-granted and has become synonymous with De Beers Corporation.[80]

De Beers and its advertisers have also developed a "shadow" campaign to sell to consumers the advice that the "appropriate" diamond engagement ring should cost at least "two months' salary" for the groom.[81] They have also adjusted this figure to address economic differences in other parts of the world. For example, European men only need one month's salary while Japanese men should commit three.[82] This advertising strategy signals to newlyweds—grooms in particular—that anything less is not acceptable. The diamond industry has effectively convinced us that purchasing a diamond engagement ring is no longer a luxury but a necessity. Not surprisingly, according to wedding industry estimates, this message is reaching its target. The average expenditure for engagement rings has risen 39 percent since 1999 to $4,146.[83] This figure translates into an annual salary of approximately $26,000 per year in the U.S, the income bracket many of these ads target.

Diamonds, from the Greek *adamas*, for unconquerable, were discovered more than two thousand years ago in India and are believed to be the most enduring and hardest natural substance known to humankind. While their pyramid-like shapes and durability have evoked much mystery, it is the labor and the technology required in the mining and processing as well as the supply controls applied by De Beers that have had the most effect on the cost of these gems. According to the diamond industry, the mining of 250 tons of earth is required to produce a one-carat polished diamond. From mining and processing to cutting and sales, a diamond touches at least five continents and involves the skills of many laborers before it is worn by the bride-to-be (Figure 2.3).

What are conflict diamonds?

Conflict diamonds are diamonds illegally traded to fund conflict in war-torn areas, particularly in central and western Africa. The United Nations (UN) defines conflict diamonds as ". . . diamonds that originate from areas controlled by forces or factions opposed to legitimate and internationally recognized governments, and are used to fund military action in opposition to those governments, or in contravention of the decisions of the Security Council." These diamonds are sometimes referred to as "blood diamonds."

While diamonds have been used to fund conflict, the problem is not the diamonds themselves but the rebels who exploit diamonds (along with other natural resources) to achieve their illicit goals. The vast majority of diamonds come from countries at peace. These countries have been able to invest the revenue from diamonds into the development of infrastructure, schools and hospitals for the good of the communities in which diamonds are found. These countries include Australia, Botswana, Canada, Namibia, Russia, South Africa and Tanzania.

Today, more than 99% of the world's diamonds are now from conflict-free sources and are officially traded under the UN mandated Kimberley Process.

—http://www.debeersgroup.com

By the fifteenth century, diamond rings were a routine feature of the weddings of kings, queens, and other royalty. The presumed rarity of these gems and the changes in cutting techniques—from styles that absorbed light to patterns that reflected light—made diamonds more beautiful, mysterious, highly prized, and available only to the elite classes. Of course, there is nothing rare at all about diamonds. They exist all over the globe and are quite plentiful. What makes them appear rare is the industry itself. Since its inception, De Beers has controlled the availability of diamonds as a strategy to create the illusion that diamonds are difficult to obtain and are exceedingly rare. With the creation of this myth, De Beers has achieved great success in manipulating and preserving supply and demand levels that have served them well even during challenging times, e.g., world wars, economic hard times.

The discovery of diamonds in Brazil in the eighteenth century increased their availability and appeal. In 1870, supply met with demand when great quantities of diamonds were discovered in Africa. With increased availability the prices of

"Centuries ago, grooms presented rings as partial payment for the bride."

—Lee 1994, p. 35

The changing face of De Beers

In 2005, De Beers announced a groundbreaking Black Economic Empowerment deal with Ponahalo Investment which saw the sale of 26% of the equity of De Beers Consolidated Mines (DBCM) to Ponahalo. The shareholders in Ponahalo represent the broadest possible cross-section of South African society. This sale is heralded to be a clear demonstration of De Beers becoming a company that truly reflects the non-racial ideals of the government and citizens of South Africa.

—http://www. debeersgroup.com

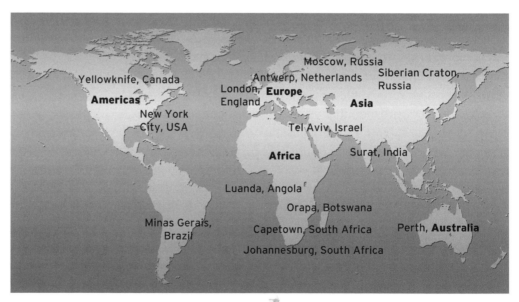

Figure 2.3 Global diamond mining and production
Source: Data from Hart 2002

diamonds declined and the diamond engagement ring became more accessible to the lower classes. What Queen Victoria did for the white wedding gown, she also did for diamonds. Throughout the nineteenth century, she purchased an enormous collection of diamonds of all sizes and values, making them the gem of choice among the royalty-following masses. Her engagement ring was a "snake ring" with diamonds in the eyes of the snake.

Following the great success of the De Beers "forever" campaign, Hollywood became enamored with diamonds and played a key role in popularizing them. By the mid-twentieth century, messages about diamond rings were popularized. Perhaps the most memorable instance of Hollywood's romance with diamonds is the film *Gentlemen Prefer Blondes* where this infamous phrase emerged: "Men grow cold as girls grow old, and we all lose our charms in the end ... But square-cut or pear-shape, these rocks don't lose their shape; diamonds are a girl's best friend."[84] This famous passage helped to make the diamond engagement ring the ultimate symbol of lasting heterosexual love. Even when we are too old to be passionate or beautiful, the diamond will still radiate. This gem will serve as a beacon of light, ever reminding the romantic of what was once bright and beautiful. Today, it is common to see celebrities with hundreds of thousands of dollars worth of diamonds at events such as the Academy Awards and the Golden Globes. Popular films still make great use of diamonds and further the public's fascination as well as equating diamonds with celebrity. In everything from *To Catch a Thief,* a famous Hitchcock thriller that features extravagant diamonds and a sexy diamond thief (Cary Grant), to *Schindler's List* where diamonds are used to save a Jew from the Nazis and certain death, diamonds have become regular features in Hollywood fare. In 2006, Leonardo DiCaprio starred in a widely popular exposé of the diamond industry, *Blood Diamond,* that dramatically illustrates the treachery involved in the diamond industry and in the destruction of African cultures and peoples in the interest of greed and power.

In addition to the purchase of an engagement ring, newlyweds have also been convinced they *must* buy wedding rings—at an average cost of $1612, a 39 percent increase since 1999.[85] Nearly 100 percent of brides receive a wedding band. Grooms, on the other hand, have not historically been required to wear a ring. The "betrothal ring" traditionally signified the pledge that the marriage contract guaranteeing the

KOIDU TOWN, Sierra Leone, Feb 28 (IPS) – "I cannot believe that in this day and age, so many children could be forced to slave away in the mines earning next to nothing; this is appalling," says UN Under-Secretary-General for Children and Armed Conflict, Olara Otunnu, who is visiting the war-scarred West African country.

"I was horrified by what I saw at the minefields," Otunnu told IPS this week.

Thousands of children, aged between seven and 16, are being engaged in the minefields of Koidu Town, the capital of the eastern diamond-rich district of Kono in what is clearly child labour in the post-war era.

—Lansana Fofana, Inter Press News Service Agency, http://www. ipsnews.net/africa/interna. asp?idnews=16367, 2003

In this world of rapid change and intense competition, the Department of Trade and Industry (DTI) plays a vital role, creating the conditions for business success; and helping the UK respond to the challenge of globalisation.

—DTI, 2006

transfer of a woman as property from the father to the groom would be honored. This ancient Roman tradition was adopted by the Christians early in the first century and became an integral part of the church ceremony. Currently, the trend in the U.S. is toward the groom also wearing a wedding band, usually made of gold. Today, 90 percent of grooms receive a wedding ring, and 20 percent wear a diamond wedding band.[86]

Of course, none of these rings are necessary or mandatory, but patriarchal history and the work of advertisers and other members of the wedding-industrial complex have been so effective in conveying their message that most newlyweds follow the norm. "May I have the rings please?" is a phrase most believe carries the authority of the church or synagogue and is integral to the wedding ceremony, making noncompliance unthinkable.

Lynn Ramsey, president of the Jewelry Information Center in Manhattan, a nonprofit association representing the fine jewelry industry, offers this rationale for purchasing expensive wedding jewelry:

> When you think about what [a diamond] represents—a union between two people that could last a lifetime—then it isn't very much money. And you can pass the ring on to your children. But you have to think about it differently than a car or fur coat, because [each] diamond is unique.[87]

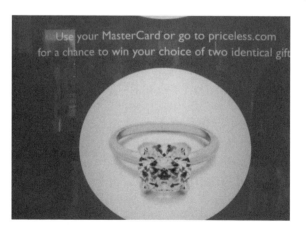

The bride also wears jewelry, and the bride and groom frequently give gifts of jewelry to the wedding party. Sold as markers of "one of life's most important rites of passage," infamous and upscale establishments such as Tiffany & Co. and Fortunoff set the standard for suitable and even "affordable" gifts. Typical choices are sterling silver cufflinks or money clips for the ushers and pearl earrings or silver or crystal necklaces and pendants for the bridesmaids. The total average expenditure per wedding on jewelry in the United States is nearly $5,000.

De Beers Diamond Minning International and De Beers Group

Hidden behind the romance with diamond rings and wedding jewelry is an industry with a history steeped in intrigue, treachery, terrorism, and vast wealth. Everyone from global capitalists to governments to political operatives to geologists to advertising agencies to jewelry stores is included. The mining, manufacturing, and marketing of diamonds have involved colonial wars, apartheid, child soldiers, racist violence, massive labor abuses, dismemberment, struggles between superpowers, the stability of nations, al-Qaeda, Hezbollah, slavery, and the hiring of mercenary armies. This section offers a historical sketch of the leading players and interests and will provide a case study of one of the largest and most powerful diamond cartels: De Beers Diamond Mining International, based in Johannesburg, South Africa.

"Diamonds are forever" the De Beers ad claims, or at least De Beers hopes so. And they're not talking about Ian Fleming's James Bond novel *Diamonds are Forever* (1956), which Fleming based on the real De Beers story.[88] Founded by Cecil Rhodes during the British colonial era in southern Africa in 1888, the modern De Beers organization was created and overseen by Sir Ernest Oppenheimer. His son, South African Harry Oppenheimer, as chairman of De Beers, went to great lengths in the 1950s to secure control of African diamond reserves,

by enlisting Sir Percy Sillitoe, one of Britain's top counterespionage agents during World War II ... Sillitoe orchestrated an intelligence

network of local informants along the smuggling trail, hired an army of mercenaries, and launched an all-out diamond war. The mercenaries laid booby traps, mined the border crossings, and ambushed the smugglers—predominantly Mandingo tribesmen and Lebanese—until they were persuaded to sell their wares to the De Beers buyers.[89]

Since that time, De Beers Consolidated Mines Limited has grown and diversified to become what has often been referred to as the Oppenheimer empire.[90] Headed today by Nicky Oppenheimer, the De Beers Group is a privately owned company with three shareholders: Anglo American owns 45 percent; Central Holdings Group owns 40 percent; and the Government of Botswana owns 15 percent. In 2005, the De Beers Group generated $6.5 billion in revenue and $554 million in net earnings.

De Beers and its partner companies "employ more than 21,000 people in 25 countries on five continents."[91] With interests in 15 African diamond mines in South Africa, Botswana, Namibia, and Tanzania, mines and production facilities in Russia, Australia, India, and South America, and new mines in Canada, its Central Selling Organisation unit (CSO)—the "diamond cartel"—controls 80 percent of the world's rough diamond production. In addition to its current holdings, De Beers's technical resources are directed toward the "discovery of world-class deposits and the investigation of known deposits in Africa, Canada, Brazil, Europe, Australia, and Asia."

In Angola, where De Beers has been working to extract quantities of diamonds for many years, civil wars and unrest have thwarted their efforts. In 2005, however, De Beers finally received approval from the Angolan Council of Ministers to enter into a Joint Venture Contract to exercise mineral rights for prospecting, evaluation, and research. In the troubled Democratic Republic of Congo, De Beers was charged by the United Nations Expert Panel on the Illegal Exploitation of Natural Resources and Other Forms of Wealth (the UN Expert Panel) as having breached their own DTC Diamond Best Practices policy and were named as having breached the Organisation for Economic Co-operation and Development (OECD) Guidelines for multinational corporations.[92]

De Beers's prime competitors include Russian, Angolan, Australian, and Canadian diamond producers. In 1997, De Beers brokered a deal with Almazy Rossii Sakha (ARS) of Russia to buy $550 million worth of uncut diamonds annually. This didn't happen without a significant struggle, however. With the bulk of Russian diamonds under the control of the republic of Yakutia, a struggle ensued involving ARS, Moscow, and Yakutia to release nearly $300 million in diamonds to De Beers.

De Beers's top two sales markets are the United States and Japan, with the United States accounting for one-third of all sales. De Beers is currently actively pursuing markets in the Asia Pacific region and in Turkey, the Middle East, Pakistan, and India (which now accounts for 10 percent of world diamond demand). De Beers's chairman reports that marketing programs targeted at China, believed to have enormous potential, are currently achieving positive results.[93]

While De Beers maintains offices and associates in many countries—in much of Africa and in Switzerland (the corporate headquarters of De Beers Centenary, which controls the company's non-South African assets), the United Kingdom, Belgium, China, Israel, India, Russia, Canada, Ireland, Japan, Sweden, and Hong Kong—De Beers's roots remain in South Africa, where its past is intricately bound up with that country's history, including its colonial and white supremacist history with apartheid. In reality, De Beers owes much of its wealth and success to the black South Africans who worked and slaved under apartheid in South African mines.

In Sierra Leone, in Africa, where civil wars and mercenary armies have been funded by the government to provide access to diamond mining by multinational corporations, the people don't think of diamonds as symbols of love, romance, and commitment. As one reporter put it:

> The diamond in Kono has always wielded greater authority than the
> local paramount chief or the state president or the foreign investors.
> Some people said that the diamond is alive, that it has a fire you can
> feel. Others said it is the fire of the devil.[94]

Diamond producer,
Amsterdam, the
Netherlands

Workers for one of the smaller mining companies earn

> [between] one and five dollars per day, plus some rice ... After all that
> labor, though, no ancient city would be discovered and no buildings would be
> erected; instead, hundreds of thousands of couples around the world would
> consecrate their engagements with the little stone ferreted out of the mud.[95]

Wedding Consulting

The older, two-income newlywed market has given rise to a growing occupation: wedding consulting. "Women with careers want elaborate weddings—and can afford them—but don't have the time to invest in planning them."[96] This means that activities formerly undertaken within the family are becoming commodified in a way that redefines social relations and the heterogendered division of labor as business transactions.

Disney's secondary
wedding market
products

"There was a Disney
wedding during our stay,
actually, to which we were
invited—via telecast. The
groom, who had proposed
here the previous year,
gave the bride a gilt-edged
Disney Cinderella book and
a shopping trip to Treasure
Island."

—Rapping, 1995

You may remember the character Franck, played by Martin Short in *Father of the Bride*. He was a caricature of an affected, upscale wedding consultant. This movie, a Touchstone production owned by Disney, was so successful that Disney modeled their wedding consulting business on it. The Walt Disney Corporation, the third largest media conglomerate in the world,[97] has become a central player in the wedding-industrial complex (Table 2.5). On one level Disney's contribution to the wedding market has been historically substantial with the production of children's animated films, many of which end with weddings, happily ever afters, and romantic promises. Starting in 1997, Disney decided to take things a step farther; they have ten wedding consultants on staff at their new Fairy Tale Wedding Pavilion in Disneyland and Disney World—already the honeymoon capital of the United States— which marries 2,300 couples per year, and employ twelve full-time and four part-time photographers. The average price for a one hundred guest wedding is $20,000.[98] The "Ultimate Fairy Tale Wedding" costs $100,000 and allows couples to reserve

Table 2.5 The Walt
Disney Company
Holdings (2007)
Source: http://corporate.
disney.go.com/corporate/
overview.html

Four major business segments
1. Studio Entertainment
2. Parks and Resorts
3. Consumer Products
4. Media Networks

Studio Entertainment
Walt Disney Pictures
Walt Disney Feature
   Animation
DisneyToon Studios
Touchstone Pictures
Hollywood Pictures
Miramax Films
Buena Vista International
Buena Vista Home
   Entertainment
Buena Vista Theatrical Productions
   (one of the largest producers of
   Broadway musicals)
Buena Vista Music Group
Walt Disney Records
Buena Vista Records
Hollywood Records
Lyric Street Records
Pixar

Disney Parks and Resorts
Disneyland Resort
Walt Disney World Resort
Tokyo Disney Resort
Disneyland Resort Paris
Hong Kong Disneyland
Disney Cruise Line
Disney Vacation Club
Adventures by Disney

Disney Consumer Products
Disney Hardlines
Disney Softlines
Disney Toys
Disney Publishing
Hyperion Books for
   Children
Disney Press
Disney Editions
Disney Adventures
Buena Vista Games
The Baby Einstein Company
Disney Stores worldwide
Disney Direct Marketing
DisneyStore.com
Disney Catalog

Disney Media Networks	Disney Channel
ABC Television Network	ABC Family
ABC Entertainment	Toon Disney
ABC Daytime	SOAPnet
ABC News	Walt Disney Television
ABC Kids	Animation
Touchstone Television	Fox Kids International
ABC-Owned Television Stations	Lifetime Entertainment Services
(10 stations in major cities in	A&E Television Networks
U.S.)	E! Networks
ABC Radio (72 stations in U.S.)	Disney Mobile
Radio Disney	Walt Disney Internet Group
ESPN Radio	Buena Vista Television
ABC News Radio	Buena Vista International
ESPN	Televisión

the Magic Kingdom for the "big event." The bride rides down Main Street in a glass carriage drawn by six white horses and is greeted by uniformed trumpeters and her "prince," who rides to the wedding on a white stallion.[99]

The wedding industry reports that wedding consulting or wedding planning has become one of the hottest segments of the industry. Independent consultants can go into business with as little as $3,000 though most report they need a minimum of $10,000.[100] With some research, promotional materials, and a link to the Association of Bridal Consultants (ABC), the National Bridal Service (NBS), or the Association of Certified Professional Wedding Consultants (ACPWC) which provide training, almost anyone can enter this field. ABC currently claims over one thousand members in 48 states and ten foreign countries and charges $200 for membership; NBS boasts eight hundred members, with a membership fee of $300; and ACPWC offers certification through its schools in Florida, Texas, and California for an entry fee of $200. Most bridal consultants or wedding planners charge from $25 an hour to 15 percent of the total bridal package, earning anywhere from $10,000 to $50,000 per year and more.[101]

In an article in *Black Enterprise* entitled "Here Comes the Money," the author presents a picture of wedding consulting as a growth industry. Targeted to the African-American entrepreneur, the article lays out the possibilities for catering to the African-American wedding market. "Wedding planners charge 15 percent of the total wedding costs, raking in, on average, $20,000 to $50,000 a year."[102] Typically in the wedding industry literature, articles targeting a black audience see the black marriage market as untapped and lucrative.

Prior to her trouble with an alleged insider trading violation and her ultimate conviction on obstruction of justice charges, Martha Stewart was considered the top wedding consultant in the U.S. She had teamed up—tied the knot—with Macy's to offer wedding-planning seminars at Macy's stores across the nation where the top lure for brides was the chance to win a personal consultation with Stewart herself.[103] Today, her *Keepsake Wedding Planner* is still placed among the top selling wedding planning books in the country and *Martha Stewart Weddings* magazine won the 2005 National Magazine Award for General Excellence (the Ellie).

Stewart shares her wedding planning fame with another famous wedding consultant, Colin Cowie, whose primary clientele are movie stars and Oprah. Referred to as "Hollywood's premiere wedding designer," Cowie charges a minimum of $12,000; his fees have often exceeded $250,000 and have on occasion reached a million. When Cowie was asked by *People* what advice he could give to the "average" bride, he responded: "Style is not related to money . . . I've spent a million dollars in an afternoon, but I've been just as happy spending a fraction of that."[104]

Destination Weddings and Honeymoons

One of the hottest new trends in weddings is that of the destination wedding— or the "weddingmoon," as Sandals Resorts calls them. Rather than invite two hundred and fifty guests to a reception that costs an average of nearly $14,000 combined with the average cost of a honeymoon at nearly $10,000, newlyweds are opting for weddings in "exotic" faraway places with a small group of family and friends. Surprisingly, the cost of the average destination wedding is about $25,800, nearly $3000 less than the average domestic wedding. Last year alone, Sandals hosted 12,000 weddingmoons at its properties throughout the Caribbean, a 10 percent increase over the previous two years.

Some couples opt for a destination wedding to avoid the emotional entanglements weddings frequently provoke with family members when they struggle over guest lists. "Listen," confides one wedding planner, "there are people who will pay anything to just get away from the politics of that."[105] Fairchild Publishing's bridal group estimates that 16 percent of couples had destination weddings in 2005, a 400 percent increase over the previous ten years. Tom Curtin, publisher of *Bridal Guide Magazine*, refers to the increase in destination weddings as "an absolute boom." "*The Wall Street Journal* ran a piece on a woman who rented a used wedding dress, but was willing to spend $65,000 on a destination wedding in the Bahamas with 250 guests. The popularity is enormous."[106]

The entire wedding party, including guests, celebrates the occasion with the newlyweds and then either stays with them for an extended vacation or leaves following the wedding, allowing the couple to have a honeymoon. The market for destination weddings doubled between 1991 and 1995 and reached a total of 200,000 in 2005.[107] While the market dictated this trend to some degree, the travel industry also played a key role, marketing destination weddings as a way to capitalize on the "recession-proof" wedding industry. The most popular locations are the Caribbean, Hawaii, and Mexico—which, coincidentally, also have the least complicated legal marriage requirements. This trend is a big business for airlines and destination hotspots, as well as wedding planners. With the growth of this trend, travel agents now refer to themselves as "wedding travel specialists."[108]

Another form of destination wedding is the currently popular post-*Titanic* cruise business, with businesses such as Carnival Cruise Lines staging more than two thousand weddings in 2006[109] and Disney Cruise Lines hosting another 2300 couples in 2006. In addition to their on-board cruise weddings, a wedding at one of Disney's theme parks also counts as a destination wedding.

Bride's magazine reports that 99 percent of its readers take a honeymoon trip. The average amount spent on foreign trips is $4,048 and on domestic trips, $3,266. Newlyweds generally stay about eight days and also pay for most of the expense themselves. *Bride's* readers tend to be white and more affluent than the average newlywed.

Brochure handed out at New York Bridal Expo—3/97

"You can run but you can't hide from the time of your life! Survival New York & Paintball Long Island Bachelor Parties. Come experience the thrill of helicopter assaults and the tank charges."

"We think wedding consultants should be right up there with doctors and lawyers. After all, they're organizing what is probably the most emotional day of your life."

—Houston wedding consultant

Generally, islands are "in" for honeymoons. Popular sites in order of popularity are the Caribbean, Hawaii, Florida, and Mexico, followed by domestic trips. Maui, Hawaii, for example, reports that it now maintains a multi-million-a-year wedding industry which creates hundreds of small and big business jobs on the island.[110] The Hawaii Visitors and Convention Bureau reported a record 19,340 weddings booked from North America through July, 2006, up 21.5 percent over 2005. The price tag for Hawaiian weddings runs from $2,500 to $20,000.

Hotels in the islands are also thriving as a growing proportion of visitors have their weddings and honeymoons at this destination. They provide flowers, video, and catering, maximizing their profits. Supplementing this successful business is the independent coordinator or wedding consultant. Since these weddings take place far from the couple's home, the services of a consultant are even more important. Couples come to Maui not only from the United States but also in large numbers from Japan, Europe, New Zealand, and Australia. Even the Hyatt Regency on Maui has just put in a wedding chapel.[111]

Sandals Group Resorts

One award-winning resort that has been enormously successful in attracting newlyweds to the Caribbean is Sandals. Marketing themselves as "luxury resorts for [heterosexual] couples only," Sandals has 16 all-inclusive resorts in Jamaica, Antigua, St. Lucia, and the Bahamas. The chairman of Sandals Group, Adam Stewart, recently received an award for "Best All-Inclusive and Best in the Caribbean" at the *Travel Weekly* Readers' Choice Awards. In accepting the award, Stewart attributed the success of Sandals to the teamwork and dedication of their four thousand employees and said that "during the recent recession, Sandals refurbished and improved its hotels."[112] The result has been a doubling of their matrimonial business. According to a Sandals wedding coordinator, Sandals's staff handled 12,000 weddings in 2006.[113]

Characterized by fluorescent orange and pink colors with splashes of yellow, purple, and brilliant green, Sandals's advertising stands out in most publications. The ads are very effective attention-getters and show collages of couples throughout. Most bridal magazines carry them, as do other magazines. Enter a travel agency or attend a bridal show and you'll find their advertising booklets prominently displayed. What also stands out in their publications is the prevalence of white couples. In one 112-page booklet describing their "ultra-all-inclusive [meaning all services included] luxury resorts for couples only," they show photographs of approximately 708 heterosexual couples; 694 are white (98 percent). Put another way, at these resort hotels for couples-only, only 14 of the couples were people of color paired with other people of color, usually of the same ethnicity. There were no interracial couples pictured.

All the servants, however—whether they are bartenders, waiters/waitresses, masseuses, drivers, hotel clerks, facial experts, or boat operators—are people of color. The extremely obvious message conveyed in these marketing campaigns is that Sandals Resorts are for white couples who can luxuriate in the Caribbean Ocean while being served by local people of color. One can only wonder what the earnings are of the workers at these resorts for which Mr. Stewart received such acclaim and what the difference is between his earnings and those of the workers who made it possible for Sandals to gain such acclaim.

In *A Small Place*, a scathing critique of the tourism industry in the Caribbean, noted author Jamaica Kincaid writes:

> [Y]ou stay in this place (Antigua) where the sun always shines and where the climate is deliciously hot and dry for the four to ten days you are going to be staying there; and since you are on your holiday, since you are a tourist, the thought of what it might be like for someone who had to live day in, day out in a place that suffers constantly from drought, and so has to watch carefully every drop of fresh water used (while at the same time surrounded by a sea and an ocean) . . . must never cross your mind.[114]

What also may never cross your mind is that these resorts are built on islands that once were centers for the slave trade, which in an earlier era of globalization, other countries referred to as their colonies. Today, nonindigenous corporations engage in a "new colonialism," taking the place of nation-states in extracting enormous wealth and resources from poor countries where the majority live in poverty. For all the claims these corporations make about bringing prosperity to these nations, the reality is that most of the citizens in these countries do not experience any significant social or economic benefit. Sociologist Patricia Hill Collins in her important work, *Black Sexual Politics* (2004), argues that the new racism is framed by global capitalism:

> People of African descent are routinely disadvantaged in this global economy in which corporations make the decisions and in which "the company is free to move; but the consequences of the move are bound to stay."[115] Within a global context, Black people and other people of color are those more likely to lose jobs in local labor markets. They are the ones who lack control over oil, mineral wealth, or other natural resources on their land; who lose their land to global [business]; and who are denied basic services of electricity and clean water, let alone luxury goods.[116]

Hill Collins describes the new racism as comprised of "a set of ideas and social practices shaped by gender, race, and sexuality" as well as by global capitalism.[117] In elaborating the central features of the new racism, Hill Collins contends that heterosexism functions as a "system of oppression similar to racism, sexism, and class oppression" and "fosters Black subordination."[118]

Imbricated in the new colonialism, the new racism serves as its organizing ideology in a way that makes the social hierarchies embedded in travel and tourism practices seem only natural. Consider the story I was told at a lecture recently about a white couple on a romantic cruise to Jamaica. They became so incensed when they found out that Jamaica was full of black people that they demanded that the cruise line refund their money.

The workings of the travel industry help to secure the legitimacy of the new colonialism. Using sacred notions of love and romance alongside those of entitled leisure, tourism reproduces the ideological privileging of First World needs over those of Third World peoples by privileging newlyweds and romantic getaways over the needs of the less fortunate. Through these practices we naturalize a sense of entitlement for privileged and usually white populations and legitimize the belief that poor nations benefit from this new colonialism. Unfortunately, the race to the bottom—the quest for higher profits by locating cheaper wages, lower taxes, and weaker environmental and labor regulations—makes these countries and their people the playground for wealthy companies and nations. All in all, the heterosexual imaginary is deeply implicated in both the new colonialism and the new racism.

The Secondary Wedding Market

Recognizing the magnitude and promise of the transnational wedding industry, businesses interested in developing a future clientele also target newlyweds indirectly. As you will see in the following section, the secondary wedding market is, for the most part, sizable and undocumented and covers everything from "My Size Bride Barbie" to Home Depot to General Motors. Advertising using wedding images to target newlyweds is virtually everywhere.

The secondary wedding market is made up of companies using white weddings to sell products that are only *indirectly* related to them. For example, while Metropolitan Life uses white weddings in its ads, life insurance is not a direct wedding item but is something that a married couple might purchase years later, after acquiring some property or having children. Numerous companies use this strategy to secure future consumption. For example, Parke-Davis now sponsors booths at bridal expos marketing family planning and birth control to newlyweds. Even Viagra marketers are targeting newlyweds of all ages.

Case Study: Mattel and the Toy Industry

The marketing of wedding products does not begin with adult women. Toy manufacturers, for one, have seized on the current wedding market and the opportunity to develop future consumers by producing a whole variety of wedding toys featuring the "classic" white wedding and sold during Saturday-morning children's television shows.

"Fashion designer Vera Wang has taken her first steps down the catwalk of dolldom with a series of designer Barbies. Known in today's world of haute couture as the premier designer of bridal gowns, Wang has extended her creative talents to include the world's top fashion doll, dressing the honey-blond fashion maven in one of her signature gowns."

—Denise I. O'Neil, *Chicago Sun-Times*, June 12, 1998

Marketing the white wedding to girls

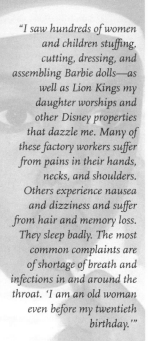

Toy companies, generally part of large conglomerates that also own related commodities such as travel or cosmetics, work to secure future markets for all their products through the selling of wedding toys. For example, Toy Biz, which was owned by the same company as Revlon, produced a product called the "Caboodles Wedding Playset" featuring not only a wedding but also "free" makeup for the future bride. And most recently, Mattel partnered their Barbie Doll with Bonne Bell Cosmetics to help regain market share from Bratz Dolls in the U.S.

Mattel, the world's largest toymaker and a major multinational corporation, has offices and facilities in 42 countries and sells products in one hundred and fifty nations. Their major toy brand, accounting for 80 percent of their profits and revenues of $3 billion per year, is the Barbie Doll—all one hundred and twenty different versions of her. They also own American Girl, TMX Elmo, Fisher-Price, Disney entertainment lines, Hot Wheels and Matchbox cars, Power Wheels, and Polly Pocket.[119] In addition to these lines, Mattel products include Sesame Street toys, a variety of Disney dolls and books, as well as other licensed items such as Harry Potter toys (Table 2.6). Mattel has also tapped into the

Table 2.6 Mattel's portfolio of
brands and products
Source: Mattel Annual Report
to Shareholders 2006.

Mattel Girls & Boys Brands—including Barbie® fashion dolls and accessories
("Barbie®"), Polly Pocket!™, Pixel Chix™, Winx Club™ and Disney Classics
(collectively "Other Girls Brands"), Hot Wheels®, Matchbox® and Tyco®
R/C vehicles and playsets (collectively "Wheels") and Batman™, CARS™,
Superman™, Radica:® products, and games and puzzles (collectively
"Entertainment").

Fisher-Price Brands—including Fisher-Price®, Little People®, BabyGear™ and
View-Master® (collectively "Core Fisher-Price®"), Sesame Street®, Dora the
Explorer™, Go-Diego-Go!™, Winnie the Pooh, InteracTV™ and See 'N Say®
(collectively "Fisher-Price® Friends") and Power Wheels®.

American Girl Brands—including Just Like You™, the historical collection and
Bitty Baby®. American Girl Brands products are sold directly to consumers
and its children's publications are also sold to certain retailers.

---

lucrative technology markets and has accessorized Barbie with a variety of pink
interactive games, software, a line of Barbie MP3 players, and a variety of interaction websites. The company even licensed the Barbie name for eyewear and
distributes nearly 45 percent of their products through Wal-Mart, Target, and
Toys Я Us.

Mattel's primary manufacturing facilities are located in low cost regions
such as China, Indonesia, Malaysia, Mexico, and Thailand where they employ
nearly 32,000 people, mostly very young women of color. Annually, Mattel
Corporation makes about 100 million Barbie Dolls and earns total revenues
of $5.8 billion for their El Segundo, California, company.[120] Their CEO,

Robert A. Eckert, age 53, earns \$3.6 million annually[121] (or 1115 times the U.S. minimum wage) and they spend approximately \$460 million per year on advertising. Compare this to the young Chinese female workers they employ, who live in dormitories, sometimes work with dangerous chemicals, work long hours, and earn \$1.81 a day.[122]

Mattel: Then and Now

The first edition of *White Weddings* reviewed media reports that Mattel was engaged in significant labor abuses in their Asian manufacturing facilities. In the late 1990s, a television broadcast featuring Stone Phillips of NBC exposed a disturbing story of a 15-year-old Asian girl who worked full-time making Barbie Dolls for Mattel. She was the sole support of her family who lived in a small dirt floor house in a desolate rural area. Asked if she would like to own one of these dolls, the young worker and her friends giggled softly and replied that at their wages they would have to save for a lifetime to be able to afford such a purchase. At the conclusion of the segment, Phillips filmed the young woman at the end of her work day, boarding a bicycle for her long ride home through farmland in the dark of night. This report was one of many that erupted in the mid-1990s. The first sweatshop scandal was precipitated by an action and exposé conducted by Charles Kernaghan of the National Labor Committee based in New York City. The NLC uncovered child labor and sweatshop conditions in the factory where Kathy Lee Gifford clothing was being produced. Kathy Lee of the then famous *Regis and Kathy Lee Show*, was a high-profile target in a campaign to end labor abuses in the textile industry. Following this episode, a host of media outlets including *Dateline NBC*, *The Nation*, and *U.S. News & World Report* all provided exposés on Asian sweatshops. "Mattel makes tens of millions of Barbies a year in China, where young female Chinese workers who have migrated thousands of miles from home are alleged to earn less than the minimum wage of \$1.99 a day."[123]

In one story about Indonesia where it was illegal to unionize and workers earned \$2.25 per day, one reporter wrote: "It would take such a worker about a month to earn enough to buy Mattel's cK Calvin Klein Barbie, and twenty-eight years to make the C.E.O.'s daily salary."[124] Another reporter quipped:

"Never married but always prepared, Barbie has about 30 bridal gowns in her closet, with new ones released each year."[125] Mattel's "My Size Bride Barbie" was a popular addition. This 3-ft-tall doll came dressed in a wedding gown that also fit young girls sizes 4–10. It retailed for $149 and featured a white, blond, blue-eyed, thin, and "pretty" Barbie doll with packaging that included a photo of a little girl who looked very much like Barbie.

In Mexico, efforts by Mattel's Mexican employees to unionize were met with extremely repressive actions:

> Upon entering the plant, Rodriguez says, her purse was searched and she was taken into a room by a security guard. She and two other workers say they were coercively interrogated, accused of passing out subversive materials, detained against their will until the next morning and prevented from going to the bathroom or making phone calls to their families. In the end . . . [they were told] they would have to quit their jobs or go to prison.[126]

While it is not illegal to organize in Mexico, the actions of company officials have a quieting effect on workers interested in protecting their rights.

Around the same time an article appeared in the *Wall Street Journal*, "Toy Business Focuses More on Marketing and Less on New Ideas,"[127] in which the author made reference to Mattel's revenues and profit margins:

> Mattel reaped $1.4 billion in sales last year from Barbie and her spinoffs, by far the biggest line in all of toy land. Gross profit margins on licensed figurines can run 50%, what with the modest cost of making them; most are produced abroad and don't require much investment in plant and equipment.

This article was only critical of Mattel's conservative approach to innovation. The bulk of Mattel's expenses, it was reported here, could be attributed to marketing, product development and design, but not to labor and production costs.

In 1988, Mattel "married" Disney. At that time, Mattel contracted to become Disney's lead toy licensee. Then again in 1996 Mattel and Disney created another alliance, a three-year licensing pact for Disney's television and film properties. This arrangement gave Mattel exclusive rights for the production of toys tied to Disney films. With Disney products viewed as highly profitable, competition by toy companies vying for such contracts was intense. Considering Disney's history in the production of "happily-ever-after" films where the heroine generally finds and marries her Prince Charming, the secondary wedding market became even stronger with this corporate "wedding."

Mattel has learned many lessons in the global economy and has engaged in a significant effort to rebuild its reputation. After all, how could a toy company that markets happy toys to children in one part of the world also be found abusing them in other parts of the world?! Today, Mattel boasts a Corporate Social Responsibility effort on its corporate website, complete with a slideshow on working conditions for their Asian employees. These photos, however, say nothing of the wages or ages of these workers or of the dormitory conditions within which they live or of the massive amount of outsourcing being utilized in the toy industry. Instead they show pristine factories with workers dressed in immaculate uniforms and safety gear. To demonstrate a commitment to socially responsible business practices, Mattel instituted an internal policy they dubbed the Global Manufacturing Principles (GMP), which they launched in November 1997. They consider these principles the cornerstone of the company's manufacturing practices around the world. Adherence to GMP seeks to ensure that wages, working and living conditions and employee access to management are just and fair, as well as to assure protection of the environment. The question becomes whether these principles function as a form of reputation management or a sincere attempt to insure that they engage in socially responsible business practices. Their website also mentions that they subscribe to GRI: Global Reporting Initiative. The GRI was formed by the Coalition for Environmentally Responsible Economies (CERES) and the Tellus Institute—both U.S. NGOs—with the support of the United Nations Environment Programme (UNEP) in 1997. This Initiative was created in response to pressures from the international corporate social responsibility movement to balance the fulfillment of human needs with the protection of the natural environment.

Subscription to the GRI by an organization or a company signals their awareness that corporate policies and practices must provide both human rights and environmental protections.

A recent article in the *New York Times* makes it clear that child slavery issues in China are far from resolved. Across the country schools and businesses are using work study laws to bypass any scrutiny with regard to child labor abuses:

> From the densely packed factory zones of Guangdong Province to the street markets, kitchens, and brothels of major cities, to the primitive factories of China's relatively poor western provinces, child labor is a fact of life, experts here say, and one that the government, preoccupied with economic growth, has traditionally turned a blind eye to . . . "In Dongguan, you can even see children of 12 and 15 working in toy factories."[128]

The reality is that multinational corporate policies are only as good as the context in which they are to be implemented. Doing "business" with China under these conditions requires more systemic changes on the part of the Chinese government and its local agents. Utilizing foreign labor as a way to reduce cost means multinational corporations are complicit in labor abuses when their policies aren't enforced by host governments. American companies are completely cognizant of labor and environmental standards that prevent them from carrying out practices that they can "get away with" in other countries. Their location in other countries indicates their willingness to turn a blind eye in the interest of lowering costs and increasing profits.

The so-called "Wal-Mart Effect"—where the race to the bottom[129] is legitimized in the name of lower prices—pressures companies to find the lowest production costs in order to yield the "lowest" retail cost to customers. The great myth in this taken-for-granted tale is that these savings are actually passed on to the consumer. In reality, a significant percentage of profit goes toward executive and shareholder compensation. Increasing wages, for example, would cut into some of the excessive executive compensation while working toward leveling the global labor field. But,

Mattel Inc. shareholders on Wednesday voted down a proposal to link top executives' pay to child labor practices at the toymaker's overseas manufacturing operations. "Our position was that not only do we have certainly the most aggressive monitor plan in the toy industry, but we are the first international consumer products company to introduce independent third-party monitoring on a worldwide basis. The initiative was essentially redundant."

—Associated Press 1998, p. B1

it would not have to increase cost to the consumer. This culture of consumerism relies on the belief that these practices are necessary for the American way of life to persist and that we are actually "helping" poorer countries. Whether it is textiles or chocolate or electronics, corporate and state abuses have shortened lifespans, increased environmental degradation, destroyed indigenous cultures, and lowered wages outside and inside the U.S. Think about it the next time you ask for a raise or you hear your job is being moved to another country. Do you really believe keeping jobs in the U.S. or paying a living wage will increase the price of goods and make them unaffordable to Americans? Is the cost of paying a living wage, employing adults for eight-hour days, preventing pollution or exposure to toxic chemicals really less expensive than buying Barbie cheaper at Wal-Mart?

Disney and the Secondary Wedding Market

One of the most dramatic examples in the wedding-industrial complex is the Walt Disney Co. Not only are they involved in the *primary* wedding market, but they are also central players in the *secondary* wedding market, serving a powerful role in securing future consumers by catering directly to both children and adults through film, television, theme parks, sports franchises, publishing companies, and new interactive media outlets. Disney is the world's second-largest media conglomerate, after Time Warner, with annual revenues exceeding $54 billion, 133,000 employees, 10 collective bargaining agreements, 32 unions, and holdings that are extremely diverse. For example, they own Walt Disney Pictures, Touchstone Pictures, Caravan Pictures, Miramax Films, Buena Vista Pictures Distribution, and Hollywood Pictures. They control the ABC Television Network, ABC Sports, a variety of television stations in major media markets, Walt Disney Television, Touchstone Television, and Buena Vista Television. Disney maintains ABC radio networks, which reach 100 million listeners each week, major market radio stations, the Disney Channel, ESPN and ESPN2, Lifetime, and the Arts and Entertainment Network. And for the adult media market Disney also owns some of the most popular primetime programs in television history: *Grey's Anatomy*, *Desperate Housewives*, and *Lost*. Because of the ratings these shows have achieved, Disney is now considered the number two broadcast television network (behind CBS). In addition to its primary network, ABC also owns 10 television stations, 225 affiliates and holds stakes in several cable channels through Disney ABC Cable. And if this weren't enough, they also own Disneyland, Disney World, the Epcot Center, Disney Stores, ABC Online, Disney Interactive, and a wide variety of magazines and newspapers, including *Women's Wear Daily* (see Table 2.5, pp. 88–89).

Founded in 1923 by Walter and Roy Disney, Walt Disney Productions established its fame with an animated film mouse called Mickey Mouse. With the enormous success of their animated short films, the Disney brothers went on to create Disneyland in 1955. Although the Disney Company stayed under family control for many years, in 1984, in the wake of a hostile corporate takeover, many modifications were made to the corporate structure. New goals were established for the company's future. It shifted its consumer focus, expanded and diversified into related fields, changed from Walt Disney Productions to Walt Disney Company, and hired CEO Michael Eisner. During his reign Eisner became one of the most powerful and controversial figures nationally with control of this media empire, stock options worth almost $200 million, and an annual salary of $750,000. Following a corporate *coup d'état* that purged Eisner, the Board appointed Robert A. Iger, former head of ABC, to be the current President and CEO of Disney Corporation. Eisner's severance package totaled $40 million and he retained his corporate governance rights.

Disney's long history with the secondary wedding market is wrapped up in its dominance of children's films, particularly animated films, for many decades. Famous examples include *Beauty and the Beast*, *The Little Mermaid*, *Snow White and the Seven Dwarfs*, and *Cinderella*. The vast majority of Disney children's films have "happily-ever-after" endings in which the (usually white) damsel-in-distress finds her handsome prince and, by the end of the film, weds. For many years, Disney films have been equated with the beautiful maiden finding her Prince Charming, marrying, and living happily ever after. As mentioned earlier, this is the foundation for Disney's success in the primary wedding market with their Fairy Tale Wedding business. Beyond their children's films, Disney has also produced *Father of the Bride* and *Muriel's Wedding*.

Tapping into the Wedding Industry to Sell Broadway Seats

New York – Producers behind "The Wedding Singer" are fueling ticket sales by tapping into the multibillion-dollar wedding industry. The musical has been negotiating advertising partnerships with big wedding Web sites like The Knot and such magazines as Modern Bride. Producers are talking with Kleinfeld, a giant New York bridal retailer, about sponsoring ticket packages and perhaps selling "Wedding Singer" branded gowns. And NBC's powerful "Today" show has agreed to play songs from the musical during its biweekly "Today Throws a Wedding" segments, which run through October.

—Barnes and Monica M. Clark, *Wall Street Journal*. (Eastern edition), New York: July 7, 2006, p. B.1

Not without controversy, Disney's role in the wedding industry is, at best, contradictory. On the one hand Disney has for decades cultivated a wedding market through their dominance in popular film. They've taken this market and turned it into a lucrative wedding and honeymoon business at Disney World and Disneyland. Their adult wedding films tend to be blockbusters, further securing their hold on the wedding industry, and their television shows on ABC are among those beginning or ending their seasons with a wedding. The Lifetime Channel, another one of their media holdings, regularly features both celebrity wedding and other reality wedding shows.

On the other hand, this same media conglomerate has been the target of numerous protests and boycotts on the part of the religious right. Because of their liberal domestic partners' policy, gay and lesbian employees are able to get a variety of benefits from the Disney Company. They also allowed the production of the first sitcom with an openly lesbian main character on a major network with the showing of *Ellen* on ABC.

But they've also been in trouble with the labor movement. In 1996, Charles Kernaghan and the National Labor Committee exposed Disney's use of sweatshops in Haiti and other parts of the world in the production of Disney products. With their alliance with Mattel, the reach of this production into other offshore locations where labor practices are less than desirable has put Disney's image of family fun and lovable cartoon characters into jeopardy. Today, evidence of extensive human rights and labor abuses in the toy industry continues to be well documented and a source of great concern with companies claiming sustainable development policies and hiding behind sub-contractors and governments to escape public scrutiny. The truth is, we have a long way to go before the feel-good fantasy provided by Mattel and Disney has any reality in the manufacturing of their products.

The Tertiary Wedding Market

The tertiary wedding market is made up of those companies that have little or no relationship to the wedding market or to newlyweds but make use of wedding imagery and the heterosexual imaginary to capture the imaginations of potential consumers. The romance, promise, and morality of white weddings

Social construction of whiteness in white wedding advertising

secure product consumption, especially by women who associate this image with something positive and trustworthy. White weddings appear in a vast array of advertising for products such as Buick, One-A-Day Vitamins, Pepto Bismol, Esteé Lauder perfume, Colgate-Palmolive products, General Electric, McDonald's, Tylenol, Bayer Aspirin, Pepsi, Ford, Chevrolet, Toyota, Verizon, and Midas Muffler, to name a few. The vast majority of television advertisers employ some form of wedding imagery at some point in their current displays.

There is no data available to measure the size and scope of the tertiary wedding market. Suffice it to say, it's worth millions, if not billions.

The State

The state plays a major role in affecting how we think about and engage in the practice of wedding. In regulating marriage materially via civil law, the state injects its presence into the wedding ceremony through licensing practices and fees, establishing who is legally "qualified" to officiate a wedding, and charges for blood tests and name changes. The state also protects its interests through miscegenation, domestic relations, and other laws regarding what constitutes legitimate marriage. For example, New York State domestic relations laws assert that a "legal" marriage can only occur between one man and one woman. But, it wasn't until 1972 that it was found necessary to include this clarification, leading us to question, after hundreds of years without this clause, what made this exclusion a necessity in 1972? Several explanations are plausible here. The lesbian and gay rights movement and the feminist movement were very active at this time, pressuring all sorts of laws for inclusive language. Foremost in these efforts was the push for an Equal Rights Amendment (ERA) to insert "women" into the language of the Constitution. The gendered division of labor was also being challenged at this historical moment *vis-à-vis* feminism, and the state asserted its interests by preserving marriage as a solely heterogendered institution.

With state domestic relations laws saying such things as "[the state considers] marriage the cornerstone of organized society" and "the state regards with a jealous eye any effort to interfere in this relation," it's no wonder similar ideas are often inscribed in the wedding ceremony and in the officiating comments of the clergy. As the point of entry to marriage, the wedding signals compliance with these regulating practices, consent to the heterogendered division of labor the traditional wedding enacts, and access to the many benefits and rewards of this institution. "Over a ten-year period, a [unmarried and partnered] worker earning $40,000 a year may earn as much as $55,800 less in benefits than a married co-worker."[130] Few newlyweds have read these laws or are aware that marriage, according to these statutes, is a relation among a man, a woman, and the state. It is well within the realm of state and federal

"The Romans had legal protections for their military soldiers who were in holy unions (same-sex marriages). In fact, Roman law had required the Jewish council, the Sanhedrin, to come up with its own law to punish Jews who stoned or defamed lesbian/gay couples of Roman citizenship."

—Rev. Timm Peterson, Ph.D. (Demian 1997)

legislators' influence, then, to engage in public debate about the morality (or politics) of marriage or the need for welfare mothers to marry. The effect of this engagement can best be seen in attempts by newlyweds to create rituals that signify their distance from lower-class practices. Regardless of their incomes, couples frequently purchase wedding services far in excess of their ability to pay. The law is a powerful vehicle to control challenges to patriarchal authority.

The state plays another significant role and one even less obvious than any previously mentioned. Through free trade agreements such as the North American Free Trade Agreement (NAFTA),[131] the state creates the conditions by which exploitative offshore labor practices are undertaken in the manufacture of products such as wedding gowns, gifts, and wedding toys. And the state features in the travel industry to the extent that it regulates tourism particularly in conjunction with transnational corporations and national security interests.

In 1997, the U.S. Congress voted overwhelmingly to pass the Defense of Marriage Act (DOMA) (see Appendix for full text), changing the role of the federal government in defining "marriage" as a "legal union between one man and one woman as husband and wife"—usually a right reserved for states—and prohibiting the legalization of same sex marriage for federal purposes and allowing states to ignore a same sex marriage from another state. "Although the marriage contract is governed by state law, the federal government uses marital status as the qualification for more than 1,096 federally registered rights and responsibilities."[132] With the passage of this law, the U.S. government essentially asserted that state and federal rights and responsibilities connected to legal marriage be denied anyone who is *not married*—singles, lesbians, gay men, cohabiting heterosexuals, siblings living together, etc. In preparation for passage of this bill, the U.S. Government Accounting Office (GAO) identified all federal laws in which marital status is a factor. They found thirteen categories: Social Security (which includes related programs, housing, and food stamps); veterans' benefits; taxation; civilian and military benefits; employment benefits; immigration and naturalization laws; Indians; trade, commerce, and intellectual property; financial disclosure and conflict of interest; crimes and family violence; loans, guarantees, and payments in agriculture; federal natural resources and related laws; and miscellaneous laws (see Appendix for listings).[133] In most cases,

"The freedom to marry has long been recognized as one of the vital personal rights essential to the orderly pursuit of happiness by free men."

—Chief Justice Earl Warren writing for the majority, Loving v. Virginia, 1967 these laws assume the presence of a marital relationship. To provide a sense for the extent to which these laws reward "legal" marriage, I've provided a few examples. Under the first category, Social Security law, benefits to domestic partners only continue if those partners are legally married. Laws pertaining to Old Age, Survivors, and Disability Insurance (OASDI) are written in terms of the rights of husbands and wives, widows and widowers. Married persons are considered "essential" to individuals receiving Medicaid benefits and are therefore eligible for medical assistance themselves. In the National Affordable Housing program intended to assist "first-time home buyers," this category is defined as "an individual and his or her spouse."[134]

The second grouping, veterans' benefits, awards husbands and wives many opportunities based on their marital status. For instance, a surviving spouse is entitled to monthly dependency and indemnity compensation payments when the veteran's death is service-connected. When the death is not service-connected, the spouse is entitled to receive a monthly pension. The spouse of a veteran is also entitled to compensation if a veteran disappears. Furthermore, spouses of certain veterans are entitled to medical care, National Service Life Insurance, preference in federal employment, and interment in national cemeteries. And, finally, spouses of veterans who die from a service-connected disability are entitled to educational assistance, job counseling, training, and placement services.

Laws pertaining to Indians (Native Americans) insert property rights into the lives of native peoples on the basis of marital status. "Various laws set out the rights to tribal property of white men marrying Indian women, or of Indian women marrying white men."[135] This group of laws also gives relocation benefits to spouses who relinquish life estates.

Particularly poignant benefits the government awards on the basis of marital status are visitation rights in hospitals and prisons, bereavement leaves, burial determination, child custody, domestic violence protection, sick leave to care for a partner, and medical decisions on behalf of a partner. These rights and privileges are only granted to "legally" married couples. Anyone living outside of this arrangement must either make costly legal arrangements or depend on the mercy and sensitivity of the governing institutions for access to these protections.

"I have been privileged on many occasions to work with a substantial number of ministers whose Washington churches today are referred to as 'African American.' I ran into one of these fine ministers. He was saying, 'Are you going home tomorrow?' I told him I thought I was. I asked him if he had a message for the folks back home. And he said, 'I sure do. Tell them that God created Adam and Eve—not Adam and Steve.'"

—Senator Jesse Helms, September 9, 1996, with regard to the Defense of Marriage Act

The centrality of marital status to "organized society" cannot be overstated given the significance of these laws to the everyday lives of U.S. citizens and immigrants. The state has a substantial stake in heterosexual marriage and protects and preserves its interests in a multitude of laws, policies, and practices. Even the U.S. Postal Service recognizes the revenue potential of the wedding market and regularly staffs booths at regional bridal shows. The postage costs for wedding and shower invitations as well as for thank-you notes are substantial.

Religion

Religions vary in the meaning they attach to the wedding, but all reserve the right to require certain practices and beliefs regarding the wedding ceremony as well as the institution of marriage. Many religions view marriage as a religious institution and not the domain of the state. Yet religious ceremonies do not carry the weight of law. Newlyweds must also obtain a state license in order to have access to the material rewards of this arrangement. While religions interact with the state in legalizing marriage, their power rests in legitimizing marriage through moral teachings.

Compliance with religious doctrine can be seen clearly in the selection of readings used during the ceremony itself as well as in the comments offered by the presiding clergy. The wedding becomes a site for the ritual enactment of religious doctrine, shoring up the stake the church has in a patriarchal social order and in a heterosexual marriage that ensures a heterogendered division of labor and women's continued function as the property of men. This is embodied especially in the "giving away" of the bride from father (son, brother, or even both parents) to husband and in the "taking" of the husband's last name. In many ceremonies, the naming exceeds just the taking of the last name. Frequently, the newlyweds are announced as "For the first time ever, Mr. and Mrs. Ralph Reed."

In June 1998, Southern Baptists voted to uphold patriarchal marriage as the centerpiece of the Baptist faith by declaring that a woman should "submit herself graciously" to her husband. Ironically, Southern Baptists who would find the greatest popular culture support for their position in Disney films, toys, and theme parks—especially Disney's Fairy Tale Wedding Pavilion at Disney World—launched

Facts About Latin Brides not Mail Order Brides

The liberal media (supported by feminists, among others) hope to discredit and sensationalize the success of this alternative method of meeting in an attempt to discourage and sell papers. Let's face it, scandalous negative, freaky news sells, while positive, "happily-ever-after" stories don't. The term "mail order brides" has not been effective in deterring interested gentlemen.

Fiction – Mail Order Brides

The men are looking for subservient women and the women are escaping misery and poverty. Both the men and women enrolled in our agency are above average in appearance, education and social skills. They simply want to meet their soul mate, and are not brides ordered through the mail.

—http://www.latin-bride. com

a boycott against the Disney Company for what they considered to be a significant decline in moral values. Prior to this vote, Disney had supported a benefits package for domestic partnerships and had through its holdings—ABC, Disney World, Touchstone, and Miramax—provided both film and television offerings that Southern Baptists considered unacceptable. Most notable of these was the television sitcom *Ellen*, which featured a lesbian lead character and lesbian and gay themes. The Church of the Nazarene and Presbyterian Church in America also voiced their concerns over Disney's moral direction and joined the boycott. "It has become clear that the Disney Corporation is on a deliberate course of promoting the homosexual agenda and marginalizing the evangelical and conservative church and making them seem irrelevant to our culture."[136] In 2005, Southern Baptists voted to end the multi-year boycott following the lead of another conservative religious group, the American Family Association, which also ended their sanctions against the company. In negotiations with Disney following the removal of Michael Eisner, religious conservatives expressed confidence that the company would provide "only those products that affirm traditional family values."[137] Gay rights organizations claimed that the failure of the boycott was the primary reason these organizations voted to change course. In fact, Gay Days at Disney continue to be enormously well attended and successful events.

Religions frequently set the rules for personal and social behavior and relationships. In particular, they organize and regulate marriage, monogamy, patriarchy, and police any violations of religious law.

Mass media

The role of the mass media is primarily ideological and comprised of what sociologist Howard Becker calls "consciousness industries."[138] In other words, their task is to provide the public with information and materials that help shape how we view the world, ourselves, and the values we live by. They provide the symbols, myths, images, and ideas by which we constitute dominant culture.

When the work they do involves weddings and marriage, what is significant is the degree to which they make use of these images, the interests they serve, and the effect they have on our imaginations and values. Given the shrinking of media ownership down to six major conglomerates and the diversity of their holdings,

"Still pregnant brides shouldn't expect widespread acceptance, especially from the clergy. [A couple from Syracuse] were married in a Catholic ceremony, but not in her family church; the priest there was known for ordering pregnant brides not to wear white. Given all the discomfort, one might wonder why brides don't just put the whole thing off. For one reason, wedding plans have their own momentum. Postponement 'was my greatest fear,' explains the bride's mother. 'We'd put down deposits, we'd sent out the invitations.' 'Given the alternative,' says Miss Manners, 'a wedding is very appropriate for the pregnant bride.'"

—Mieher 1993, p. A1

these messages tend not to vary much. Disney is a perfect example of this, with its control of multimedia, home video, book publishing, motion pictures, magazines, TV and cable, retail, sports teams, newspapers, music, insurance, petroleum and natural gas, and theme parks and resorts. Mass media are used by the privileged to define or legitimize entitlements by producing certain belief systems, based largely on myths and stereotypes. These entitlements refer to the rights of certain groups within society to have more or less access to resources and institutions.

The staging of weddings in television shows, weekly reporting on weddings in the press, magazine reports on celebrity weddings, advertising, and popular adult and children's movies with wedding themes or weddings inserted all work together to teach us how to think about weddings, marriage, heterosexuality, race, gender, and labor. Through the application of the heterosexual imaginary, the media—television, magazines, internet, all new media—cloak most representations of weddings in signifiers of romance, purity, morality, promise, affluence or accumulation, and whiteness. Many newlyweds today experience their weddings as stars of a fairy tale movie in which they are scripted, videotaped, and photographed by paparazzi wedding-goers. Even Kodak and Fuji offer disposable "wedding" cameras for placement on reception tables, ensuring that no moment in this spectacle will be overlooked.

In Chapter 3, I discuss the key role of bridal magazines in the primary wedding market and the wedding-ideological complex. As you will see, these periodicals depend upon signifiers of elegance, opulence, and traditional femininity and, with the exception of those few that target women of color, e.g., *Signature Bride*, also emphasize whiteness. Bridal magazines are a central site for demonstrating how the wedding industry is bound up with the accumulation of wealth and the perpetuation of class, gender, and racial hierarchies.

Conclusion

The contemporary white wedding under transnational capitalism is, in effect, a mass-marketed, homogeneous, assembly-line production with little resemblance to the utopian vision many participants hold. With enormous profit-making ventures dependent upon this market and newlyweds caught up in

"Across the street from the church, more than a dozen anti-gay protesters waved signs with messages such as 'God Hates Fags.' 'I came to spread some truth in this orgy of lies,' said [one protester] from a Baptist church in Topeka, Kan., whose members regularly engage in anti-homosexual picketing at funerals. One protester yelled: 'Mathew was wicked!'"

—Associated Press Report on the funeral for Mathew Shepard, the young man who was murdered in Wyoming for being gay. http://www.mathewshepard.com

the machinery of the wedding production, the focus is on the spectacle of accumulation being created. "The whole life of those societies in which modern conditions of production prevail presents itself as an immense accumulation of *spectacles*. All that once was directly lived has become mere representation."[139] The engine driving the wedding market has mostly to do with the romancing of heterosexuality in the interests of capitalism. The social relations at stake—love, community, commitment, and family—become alienated from the production of the wedding spectacle, while practices reinforcing a heterogendered and globalized racial division of labor, white supremacy, the private sphere as women's work, and women as property are reinforced.

The design of these rituals secures a heterogendered division of labor with the bride, socialized since childhood, as the domestic planner, showpiece of the groom's potential wealth and producer of future workers, while the groom represents the final decision maker—patriarchal authority—and passive recipient of the bride's service. He's in charge of the honeymoon travel (adventure) plans. The system also sets up the bride as primary consumer and the marriage promise as integral to the accumulation of private property, particularly for whites, who have significant economic advantage in American society. Ruth Frankenberg, in her ground-breaking book *White Women, Race Matters: The Social Construction of Whiteness*, defines whiteness as:

> a set of locations that are historically, socially, politically, and
> culturally produced and, moreover, are intrinsically linked to
> unfolding relations of domination. Naming "whiteness" displaces it
> from the unmarked, unnamed status that is itself an effect of its
> dominance. Among the effects on white people both of race privilege
> and of the dominance of whiteness are their seeming normativity,
> their structured invisibility . . . To look at the social construction of
> whiteness . . . is to look head-on at a site of dominance. [140]

The heterosexual imaginary circulating throughout the wedding-industrial complex masks the fact that global, racial, class, and sexual hierarchies are

International attention for mass wedding 21 March 2007

BRUSSELS – The mass wedding planned for tonight in Sint-Niklaas has attracted the attention of the world press. Dutch, French and British media, and even Arabic television station Al-Jazeera are reporting on the festivities as 600 couples prepare to be married by black municipal official Wouter Van Bellingen, the Standaard reports.

The event was planned as part of Europe's action week against racism. Three couples refused to be married by Van Bellingen earlier this year because he is black.

—Expatica News 2007

secured. For instance, in nearly all of the examples offered here, the wedding industry depends upon the availability of cheap labor from developing nations with majority populations made up of people of color. The wealth garnered by white transnational corporations both relies on racial hierarchies, exploiting people and resources of communities of color (Africa, China, Haiti, Mexico, South Asia), and perpetuates them in the marketing of the wedding industry.

With 43 percent of all marriages ending in divorce, the number of marriages declining by 31 percent, and the historical necessity of marriage diminishing, the wedding market "needs" the fantasy of the once-in-a-lifetime extravaganza/spectacle or it would cease to exist. How this fantasy is created is the work of the wedding-ideological complex and the focus of the next two chapters.

"Never mind that people who've been divorced by 30 blithely refer to those aborted unions as their 'starter marriages,' that the rate of divorce tripled between 1970 and 1995, that a third of all babies today are born 'out of wedlock' . . . People still love a good party."

—Bart Nagel and Karen Huff, "Something Old, Something New," *Might*, March/April 1997, 48

Chapter Three

Romancing the Clone

The *White* Wedding

"Match a pretty girl with a handsome guy. It's true love, now don't be shy. Dress them in a tux and a wedding gown.... They're the happiest couple in town! Next a chapel wedding for the bride and groom, then send them off on their honeymoon. Now move them into their family home... add special stickers to make it their own! The time has come for a sweet surprise... a dear little baby with love in her eyes! Inside! A baby for you after saying 'I do!'."

—*Family Corners toy by Mattel*

"People who are ugly are not worthy of a wedding!"

—*the wedding singer in the film The Wedding Singer*

"Mirror, mirror on the wall . . . who's the fairest of them all?"

—*The Queen in the film Snow White*

The first quote opening this chapter comes from the back of a box for a doll named Ryan of the *Family Corners* series made by Mattel. Ryan is one of four potential groom dolls children can select to go with any one of four bride dolls. In addition to the family values position in this passage, the four male dolls and the four female dolls each represent different ethnic groups. While the option is available for children to pair the bride and groom whichever way they choose, Mattel doesn't want to leave anything to chance. The photos on the back of the box show each of the four male dolls by name and clothing, the four female dolls by name and clothing, and then provide "appropriate" pairings of each of the grooms with the corresponding bride of the same race or ethnicity. Since all the dolls represented are relatively light-skinned, their pairing by the more easily discernible hair color differences—blonds with blonds, brunettes with brunettes, redheads with redheads—masks the racial pairings in evidence in these photos. In this example, children are discouraged from imagining interracial or interethnic marriage and same sex pairings. Instead, the mythology of sameness concerning what counts as a family is instilled, making all other manifestations or configurations unimaginable. Nicola Field, in her book *Over the Rainbow*, explains the motivation and consequences of perpetuating this notion of family:

> The idea of the family as a protective haven is a myth; the family unit cannot provide the haven it promises. On the contrary, we can never isolate ourselves from social and political relationships in the world. The places we choose to hide are always inseparably connected to the real world, the world they actually might encounter in school, and for some, in neighborhoods. It is not the failure, or the breakdown, of the family which causes our alienation, but the ever-disappointed hopes instilled in us as children. These hopes are false dreams of being cocooned and of belonging.[1]

The cocooning Field refers to in this passage is a form of romance, living within the imaginary. This illusion of insularity and well-being is recreated through romantic mythology, keeping children from seeing and living in the real world. In actuality, gender and sexuality are highly variable over the lifespan and love is not about one's melanin content or appearance, yet truths such as these are masked by illusory images that make the variability in life unimaginable. Romancing heterosexuality in a manner such as that of the *Family Corners* toy—images common to a wide variety of children's toys—ensures an ongoing wedding market that also preserves patriarchal authority, racial separation, and a heterogendered view of the world. These images perpetuate the myth that housework and family are the exclusive domain of women and they keep in place an expectation that women must be dependent on men for the survival of the family. These constructions of social relations conceal from children an awareness of real life and the opportunity to develop some of life's most valuable survival skills—the ability to live with difference and to imagine alternatives.

The second quote at the beginning of this chapter is taken from the movie *The Wedding Singer* and sets up one of the key organizing principles of the wedding market. All brides are beautiful! Estée Lauder has long used an advertising campaign for its perfume depicting a white, blond flower girl in a white dress looking up into the eyes of a white, blond bride in a white wedding gown. The only text in the ad says

"Beautiful," establishing the white bride and the future bride as standard-bearers of what counts as beauty.

What's not said but is implied in bridal magazines, children's toys, popular film, television, and advertising is that something is wrong with people who do not marry. *The Wedding Singer,* the *Family Corners* toy, and the Estée Lauder ad are but a sampling of a pervasive cultural depiction that reinforces the same message: brides are beautiful, grooms are handsome, and anyone who doesn't marry is ugly. With a few notable exceptions covered later in this chapter, what counts as beautiful in mainstream popular culture is a white, fair, thin, and female racial stereotype.

In the examples above, the effect for anyone who doesn't meet these standards can be moderate to severe, manifesting in everything from eating disorders to the toleration of domestic violence to labor abuses. Additionally, examples such as these perpetuate gender, racial, class, and sexuality hierarchies, setting up some groups to fare poorly in relation to dominant constructions of heterosexuality. The beliefs emanating from these sites legitimize oppressive treatment of those who do not mirror these images through the objectification and trivialization of those who don't fit the script. In other words, the institution of heterosexuality as it is currently organized functions as a form of social control and depends upon the heterosexual imaginary to conceal its regulatory function and effects.

Women are taught from early childhood to plan for "the happiest day of their lives." (Apparently, everything after that is downhill!) Men are taught, by the absence of these socializing mechanisms, that their work is "other" than that. A brief stroll through toy catalogs conveys this message quite clearly. The pages for girls are easy to locate. They are the ones little boys distance themselves from, and they are coded with Barbie pink. This same color permeates most products targeted to female children, including bicycles and other toys that have no particular gender distinctions. The possibilities children learn to imagine are only as broad as their cultural exposure allows. Children are socialized to understand the importance of coupling—appropriate coupling—and what counts as beauty, what counts as women's work and men's work, and how to become good consumers by participating in those institutions that stimulate their interests and emotions and reap the most rewards. Many people believe that the advances of the women's movement have

"'Arm Candy': One-Night Stun. The accessory of the 90's walks and talks (preferably only in monosyllables). The most important criteria are good looks and an absolute lack of expectations.

Arm candy. The phrase is bracing in its candor, implying a beautiful object to attach to your arm, for others to feast their eyes upon. In the image-obsessed 1990's, when a dominant mood is the desire to inspire fits of envy in one's friends, a woman (and sometimes a man) in the role of arm candy expresses the quintessential modern relationship. It's a one-night thing, a post-sexual image enhancer and ego booster. In the conventional pairing—powerful older man, stunning young woman—her presence assures the seething jealousy of other men and guarantees the intrigued interest of women."

—Kuczynski 1998, p. 9.1

been absorbed and are no longer necessary. There is ample evidence to the contrary. Examining these markets shows that there is still an enormous amount of ideological weight placed on gender and race differentiation and hierarchies.

Gender does not exist in a social vacuum. It is the central organizing concept for the institution of heterosexuality, setting the standards for male/female relations at all levels—heterogender. Heterogender differentiation will not disappear or change until a transformation in its organizing institution—heterosexuality and the interests it serves—occurs.

"Movies, the fashion industry, magazines and television have discovered that weddings sell."[2] But more than that, they've discovered that we'll consent to their messages. In order to give consent, one must be assured that there will be certain rewards. One of the central ways the industry succeeds is by convincing consumers that romance is both necessary and sacred and far outweighs the realities of the marketplace and its consequences for consumers, labor, communities, social groups, and countries.

In order for the wedding industry to be "recession-proof"—that is, that people will pay for a wedding no matter what—it must rely on a very powerful meaning-making apparatus guaranteeing our compliance and consent to participate. This *wedding-ideological complex* is made up of those sites in American popular culture—children's toys, wedding announcements, advertising, film, internet, television, bridal magazines, jokes, cartoons, music—that *work as an ensemble in creating many taken-for-granted beliefs, values, and assumptions within social texts and practices about weddings* (see Figure 3.1).

One of the central functions of this complex is to create the conditions that allow us to imagine possibilities in relation to weddings, marriage, heterogender, race, class, and heterosexuality. The beliefs we hold about weddings and marriage emanate from a variety of historical and material sites and are made use of daily in the wedding market. These meanings rely on romantic and sacred notions of heterosexuality (or a heterosexual social order) in order to create and maintain the illusion of well-being—the heterosexual imaginary. This romantic view of weddings, marriage, and heterosexuality prevents us from seeing the powerful arrangements these meanings serve as well as the consequences they produce.

"It is estimated that the additional cost of achieving and maintaining universal access to basic education for all, basic health care for all, reproductive health care for all women, adequate food for all and clean water and safe sewers for all is roughly $40 billion a year—or less than 4 percent of the combined wealth of the 225 richest people in the world."

—Annan 1998, p. 16

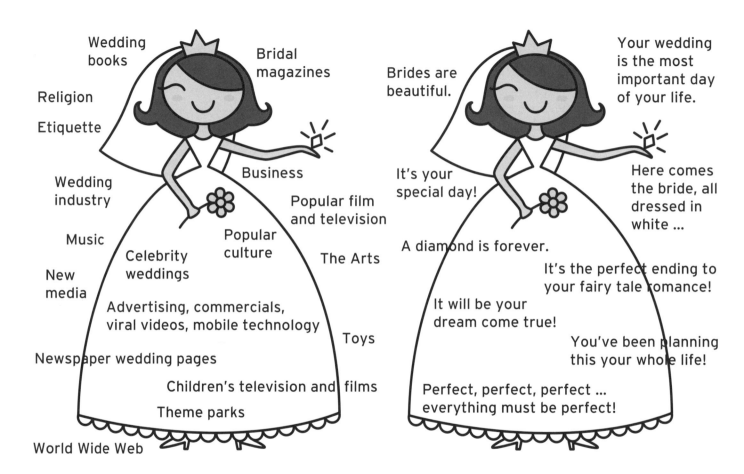

Figure 3.1 Wedding-ideological complex and messages

The prevailing national and state interests of this historical moment are those of transnational capitalist patriarchy. But what does that mean in terms of our everyday lives? In part, it means we live in a country that is highly stratified: where the rich control most of the income and wealth, consume the largest amount of goods and services, receive the highest quality schooling, have the greatest influence over public policy, enjoy the best health care money can buy, and where men and whites are privileged.

What does this have to do with the portrayal of weddings in popular culture? In recent years we have been watching the rich get richer and the poor get poorer. In fact, as of 2006, the richest 20 percent of American families earned 48.1 percent of all available income and controlled 84 percent of the country's wealth—stocks, bonds, real estate, automobiles, businesses, and other private property. The wealthiest 5 percent of families "own 60 percent of all wealth, and the super-rich, in the top 1 percent, control 40 percent of all private assets."[3] If 20 percent of the population controls 84 percent of the wealth and resources, that leaves the rest to be divided up among the remaining 80 percent of the population (see Figure 3.2).

Distribution of Wealth 2004

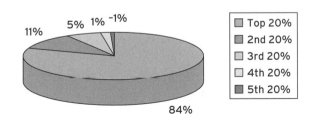

Distribution of Income 2004

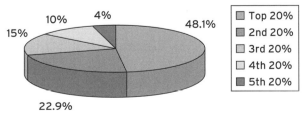

Figure 3.2
Distribution of income and wealth among families in the United States, 2004
U.S. Census Bureau (2006) and Macionis (2008)

As you can see from Figure 3.2, the rich control significant portions of the country's income and wealth, leaving the remainder to be divided among the lower classes. Given that much of the lower classes' income and wealth comes from the labor of those working for the richest 20 percent, it is the role of capitalist institutions and ideologies to justify this uneven economic distribution and to gain the consent of the lower classes who participate in these arrangements. One of the dominant ideologies of capitalism, disseminated through a wide variety of institutions (e.g., education, law, media, family, science, medicine, government, and religion), is the belief that inequalities of wealth and income are socially just. In other words, to legitimize the concentration of wealth and income among a small number of Americans and to determine how the remainder will be distributed among the masses, ways of thinking about difference and value are necessary.

Competition, another central organizing principle of capitalism, combined with meaning-making systems circulating in an array of social practices including weddings, sets the terms for consenting to the ruling order and to its mechanisms for distributing what is left over. This is the primary rationale for belief systems organizing heterosexuality, race, class, gender, and age. Popular culture plays a crucial role in this regard by both justifying the dominant social order and binding us to it. As John Storey explains in his summary of Althusser's theory of ideology, prevailing rituals and customs

> offer pleasure and release from the usual demands of the social order, but . . . ultimately, they return us to our places in the social order, refreshed and ready to put up with our exploitation and oppression until the next *official* break comes along. In this sense ideology works to *reproduce* the social conditions and social relations necessary for the economic conditions and economic relations of capitalism to continue.[4]

The role of popular culture and of weddings within that setting is to provide that "official break." French sociologist Pierre Bourdieu further elaborates on this idea by linking cultural distinctions with class distinctions. Notions of style and taste become markers of class and status, "predisposed, consciously and

"The richest fifth of the world's people consumes 86 percent of all goods and services while the poorest fifth consumes just 1.3 percent. Indeed, the richest fifth consumes 45 percent of all meat and fish, 58 percent of all energy used and 84 percent of all paper, has 74 percent of all telephone lines and owns 87 percent of all vehicles."

—Annan 1998, p. 16

"The three richest people in the world have assets that exceed the combined gross domestic product of the 48 least developed countries."

—Annan 1998, p. 16

deliberately or not, to fulfill a social function of legitimating social differences."[5]

Popular culture, which is also mass culture and dominated by the mass media—television, film, magazines, newspapers, radio, and the internet—is controlled by the same owning class that controls the country's wealth and income. Six major corporations control most of America's global media: General Electric (NBC), Disney (ABC), CBS Corporation (CBS), News Corporation (Rupert Murdoch) (Fox), Viacom, and Time Warner (CNN). Consequently, their role in ruling and the production of meaning is significant. The next two chapters will focus on the meaning-making processes of the wedding-ideological complex organizing the portrayal of weddings and the "recession-proof" wedding industry. Several sites within American popular culture will be examined for the ways they exploit utopian desires for community, love, and belonging by using the ideology of romantic love to secure particular class and race interests.

"Isn't It Romantic . . . ?"

One of the central organizing concepts of the wedding-ideological complex is the notion of romance or romantic love. But what is *romance* or *romantic love* and how do they work to organize how we think about weddings? To begin, romance is ideology in action. Ideology manifests in words and images that establish and regulate meanings and beliefs justifying dominant interests. Ideologies naturalize our socially created world, replacing realistic perceptions with idealized notions of that world. Romance ideology works to secure in the popular imagination the notion that enthusiasm or the promise of love, lust, and passion are what constitutes real love. Our national romance with engagement practices offers a dramatic example of this. We perceive the *promise* to marry and the act of marrying (the wedding) as instances of love and commitment. It isn't until the real experience of living, loving, and caring for another that couples discover what love requires. I promise to love, honor, and cherish becomes tested by the realities of "in sickness and in health, till death do us part." Frequently, the period following the promise and the enthusiasm manifests as disillusionment and the end of the marriage commitment. Loving is hard.

In the instance of romantic love the focus is on what is commonly thought of as a private or personal emotion that mysteriously manifests as "chemistry," "a crush," or "falling in love." It is thought of as an unexplainable and natural emotion—as long as it is heterosexual—as opposed to one that is socially produced and organized. The ideology of romantic love is a belief in a social relation disconnected from real conditions of existence—a social relation that masks or conceals contradictions in favor of reproducing a reassuring illusion or the promise of well-being and bonding. This ideal depends upon a belief in monogamous coupling as the preferred manifestation of love relationships, making all other possibilities unimaginable or unacceptable. It also elevates the individuals in the couple to the status of unique and exclusive, bestowed with the mantle of "chosen one" or "one and only" from "now until forever," "'til death do us part." It is here that the ideology of romantic love incorporates property relations, naturalizing love with ownership, a pervasive belief about romance, commitment, and marriage. The extension of these beliefs manifests in feelings of possessiveness, jealousy, and, in many cases, violence. For example, the majority of cases of all forms of violence against women are committed by current or former intimate partners. In the words of the popular song "End of the Road," from Boyz II Men:

> Although we've come
> To the end of the road
> Still I can't let go
> It's unnatural
> You belong to me
> I belong to you.

Patriarchal heterosexuality makes use of the ideology of romantic love to serve the interests of male dominance and capitalism. It reinforces a heterogendered division of labor that subordinates women's needs to men's desires, notions that are central to the heterosexual imaginary. Creating the illusion of plenitude and fullness, the ideology of romance produces a belief that sexual objectification and subordination are both natural and justified. Enormous inequities are overlooked when the promise of love—romance—presents itself. And women are more subject to this outcome than men, given their heterogender socialization and their positioning by the wedding-ideological complex. For example, from early childhood women are taught to accept these practices and beliefs. The alienation from the real that these arrangements produce is significant. Consider, for example, the high frequency of responses women give to their experience with domestic or sexual violence, using rationalizations for staying in abusive relationships–"but I love him" or "I don't know how to live without him" or "he doesn't really mean it, he loves me." All too often, "falling in love" with the fantasy of romantic love becomes the aphrodisiac, rather than learning to love the real person and in real conditions of existence.

The political spectacle of former President William Clinton's affair with White House intern Monica Lewinsky illustrates how this works. Independent counsel Kenneth Starr conducted an in-depth investigation into the dealings of the Clinton White House. While this investigation yielded no wrong-doing by anyone for the majority of the years under investigation, it did uncover a brief sexual impropriety committed by then-President Bill Clinton. The detailing of this investigation appeared in book form in what was called *The Starr Report*. In the following excerpt, Starr paraphrases and quotes Ms. Lewinsky's description of her relationship with President Clinton:

> The President was the "most affectionate with me he'd ever been," Ms. Lewinsky testified. He stroked her arm, toyed with her hair, kissed her neck, praised her intellect and beauty . . . He remarked . . . that he wished he had more time for me. And so I said, well, maybe you will have more time in three years. And I was . . . thinking just when he wasn't President, he was going to have more time on his hands. And he said, well, I don't know, I might be alone in three years. And then I said something about . . . us sort of being together. I think I kind of said, oh, I think we'd be a good team, or something like that [he responded with a reference to being significantly older than her] "I left that day sort of emotionally stunned," for "I just knew he was in love with me."[6]

"Looking for Love in the Feds Funds Rate"

Like a love-struck intern parsing the boss's every word for a sign that the feeling is mutual, world markets hunted obsessively last week for reasons to believe that the Federal Open Market Committee would cut interest rates at its meeting on Tuesday.

Hearts skipped beats at midweek when Alan Greenspan suggested to Congress that action was needed "shortly" to keep the contagion of economic instability now afflicting emerging markets from "really spilling over and creating some very significant further difficulties." The remark apparently sounded enough like "Will you marry me?" to send stocks soaring for a day. By week's end, the main question seemed to be how big a diamond, er, rate cut would be forthcoming.

—New York Times 1998, p. 3.4

In this passage the ideology of romantic love is evident in Lewinsky's translation of a moment of affection intended to romance the ending of their relationship into her fantasy of a lifelong romantic bond. Lewinsky's fetishizing of the President works to obscure the enormous complexities and contradictions of an extramarital affair between the most powerful man in the world and an intern, a fifty-year-old and a twenty-year-old, in the context of a significant political struggle for control of the White House. More reminiscent of fairy tales or romance novels, this story exemplifies the crises romantic mythologies yield when confronted with reality.

As Nicola Field argues in her theory of romance, "The ideology of romance overrides contradictions and simplifies overwhelming complexities. Romance is there to blur the past, and fudge over the real contradictions of the present, in order to control the future."[7]

In a satirical article in the *New York Times Magazine,* the Sunday after the *Starr Report* was released, the use of the white wedding to erase the taint of scandal is suggested.[8] Titled "Miss Lewinsky: Are You Ready for Your Makeover Now?," this article offers three options for blurring the past and getting her "life back": "quiet respectability," "marrying well," and "questing for fame." Each recommendation is accompanied by a photo overlaid with a paperdoll outfit to exemplify the option being offered. The second choice, "marrying well," features Lewinsky in a wedding gown. Lisa Johnson, author of *How to Snare a Millionaire,* is quoted as recommending that Lewinsky "slim down at a Palm Springs spa, where she can 'learn the rich man's sports of tennis and golf under the tutelage of gorgeous foreign pros'" on her way to finding a wealthy man to marry her. After several tongue-in-cheek recommendations for associating with the upper class as a way to recuperate her reputation, this section quotes Geraldo Rivera as saying, "Monica will make the perfect trophy wife for the next millennium." Clearly, weddings certify more than whether a woman is "pretty enough."

In the wake of a similar scandal portrayed in the film *The Birdcage,* the senator's wife recommends a high-status wedding for their daughter as a way to cleanse away the shame of the past. She exclaims,

> What about a wedding? A big white wedding! Why not? It would restore
> your image. A wedding is hope, a white wedding is *family and morality*

and tradition and it would be such a special marriage . . . and to a cultural attaché's son. It would be *love and optimism versus cynicism and sex!!* It would be an affirmation!

These examples reflect the success of the wedding-ideological complex in guaranteeing future markets and preserving ruling-class interests by securing in the collective consciousness the association of weddings with whiteness and wealth, morality and optimism. Whiteness, wealth, and weddings become central features of the ideology of romantic love, communicating a sign system that collapses them into one package. The way the heterosexual imaginary works is by making use of both fantasy and nostalgia. The effect is a masking of the very real, contradictory, and complicated ways institutionalized heterosexuality works in the interests of the dominant classes. Through the use of nostalgia, romance renarrates history and naturalizes tradition. For instance, to help the new bride imagine her marriage will be a success, *Bride's* published a story called "Dangerous Liaisons: Rewriting History for Hollywood's Classic Couples," in which they rewrite sad movie endings as "happily-ever-afters."

As you look forward to your own happily-ever-after, consider the fate of some of Hollywood's most famous lovers . . . Devoted fans were left wondering "What if?" To give everyone closure, we've rewritten history for five beloved couples from both the small and silver screen. Because, frankly, we die-hard romantics still give a damn.[9]

Following this introduction, *Bride's* goes on to rewrite endings for movies such as *The Way We Were, Casablanca, Star Wars,* and *Batman,* providing brides with messages about which romances *should* have failed and which should have been given another chance. *The Way We Were* ended properly, in that Katie and Hubbell divorced. They were a mismatch to start—but particularly because of Katie's "perfectionism" and "nagging." In the rewriting of *Casablanca,* Ilsa divorces her "boring husband," finds Rick, and marries him. Clearly, women like Ilsa deserve men like Rick, but "nagging" women don't earn a second chance. The message to new brides: exemplify the Ingrid Bergman type of femininity, be the good wife, and don't nag! It's your responsibility to make the marriage work!

This rewriting of Hollywood history provides a simulation of the celebrity wedding, using fairy tales as substitutes for the real. Once again the ideology of romantic love works to erase history in the interests of the illusion of heterosexual stability. To secure the ideology of romantic love, lessons on romance, romantic settings, and how to keep the romance alive are offered. In the end, tradition is left unquestioned, leaving a vehicle and a rationale for ruling-class interests to be desired, emulated, and legitimized.

Brides and Barbies: Romancing the Clone

Central to the primary wedding market and to securing dominant class and race interests are bridal magazines. While the magazine industry as a whole has suffered significant losses in proportion to the growth of online publications, many in the industry have turned to web development to offset this decline. Long dependent upon advertising pages to offset the costs to consumers, magazine companies are finding new and provocative ways to attract readers. *Bride's* magazine, for example, is currently the largest magazine in the United States in terms of ad pages (seven hundred per issue), has a circulation of 360,688 per issue, down by 11 percent since 1999. Even so, they can claim a total audience of 6,448,000, largely due to increases in subscriptions and to their sister website, Brides.com. With an audience whose median age is 30 and household income is $49,608, *Bride's* maintains a bi-monthly publishing schedule, producing six issues per year, at a cost of $5.99 per copy. Their February/March 2006 issue—traditionally their largest issue—featured 564 pages of ads, weighed 3 pounds, and had 860 pages—down 25 percent since 1999. On average, *Bride's* magazine devotes 80 percent of its coverage to advertising and it set a world record three years in a row for most magazine advertising pages.[10] Owned by Condé Nast Publications, *Bride's* is a key link in a corporation whose holdings include *Modern Bride, Elegant Bride,* and *Brides.com.* Catering to the primary and secondary wedding markets, their other publications also provide links to the wedding industry. *Traveler,* for example, caters to honeymooners while *Allure, Details, Glamour, Gourmet, GQ, House & Garden,*

Vanity Fair, Vogue, and *W,* popular in their own right, provide advice on trends, fashion, food, and home decorating, interests that are prominent among newlyweds.[11]

In the 1990s, *Bride's* adjusted their marketing to appeal to a rising median age among newlyweds. To accommodate their new target audience with its increases in higher education and career opportunities, they changed their masthead to *Bride's and Your New Home,* and added regular sections on "Brides," "Weddings," "Honeymoon," and "Home." During this period, the editors acknowledged that because newlyweds were older, they often already had careers and homes and required a different approach on the part of the wedding industry. It wasn't uncommon during this period to find ads for power tools and automobiles in addition to the usual kitchenware and china offerings.

Today, the average combined income of *Bride's* couples has risen to $65,076.[12] Newlyweds are older at 25 for women and 26.8 for men, better educated, and more accomplished. They are 40 percent more affluent than the average U.S. household ($46,326)[13] and they are primarily members of the owning class and the professional-managerial class.[14] Further, the current wedding market is rapidly becoming more globalized and the internet is now a key player. As a result of these trends, *Bride's* once again changed its masthead and removed the apostrophe (*Bride's*), taking its name from possessive to plural and inclusive (*Brides*). They also removed the phrase "and your new home" and incorporated http://www.brides.com and the phrase "The World's No. 1 Bridal Magazine" into their cover. With these changes, *Brides* signals that they have actively entered the globalized wedding market and intend to secure their place as a primary stakeholder in this industry.

In the mid-1990s former editor-in-chief Barbara Tober retired from *Bride's* magazine after thirty years. In an interview with the *Los Angeles Times,* Ms. Tober outlined her business philosophy in making *Bride's* a leader in the wedding industry. "'When people marry, other people work ... A wedding brings economic health ... It is a great banquet from which everyone can derive a living. It makes enormous sense to me.'"[15] *Bride's* survived many changes in American society and established itself as not only the standard-bearer of wedding culture but also as critical to a healthy economy. While many would characterize a magazine such as this as dealing only with the trivial in

Millie Martini Bratten, the editor-in-chief of Brides *magazine, said that over the last five years the interest in green weddings has blossomed from a desire to incorporate a few green elements, like a vegan menu, to making sure the entire celebration won't contribute to the depletion of natural resources. This may include finding halls that recycle, hiring caterers who use locally grown ingredients, decorating with potted plants that can be transplanted and using soy-based candles, rather than those of petroleum-based wax.*

—Mireya Navarro, *New York Times,* February 11, 2007

life, *Bride's* viewed its mission as stimulating the economy, providing jobs, and servicing newlyweds and the future of the American family. In other words, the publishers were keenly aware of their role in attending to class interests, and achieved their goals largely by romancing heterosexuality.

Tober's successor, Millie Martini Bratten, continues today as editor-in-chief and has also made a lasting mark on the wedding industry, guiding her magazine through the global age of the wedding industry. *Brides*, founded in 1934, persists in an industry characterized as "recession-proof," rapidly changing, and highly competitive. In addition to the explosion of wedding industry sites on the internet, post-9/11 wedding market trends include a focus on wartime weddings, an aversion to the once popular September wedding, environmentally-conscious weddings, and destination weddings. "'In general, more people have a greater sense of the world around them and how their actions affect that world', said Millie Martini Bratten, the editor-in-chief of *Brides* magazine. She said there's an attitude 'not to have a wedding that's all about me.'"[16] Bratten has kept pace with changing trends and has produced a magazine that appeals to magazine readers, internet consumers, the wedding industry, as well as mass media audiences.

The second leading bridal magazine in terms of subscriptions is *Modern Bride*. For single issue purchases, however, *Martha Stewart Weddings* exceeds both *Brides* and *Modern Bride*. *Modern Bride*, also owned by Condé Nast, publishes six issues per year, averaging 350 pages in length, at a cost of $5.99 per copy. Their total circulation is down from 371,294 in 1999 to 331,049 readers including subscriptions. Breaking away from the primary bridal market, *Modern Bride*'s readers are slightly older with an average age of 29 and have a median household income of $55,421.

Similar to *Bride's*, *Modern Bride* has altered their delivery to meet the changing landscape of magazine consumption. They've even changed their mission to reflect today's "modern" bride:

> **Creative and provocative *Modern Bride* is a smart, funny, slightly irreverent magazine that approaches the bride in a fresh new way.**

> Speaking girlfriend to girlfriend, *Modern Bride* shares insights and
> ideas about the things readers want to know in a witty, friendly
> manner (maybe even breaking a few rules along the way!). *Modern
> Bride* embraces and celebrates this exciting lifestage with every
> issue.[17]

Key in this mission statement are the descriptors "creative and provocative,"
"irreverent" and "breaking a few rules." *Modern Bride* makes every effort to
carve out a niche market among more resistant, non-traditional, or multicultural
brides. Unlike their counterpart *Brides*, *Modern Bride* now (this was not always
the case) occasionally provides images of women of color on their cover and
throughout the magazine, although their opening advertisements still include
iconic white bride images, e.g., Esteé Lauder's Beautiful campaign. Recent
issues have included a cover photo of celebrity Kelly Rowland of Destiny's Child,
Olympic gold medalist Jennie Finch, and multiple pages on same sex weddings
and brides. Given the current decline in magazine consumption, *Modern Bride* is
also expanding their reach by targeting a non-dominant audience while keeping
the interest of the white middle-class reader. For example, if you search for
the *Modern Bride* website, you are immediately linked to http://www.brides.
com, the more traditional bridal site. At the same time, they have also launched
contests to attract ordinary or "real" brides for cover girl photos. As their contest
announcement proclaims:

> "It's the first time we're going to put a **real** bride on our cover, and
> we are just so excited about it," says *Modern Bride* Editor-in-Chief
> Antonia Van Der Meer. "We want a girl who's modern, not only in the
> way she plans her wedding, but in her relationship approach to others
> and her sense of style."[18]

Mirroring *American Idol* approaches that make use of interactive marketing
techniques, *Modern Bride* involves readers by inviting them to submit applications
to become cover girls or to vote for their favorite real-world bride.

Following the success of *Martha Stewart Living,* and of other major magazines that feature special wedding issues such as *Vogue, Living,* and *InStyle,* Martha Stewart Living Omnimedia, Inc. launched *Martha Stewart Weddings* as a special issue in 1990. By 1999, *Weddings* had become a quarterly publication of Stewart's growing media empire and regularly vies for first place sales among the leading bridal magazines.

Beyond merely exceeding expectations in the marketing of her wedding magazines and products, Stewart has become an exemplar of the twenty-first-century entrepreneur. Throughout the 1980s and 1990s, Stewart made herself the primary brand for her enterprises and grew her business as the central site for American consumers. In 2002, Martha Stewart and her signature brands experienced a significant setback. Stewart was convicted on charges of insider trading and obstruction of justice. Surprising everyone, she opted to serve a five-month sentence while her case was being appealed, thereby shortening the time it would take to recover from this scandal. She exited prison masterfully regaining the public's attention and esteem. While she never admitted guilt, Stewart wisely expedited her way through this ordeal and has re-emerged stronger than ever.

Stewart's story offers many lessons about the state of the wedding industry in today's world. A canny observer of American culture who understands the paradigm shift occurring in today's media, Stewart has rebuilt her enterprise from this setback and has expanded her interests to take center stage in today's new "convergence culture." As media scholar Henry Jenkins outlines in his recent book, convergence is

> The flow of content across multiple media platforms, the cooperation between multiple media industries, and the migratory behavior of media audiences who will go almost anywhere in search of the kinds of entertainment experiences they want. Convergence is a word that manages to describe technological, industrial, cultural, and social changes depending on who's speaking and what they think they are talking about ... In the world of media convergence, every important

story gets told, every brand gets sold, and every consumer gets
courted across multiple media platforms.[19]

What separates *Martha Stewart Weddings* from the other magazines is that
Stewart also features a "wedding week" on her daily television show to correspond
with the publication of each wedding issue. Her creative vision extends across a
wide variety of media including her award-winning *Martha Stewart Living; Martha
Stewart Weddings; Bluepring* magazine; Martha Stewart Flowers; Martha Stewart
Colors from Lowe's; Martha Stewart *Crafts*; her nationally syndicated, Emmy
Award-winning television show *The Martha Stewart Show*; Martha Stewart Living
Radio on Sirius Satellite Radio; *Body & Soul* magazine; more than 25 best-selling
books including three on weddings; Martha Stewart Everyday Food, sold at Kmart;
Martha Stewart Furniture with Bernhardt; Martha Stewart-designed homes and
communities with KB Home; Martha Stewart cards published online by Kodak;
Martha Stewart Rugs with Safavieh; the Martha Stewart Collection of home products from Macy's; and, her deal with NBC's *Today Show* to offer some fortunate
viewers an on-air Martha Stewart Wedding. Convergence culture also incorporates
interactive media and Stewart's on-air project with NBC involves viewers who will
vote for the best couple and the best products for the chosen newlyweds. And, of
course, her website, http://www.marthastewart.com, provides links to all of her
projects, archives of past recipes and crafts, and tips for the perfect wedding.

Recent entrants into the highly competitive bridal magazine market include
Condé Nast's *Elegant Bride* (200 pages and 143,966 readers per issue) which
targets an older, more affluent, primarily white audience. The median income
for *Elegant Bride* readers is $99,516, and the median age is 38. *Bridal Guide*
(400 pages and 250,000 readers per issue), another recent publication, owned
by RFP, LLC, has also claimed a significant share of the wedding magazine
market, packaging the *Honeymoon Guide* and wedding catalogs with each issue
and rivaling single copy sales on a par with *Martha Stewart Weddings*.

Lesser known—and formerly the only publication that catered to African-
American brides—is *Signature Bride*. Privately owned by Deb Kronowitz and
published online, this magazine features contributions from wedding consultant

Diann Valentine and proclaimed wedding diva Linnyette Richardson-Hall. The property of Fusion Media Properties, *Signature Bride* appears to be shifting from an in-print publication to an online magazine. More recently *Black Bride & Groom*, the official magazine of the National Black Bridal Association, published online and in print since 2005, is attempting to meet the needs of this market. They currently report a circulation of 90,000 but have yet to provide an in-print magazine for 2007. Their website, however, still provides listings of services by state for prospective newlyweds.

Seeing the enormous success of bridal magazines, many others have joined the market. Magazines such as *People, In Style, Star,* and *Town & Country* have all published special wedding issues. *Vogue* also publishes a special wedding issue in February each year. Since their company also publishes *Brides,* their features are primarily in keeping with *Vogue*'s fashion mission, with the brief but entertaining addition of a "Puppy Love" section featuring canine brides and grooms. There are also numerous regional wedding or bridal magazines such as *New England Bride's Wedding Guide, Cape Cod Wedding, New Jersey Weddings,* and others (see Table 3.1).

Book publishers have provided an onslaught of wedding guides. Most bookstores, regardless of size, feature a wedding section full of everything from etiquette guides to planners. Titles such as *Alternative Weddings, Colin Cowie Wedding, Jumping the Broom, Knot Ultimate Wedding Planner, Martha Stewart Wedding Planner, Somebody is Going to Die If Lilly Beth Doesn't Catch that Bouquet, There Must Be Something for the Groom to Do, Weddings for Grown-Ups, Weddings for Complicated Families, Wedding Plans,* and etiquette manuals from Emily Post and Amy Vanderbilt are regularly featured. While summer is usually the peak wedding season, preparation for the wedding begins months earlier. The prime wedding or bridal publication is usually released in February or March. Displays in bookstores are prolific in the spring months although they dominate many bookstore and grocery market shelves throughout the year. And, if this weren't enough, there is now wedding-planning software and a whole host of wedding websites where you can get advice on every feature of weddings, see what others have done, create your own site to share with friends

Asiana Wedding	Here Comes the	Portovert Magazine:
Bibi Magazine (South	Guide	for Eco-Savvy Green
Asian)	Idaho Weddings	Weddings
Black Bride & Groom	Inside Weddings	Premier Bride
Bridal Guide	In Style Weddings	Sarasota Magazine
Bride and Bloom	Manhattan Bride	Seattle Bride
Brides	Martha Stewart	Signature Bride
Brides to Remember	Weddings	Southern Bride
Cape Cod Bride	Modern Bride	The Knot Magazine
Magazine	Modern Wedding	Vermont Vows
Chicago Bride	New England Bride	Wedding & Home
Cosmopolitan Bride	New Hampshire	WeddingBells
Elegant Bride	Wedding Magazine	Wedding Dresses
Elegant Wedding	New Jersey Bride	Magazine
Magazine	New York Weddings	Weddings in
For the Bride	Occasions Wedding	Cleveland
Grace Ormonde	Magazine	Weddings with Style
Hawaii Bride & Groom	Pacific Rim Weddings	World Class Weddings

Table 3.1 Current listing of bridal/wedding magazines

and family, and even contract with or purchase various wedding services. Further, there are a host of interactive internet sites including wedding and bridal blogs, sites where you can share your wedding photos and experiences, and plenty of interactive web contests in which to participate.

Bridal magazines rely heavily on fairy-tale and storybook-romance themes in advertising, articles, and organization to sell everything one needs to produce their own wedding spectacle. As French theorist Guy Debord argues, the spectacle works symbolically: "The spectacle appears at once as society itself, as a part of society and as a means of unification. As a part of society, it is that sector where all attention, all consciousness, converges."[20]

Examining bridal magazines for evidence of the role they play in the wedding industry and in the production of the wedding spectacle provides insight into the consciousness organizing these events. The images bridal magazines present distort reality and unify particular beliefs about heterosexuality, race, class, and gender. In *Bridal Gown Guide*, Denise and Alan Fields offer an observation about bridal magazines and race:

> Only white people get married. Well, the major bridal magazines would never *say* that, but just take a look at the pictures. Page after page of Caucasian, size 8 models in $2,000 dresses. Just try to find a bride who's black, Hispanic or Asian. Go ahead, take as long as you need to search. While you're at it, try to discover an ad that features a bride who's a size 22.[21]

Three such industry distortions are revealed by this quote: race, class, and body size. To verify this assertion by Denise and Alan Fields, I conducted an in-depth study of the flagship of all bridal magazines, *Brides,* and reviewed a number of other regularly published national bridal magazines: *Modern Bride, Elegant Bride,* and *Bridal Guide. Martha Stewart Weddings* focuses primarily on the wedding production and is not covered in this study since it does not qualify as a "bridal" magazine.

For *Brides,* I visited the magazine archive at Condé Nast headquarters in New York City and surveyed every issue from 1959, when Newhouse purchased the 25-year-old magazine, to February/March 2007. Several interesting patterns were evident, including verification of what the Fieldses asserted about race. Since 1959, *only six covers had women of color as the cover brides.* The more typical cover representation was that of the thin, white, fair-haired—usually blond—blue-eyed young woman. The first woman of color bridesmaid appeared in August 1972 on page 165. In the February/March 1976 issue, the first African-American bride was featured in an article, and in April/May 1977 the first black wedding party was displayed, on page 135.

Inside the magazine the representation of women of color varied depending upon prominent events in a particular historical period. For example, from 1959 to the late 1960s the magazine was completely white and made use of signifiers such as "empire," "princess," and "royalty" in relation to anything bridal. The magazine's primary focus was on the new wife and her domestic responsibilities, i.e., cooking.

During the late 1960s through the 1970s the magazine nearly disappeared. Marriage was extremely unpopular in these years as the "free love" movement and feminism asserted that it was a form of female servitude and male exploitation of women. For the first time, *Bride's* offered advice on relationships, sexuality, and on how to balance career and "wifestyle." The Vietnam War was an issue in feature articles on advice to brides. "How to" articles were present for brides planning a wedding when their fiancé could be drafted. With the civil rights movement at a peak during this same period, an increase in the visibility of African-Americans occurred.

By fall 1976, *Bride's* announced that "Romance is Back" and boldly referred to divorce on their cover. With the return of romance and the beginning of the Reagan era, the magazine thrived once again. The Reagan revolution of the 1980s and the myth of national prosperity as well as Diana and Charles's wedding in 1981 provided the backdrop for a significant increase in the size, quality, cost, and representations of expensive, upscale weddings. Work disappeared as a central topic and the magazine abounded with messages about "joy," "verve," "fun," "happiness," and "romance." As these markers of class interest increased, inclusion of women of color nearly disappeared again.

In the early 1990s, the national trend toward multiculturalism and ethnic ambiguity coincided with a significant increase in the number of women of color from a range of ethnic groups in each issue of the magazine. While the presence of women of color is greater today than ever in the history of *Brides* magazine, the numbers are still extremely low. Since 1990, the average percentage of black brides per issue in *Brides* is 3.2 percent. This figure does not include women of color models who are of Latina, Asian, or Middle Eastern descent. With the dominant trend toward using light-skinned models, it is often difficult to ascertain if a bride is from one of these groups. Women of Asian descent are slightly easier to identify but are rarely used. The dominant icon of beauty, the white bride with blond hair, however, has averaged 30.7 percent of each issue during the 1990s and 29.1 percent in the 2000s.

"Each pale yellow wrapper has a picture on it. A picture of little Mary Jane, for whom the candy is named. Smiling white face. Blond hair in gentle disarray, blue eyes looking at her out of a world of clean comfort. The eyes are petulant, mischievous. To Pecola they are simply pretty. She eats the candy, and its sweetness is good. To eat the candy is somehow to eat the eyes, eat Mary Jane, Love Mary Jane. Be Mary Jane."

—Morrison 1970, p. 43

While a small percentage of black brides are used in *Brides* advertising, at least two to three times as many black women are used to advertise bridesmaids' dresses. In the first study that covered the magazine up to 1998, it was noticeable that no black bridesmaid appeared until after an average of one hundred and twenty white bridesmaids had appeared, a back-of-the-magazine phenomenon for both black brides and bridesmaids. In one issue with few black brides, a photo spread in the rear of the magazine featured several large-size bride models; at least 50 percent of those represented were black women. As for bridesmaids, in the 1990s, the number of blacks was two to three times greater than that of black brides, raising the question whether the phrase "Always a bridesmaid, never a bride" was really meant for black women. Or is it that the stereotype concerning who qualifies to be married excludes black women? One is left to wonder if the editors work to preserve the whiteness of this magazine by assigning black women to the later pages as a way to preserve the race and class base of their readers.

In examining the other national bridal magazines, similar patterns appeared. Except for *Signature Bride*, which targets African-Americans, *most* magazines foregrounded white women as both brides and bridesmaids. Generally, black women didn't appear in bridal magazines until at least halfway into each issue, and portrayals of bridal parties typically featured one black bridesmaid in a wedding party made up of several white women. For those brief displays of tuxedos for grooms, the same pattern held true in that the groom was usually white with one black usher in the wedding party. Rarely do any of the bridal magazines feature predominantly black, hispanic, or Asian weddings and wedding parties with one or two whites. Consistent with this pattern, nonwhite weddings are almost never portrayed.

An examination of *Brides* from 1998 to the present indicated some slight shifts in these patterns. While the lack of women of color is still significant, it is less so than in earlier years. *Brides* now has people of color on staff in prominent roles and has increased the presence of women of color, primarily women of African descent, to occupy about 7 percent of the magazine. Still women of color from other groups are barely in evidence. And the back-of-the-magazine phenomenon continues with layouts that focus almost exclusively on black brides. In interviews conducted with advertising executives, they reported that this practice exists primarily so that the main reader of *Brides* (and other bridal magazines) isn't discouraged from buying this magazine.

Girl dressed up
as Barbie bride
for Halloween

Bridal doll in store
window

As the trendsetter for bridal magazines nationally, *Brides* set the standard for most of the other leading bridal magazines, which now also include sections on gifts for the home, interior decorating, destination weddings, or green weddings. The assumption these magazines are based upon is that their primary market is middle- to upper-class readers who have the desire and means to own a home, travel, and attend to the environment. This change in format, combined with the racialized patterns of representation in bridal gown ads, suggests that the intentional or unintentional target wedding market for bridal magazines is white, middle- to upper-class, and propertied.

The dominant image of Mattel's Barbie doll is similar to that used in bridal magazines. Historically, Barbie and her corresponding Bridal Barbie are white, blond, blue-eyed, thin, and "pretty." Contrasted against the images in *Brides,* model, real, and toy brides all seem to look alike, sending the message that to be a bride is to look this way, to buy these products, and to participate in a heterogendered, racial, and class division of labor in keeping with these images.

The packaging containing the bridal gowns for Barbie all feature ads on the back of the carton. Four dolls appear in these ads, illustrating the range of options available for dressing Barbie. Three of the featured dolls are light-haired, white, and blue- or green-eyed, and each is dressed in a white bridal gown. The fourth, a brunette with brown eyes, is wearing a bridesmaid's gown, repeating the ethnic distribution pattern seen in the bridal magazines.

Marketed to 4- to 7-year-old girls, the "My Size Bride Barbie" mentioned earlier is clad in a white wedding gown that can be worn by the child who owns the doll. Little girls of all races get to dress like Barbie and imagine themselves as white, blond, thin, and pretty Barbie, even if they don't fit into any of these categories. Barbie products, which are wildly popular with young girls, teach children many powerful messages, the least of which is what race is the most important. While Mattel offers a range of "multicultural" Barbies, there is little variation in the facial or body characteristics of these multiethnic dolls, and the default Barbie is still understood to be white. The effect is that these products and bridal magazine marketing privilege middle-class whites. For children of color, the message is one of assimilation. Considered in relation to the images portrayed in bridal magazines, the expectation that women of color emulate white women is clearly reinforced. As bell hooks argues in her essay "Overcoming White Supremacy," "Assimilation has provided social legitimation for this shift in allegiance. It is a strategy deeply rooted in the ideology of white supremacy, as its advocates urge black people to negate blackness and imitate whites."[22]

Mattel, Disney, Hasbro, and other toy companies market a variety of children's products that feature the same dominant images of the pretty white bride whose greatest achievement is in wedding her handsome prince. The wedding becomes both the object of a young girl's dreams and the site of closure, rendering the marital relationship invisible.

Women's experience with weddings and the wedding industry is racially structured. Over and over again the icon of the beautiful white bride in the beautiful white bridal gown is replayed and reinforced, sending a clear message to young and old alike that what counts as beautiful and marriageable is white. Not only does this process secure the consent of white women in participating in the commodification of weddings, but it also contributes to the production of white heterosexual privilege.

In fall 1998, President Clinton's Initiative on Race resulted in an assessment of American attitudes and practices that reinforce white privilege. In the summary report, the committee concluded that Americans need to be educated about "'white privilege' and how it disenfranchises every group that came here without it." Both the primary and secondary wedding markets are rife with instances in which "whites tend to benefit, either unknowingly or consciously, from this country's history of white privilege."[23]

"Fairy Tales Can Come True, It Can Happen to You . . ."

In bridal magazines and in children's toys, references to fairy tales and princesses dominate, although less so today than in the 1980s. In bridal magazines since the 1950s, advertisements have frequently made reference to the bride as "princess," "royalty," or as having an "empire." Along with the demise of the British Empire, colonial references have also disappeared, but the ideology of romantic love linked to fairy tales and princesses prevails. Children still pretend to be princesses waiting for their handsome prince to arrive, the story of Cinderella continues to be popular, and Cinderella themes continue to echo through the wedding market. Even "My Size Bride Barbie" also comes in "My Size Princess Barbie." And, with the exception of the 1997 release of Disney's multicultural *Cinderella* movie, produced by Whitney Houston, all the instances of brides and princesses in children's culture are white.

In the past few years, bridal gown advertisers have abandoned the use of captions and have, instead, relied upon elegant settings and luxurious accessories such as diamond tiaras to signify princess bride and couture. Princess Diana's reputation with couture designs was most noticeable in the linkage of romance to class through references to "couture" in bridal gown advertising, e.g., Jim Hjelm Couture Collection, Carol Hai Designs, and Carmi Couture Collection. By allowing brides to imagine themselves as having access to high-fashion and "couture" gowns, advertisers create the perception that there is little difference between the average bride and the princess bride. "Style" becomes something disconnected from class and wealth and thus available to most women, regardless of income. One effect of

"The most common type of heterosexual marriage in all Mediterranean societies (and the only legal form at Athens and Rome) was monogamy: a male-female couple. Such unions were often officially possible only for the propertied classes, but the monogamous permanent relationships of the lower classes were apparently understood as analogous."

—Boswell 1994, p. 32

this practice is that most women spend beyond their means to purchase their dream gown. They can't even imagine getting married without one.

When these patterns are considered in relation to the history of marriage, the interests served by weddings and marriage have not changed much. Throughout the history of Western marriage, certain groups have been excluded from participation. As a property-based relation established for the protection of wealth, the creation of heirs, and the reproduction of the division of labor, certain groups did not qualify.

For example, in some locations in medieval Europe, the poor were not allowed to marry.[24] It was a practice reserved for the propertied classes, and in some cases only for the royal family. Not until the rich realized the need for the reproduction of working-class labor were the poor allowed to marry.

In colonial America, marriage was also a patriarchal arrangement, with fathers regarded as the head of the family and women and children part of his property holdings. Unpropertied whites and free blacks could marry, but they were still under the rule of the propertied class.

> Although unmarried women had the right to own property, enter into
> contracts, and represent themselves in court, after marriage the
> English concept of coverture was evoked, whereby the wife's legal
> identity was subsumed in that of her husband, giving him the authority to
> make decisions for her.[25]

White slave owners did not allow African slaves in the United States and the Caribbean to "legally" marry. This right was reserved for whites and was linked to both white supremacy and the passing of property from father to son. In the following passage, bell hooks describes the relationship of marriage to assimilation practices where blacks imitated whites:

> As the displaced African assimilated American values, they wanted
> to have the ecclesiastical and civil ceremonies their masters and
> mistresses had; they desired public acknowledgment of their union.
> Although there were never any legally acknowledged marriages between

slaves, they wanted the same marriage rituals their white owners enacted.[26]

As a way to effect a symbolic union similar to marriage, African slaves from a variety of African cultures combined their knowledge to create new rituals. The significance of brooms and of sticks in various African cultures combined with the once-popular ritual among white American colonists of holding hands and jumping over a broom to make the practice of "jumping the broom," a ritual sanctioned by some white plantation owners who allowed African slave marriages. Even though some slave owners permitted a marriage ritual, it was not legally binding and could be dissolved at the master's request.[27]

With the emergence of capitalism, these images shifted according to the needs of the marketplace and the division of labor. With this history, it is not surprising to see the emphasis placed on wealth and accumulation in today's wedding industry, effectively putting the traditional white wedding out of reach particularly for the poor, even though they might make every effort to locate a wedding gown that would allow them to "fit" with dominant cultural depictions of the "legitimate" white wedding. To accommodate this need, even thrift stores provide significant offerings for potential brides.

Gown in window

"Thank Heaven for Little Girls . . ."

The cultural codes of traditional femininity permeate bridal culture, from Barbie and other wedding toys to messages in bridal advertising, even though marketers are aware that they are catering to women who occupy positions of privilege and power. Many women have commented in bridal magazines and other sites that even though they typically don't participate in traditionally feminine behavior, they will deviate from this norm in order to have the wedding they've been imagining and preparing for since they were children. While the trend in bridal gown advertising has been toward the marketing of the couture dress, many gown-sellers rely on codes of femininity to attract a buyer. For example, David's Bridal, the discount gown outlet, runs a twenty-page ad highlighting little girls and grown-up brides. David's ads begin with a page of flower girls with the caption "Thank heaven for little girls . . ." followed by a corresponding page of adult brides with the text, "They grow up in the most delightful ways." These messages portray the bride as feminine, innocent, child-like, and youthful. It is commonplace in these ads to see reference to childhood dreams and desires. Listed below are some of the messages David's Bridal uses:

> "Sugar and spice and everything nice"
> "Girlish charm knows no boundaries"
> "From innocence of child to the radiance of a bride"
> "Playing dress-up was never like this"
> "Little girls aren't the only ones who love pink"
> "As soft as your first teddy bear, as tender as your first kiss"
> "Girls just want to have fun"

The ideal of femininity reproduced in these quotes reflects middle-class standards for "appropriate" heterogendered behavior, resecuring women's role as subordinate to men.

In a racialized context, such as that of bridal magazines or wedding toys, this standard also reflects white interests. Sociologist Rose Brewer theorizes the race, class, gender connection by demonstrating the ways these categories benefit the "white power elite":

> Cultural practice, beliefs and ideology also structure female labor. The ideology of what is appropriately Black women's work is played out in the arena of the public social reproduction of labor. Kitchen and cafeteria workers, nurses' aides: these are defined as appropriate jobs for Black women, very much as the domestic labor of a generation ago was defined as "Black women's work."[28]

The images of femininity and whiteness that so pervade popular cultural sites serve to secure in the collective imagination the place of women from particular classes and racial groups. It is much easier to imagine a black, working-class woman as a token collector in the New York subway system than it is to imagine a white, middle- to upper-class woman who is as "soft as her teddy bear" and full of "sugar and spice." The *absence* of women of color from popular cultural sites does as much to racialize relations of production as the *presence* of white women as classic brides.

In addition to securing class interests in relation to labor, these images play a key role in establishing patterns of social reproduction. Signifiers of femininity vary from class to class because women in each class have different responsibilities for socializing their families to take their "place" in capitalist patriarchy. For example, feminine training for children from the professional-managerial class is significantly different than for children from the working or middle classes. Barbie is a classic example of this. While she can be a mother, a wife, a hairdresser, and a makeup artist, she can also venture out of her class, albeit briefly, to be a veterinarian—all the while maintaining her femininity, never in doubt, as the hyper-compensating pink that marks all Barbie products reminds us. The roles "allowed" for Barbie don't cross over into upper-class or professional-managerial practices. (There is no "Debutante Barbie" or "CEO Barbie.") Barbie will most likely grow up to marry, have a house, be a homemaker and mother, and be skilled to do the work of raising children like herself. Verena Stolcke's succinct analysis of this process sees this as an issue of social control:

> [While] class oppression and the social division of labour have their origins in unequal access to the means of production, it is social reproduction, i.e., the perpetuation of class relations and domination—mediated directly by the institution of marriage, the family and inheritance—which requires (and thus determines) both women's primary assignment to domestic labour and the undervaluation of this function . . . [T]he social control of women through marriage differs by class and has different implications for economic roles in different classes.[29]

Mary to Tyrone:

"Do you remember our wedding, dear? I'm sure you've completely forgotten what my wedding gown looked like. Men don't notice such things. They don't think they're important. But it was important to me, I can tell you! . . .

—Eugene O'Neill, *Long Day's Journey Into Night*

While marriage is not specific to capitalism, the particular way it is organized through rules of conduct and inheritance is reinforced by the wedding industry, particularly in relation to the accumulation of property. This is where monogamous marriage is critical to capitalism and patriarchy; it secures women's subordination to men, preserves heirs, ensures that property passes within the family, and maintains class supremacy. Even biblical definitions of adultery reflect the historical need to know who fathered a child. Leviticus 20:10 identifies adulterous behavior as sexual intercourse with another man's wife. It does not specify that an adulterous man also be married, since the violation is of another man's property—the wife—and claims to fatherhood (heirs).

While many people subscribe to broader interpretations of adultery, this history of patriarchal interests still informs today's practices. For example, social sanctions against married women who "stray" are more severe than for men. Women who don't comply with dominant monogamous marriage are far more threatening to the dominant social order than are men who marry and engage in extramarital affairs. In a recent article in the *New York Times,* Gustav Niebuhr discusses the role of women in relation to monogamous marriage:

> As the magisterial *Anchor Bible Dictionary* (1992) puts it, the man's marital status was "inconsequential since only the married or betrothed woman" was "bound to fidelity." The prohibition was not so much about a husband's feelings as about knowing who had fathered a baby.

Thus, it worked to safeguard issues of family succession and property rights.[30]

The history of the wedding ring is rooted in these understandings as well. Even today, only the bride is "required" to wear a wedding ring, signifying her monogamous bond to the husband. Historically grooms weren't required to wear a wedding ring. While this has become more common, it is still optional for men.

Creating the idealized notion of monogamous marriage is one of the central roles of the heterosexual imaginary. The wedding industry and its wedding-ideological complex display images that secure women's consent to participate in these arrangements.

The Spectacle of Accumulation

A Macy's ad in *Brides* magazine proclaims, "You're getting married, you want the whole world to know." A Bed Bath & Beyond ad says, "You said 'Yes' and the whole world wants details." But why? What is the appeal of this public display?

American institutions and popular culture begin preparing women from childhood for their eventual role as the center of attraction and producer of the public wedding spectacle. Over and over again women proclaim they have been waiting for this moment since they were young children. Barbie dolls with bridal gowns and bridal parties, "My Size Bride Barbie," which allows girls to try on the wedding gown, Disney films, television cartoons and sitcoms, soap operas, messages from family members, roles as flower girls and junior bridesmaids, and wedding toys that invite little girls to plan a pretend wedding all contribute to this effort. Even computer games target girls and young women offering interactive fantasies about their future wedding.

Plan a Dream Day Wedding for your best friend Jenny in this beautiful, fun and romantic game! Find items at the gown boutique, bakery and other stylish shops to help make Jenny's special day a dream! Play Perfect Match to unlock the secret honeymoon level, or try Choose A Story where you decide what happened at Jenny and Robert's first

Where is my wedding gown now, I wonder? I kept it wrapped up in tissue paper in my trunk. I used to hope I would have a daughter and when it came time for her to marry—She couldn't have bought a lovelier gown . . . It was made of soft, shimmering satin, trimmed with wonderful old duchesse lace, in tiny ruffles around the neck and sleeves, and worked in with the folds that were draped round in a bustle effect at the back. The basque was boned and very tight. I remember I held my breath when it was fitted, so my waist would be as small as possible . . . Oh how I loved that gown! It was so beautiful! Where is it now, I wonder? I used to take it out from time to time when I was lonely . . . ."

—Eugene O'Neill, *Long Day's Journey Into Night*

> meeting, on their first date, and of course the proposal! Solve each
> wedding crisis along the way to pick the flowers, cake and dress for
> Jenny's big day![31]

In this computer game and in other sites, popular culture plays a central role in producing the desire for a big white wedding extravaganza. In addition to bridal magazines, celebrity magazines such as *People, In Style,* and *Jet* and the *Sunday New York Times* "Celebrations and Ceremonies" pages—formerly the Wedding pages—participate in the wedding-ideological complex.

Bridal magazines make it their business to prepare the bride for her part in "the most important day of her life" and for planning "her day." Using slogans such as these is common throughout bridal literature. By producing and exploiting the bride's well-developed and well-orchestrated fantasy of the "perfect" wedding with her as the "perfect" bride with the "perfect" romance, the wedding industry is able to promote accumulation. Everything—from advice on cosmetics to planning and timetable checklists—is provided. Headlines such as "Create the most romantic wedding ever: Brilliant bouquets, Storybook sites, and details that make a difference," "20 gorgeous hair ideas," or "Princess Diana—Her Wedding Remembered" offer advice and fodder for the imagination.

Displayed as the exemplar of the ultimate wedding, Princess Diana's ceremony helps the new bride imagine her own, inviting her to emulate and legitimize upper-class practices, as though the average middle-class bride could ever achieve anything remotely similar to this pageant. While the "how-to" columns provide brides-to-be with information on planning their wedding and choosing their wedding gown, one of the most important roles bridal magazines play is in capturing the bride-to-be's imagination. Real wedding stories about celebrities support advertisers' efforts to reach their audience, secure the economic health of bridal magazines, and ensure that the consumption-based wedding market imagines itself emulating royalty and wealth.

As part of the wedding-ideological complex, media constructions of celebrity weddings play a powerful part in linking romance with accumulation. Represented as the "real," celebrity weddings appeal to readers as actual manifestations of the fairy tale or storybook romance. In a recent special issue of *People* magazine, entitled *People*

Extra: Real Life Weddings,[32] they devoted an entire section of the magazine to stories and photos of ordinary weddings that were modeled on specific celebrity weddings. In one instance, the bride spent even more money than the celebrity in the hopes of outdoing her.

Princess Diana's wedding, the most retold of all celebrity weddings, frequently serves as the ideal. In recognition of the one-year anniversary of her death in 1997, numerous television networks aired video footage of Diana and Charles's wedding, *Bride's* magazine offered a retrospective, and *People* put out a special issue called *Unforgettable Women of the Century* with a small photo of Diana in her wedding tiara featured on the cover next to the other princess bride, Princess Grace, displayed prominently in the center of the cover.

MSNBC's *Time & Again* replayed Prince Charles and Lady Diana's wedding telecast, complete with narration from then and now. Jane Paulie and Tom Brokaw were the co-anchors on July 29, 1981, who provided commentary for this momentous occasion. Jane Paulie referred to this as "the day [Diana] became a wife and a princess." Tom Brokaw certified the importance and size of the royal spectacle by mentioning that 750 million people, according to BBC estimates, in sixty-one countries would be viewing the event. Descriptions from both Paulie and Brokaw alternated between fascination with Charles and Diana's romance and amazement at their wealth. Brokaw reported that the wedding presents "have been presided over by none less than a rear admiral." He commented on two of the gifts, a $20,000 fully equipped kitchen, "which they accepted," and a special bed named for Lady Diana. The bed was made with twelve hundred springs, which, according to the bed maker, were useful "just in case [Charles] comes home late so she won't be disturbed."

Jane Paulie commented on Diana's demeanor during the ceremony as the "bride's sweet timidity . . . [in this] utterly traditional twentieth-century wedding." Of course, Paulie had no idea if, in fact, the bride was feeling timid, but read these classic codes of femininity into what she perceived as a feminine event. It came out years later that Diana was very disturbed during this event about the presence of Camilla Bowles, Charles's former love interest with whom he had recently made contact.[33]

As the ceremony began Brokaw exclaimed that soon the "glass coach bearing Lady Diana" would appear. What did appear didn't seem to be glass but was a black and gold coach with coachmen dressed in full red and gold uniforms with tri-point hats of black and gold. While the carriage was extremely ornate and expensive, the idea of a "glass coach" called up images of Cinderella and fairy tales.

Both commentators were very concerned with what appeared to be a lack of romantic display following the ceremony. Paulie kept commenting on how she was waiting for Charles to look into Diana's face as a signifier of their romantic bond. Both Brokaw and Paulie repeatedly referred to this and waited for some public display of affection which could be construed as romance. Finally, from the balcony of Buckingham Palace, Diana and Charles looked into each other's faces and smiled. Brokaw and Paulie were gratified.

In keeping with the tenets of patriarchal religious ceremonies, the presiding clergy outlined what marriage is, proclaiming it to be "an honorable estate . . . signifying the mystical union between Christ and his church." He also offered three reasons why marriage is important: (1) for the "increase of mankind" where children will be brought up in "fear and nurture of the Lord"; (2) to honor the "natural instincts and affections implanted by God" which should be "hallowed by God"; and (3) to serve the interests of "mutual society, health and comfort in prosperity and adversity." After reciting these religious ideological messages concerning marriage, the priest asked, "Who gives this woman to this man?" At that point, Lady Diana's father literally gave Diana's hand to Prince Charles. Charles then placed a ring on Diana's finger and did not receive one for himself. This striking display of patriarchal tradition resecures the upper-class role of Princess Diana as wife, future mother, and future queen. This act of placing her hand into Charles's so that the ring can be placed there boldly demonstrates the transference of daughter as property of the father to husband as the new proprietor, signified by the wedding ring. Her labor will serve the interests of the British crown in providing heirs and in socializing them appropriately for their life as royalty.

This display reflects a powerful relationship among romance, religious ideology, property, and wealth or accumulation. The spectacle of wealth is never called into question but is, instead, romanticized by the emcees. The conditions upon which any of these vast holdings have been amassed are rendered invisible by the heterosexual imaginary that collapses the romantic and the material world together.

In his book *Society of the Spectacle,* Guy Debord discusses the role of celebrities in the production of the spectacle:

> Media stars are spectacular representations of living human beings, distilling the essence of the spectacle's banality into images of possible roles. Stardom is a diversification in the semblance of life—the object of an identification with mere appearance which is intended to compensate for the crumbling of directly experienced . . . activity.[34]

The spectacle—especially the media or celebrity spectacle—works ideologically, conveying to the observer/reader what they *should* believe about romance, weddings, marriage, and heterosexuality. Celebrity spectacles become the vehicles through which the masses not only imagine the possibility of wealth and fame but seek to emulate it as well, thereby legitimating the accumulation practices of the rich and famous.

People magazine's annual special issues on celebrity weddings as well as their ongoing reporting teach us not only what counts as celebrity but also the importance of romance and the wedding in American society. To qualify for a wedding announcement in *People,* one must be either famous or notorious. Included in their coverage are royalty, celebrated and successful athletes, athletes who have fallen from grace and have been "saved" by marriage, film, television, and theater stars, politicians and those who have had affairs with politicians, and music celebrities.

The reporting of celebrity weddings follows many of the same patterns visible in the presentation of Princess Diana's wedding. Of course, central to all of the coverage, regardless of status, ethnicity, or religion, is the image of the bride in her white wedding gown. Except for a couple of notable and predictable exceptions—Roseanne, for instance, marries in red—the vast majority of celebrity weddings feature a white bride with a white wedding gown. Periodicals that serve predominantly black, hispanic, native, or Asian audiences feature women of color as brides, also clad in white wedding gowns. Even when one wedding took place in Shanghai, the bride still wore white in what is becoming more normalized around the world. In a wide variety of countries today, two weddings are occurring—where the bride and groom wear traditional clothing in one and white gowns and western tuxedos in the other.

Traditional plus
western wedding
rituals for Hindu
American couple

Evidence of accumulation is also present in the reporting of celebrity weddings. While some weddings are certainly small and simple, the vast majority are sites for spectacular display. For instance, Gina Marie Tolleson rode to her wedding in a white carriage drawn by a white horse to marry Alan Thicke. Céline Dion needed a "month to plan" her hairdo and "1,000 hours to make her pearl-encrusted gown." Wed in Notre Dame Basilica in Montreal, Dion and her groom René Angélil had some nine hundred people "working for [their] wedding to happen." Emulating the attire of a queen, Dion wore a tiara that weighed twenty pounds.

People magazine's wedding annuals are extraordinarily popular among readers. They are filled with photographs and brief descriptions of weddings. The format they use for reporting these events fits with the notion of media star as spectacle and foregrounds the exceptional about these events. All descriptions include ages of the bride and groom. Interestingly, when someone refuses to give their age *People* comments on this noncompliance. Of course, we're left wondering why the ages of the newlyweds are significant for these reports.

While the vast majority of people marry someone of a similar age, the effect is that significant age differences are more noticeable. In a section called "Wedding Shockers," *People* offers the equivalent of the wedding freak show, highlighting those marriages that break from the norm. For example, they focused their attention on the Michael Jackson–Lisa Marie Presley wedding and contrasted it with Jerry Lee Lewis's marriage to an eighth-grader in 1957, suggesting by association that both marriages were deviant. Most significant of those listed in this section was the wedding of Guess model and reality TV star Anna Nicole Smith, 27, to J. Howard Marshall II, 90.

> "I'm very much in love," Smith told an interviewer, flashing her asteroid-size 22-carat engagement diamond and her diamond-dusted wedding band . . . "I could have married him four years ago if I'd just wanted to get rich . . ." His mistress of 10 years during his second marriage was a flamboyant Texas socialite named "Lady" Walker. (She died while undergoing cosmetic surgery in 1991.)[35]

Up to her premature death in February 2007, Smith claimed that she had truly loved Marshall. The media, however, continued to question her credibility. The effect of reports like these is heteronormative. Stories of the unusual or the odd serve to secure the "normal," the center, making all who occupy this space feel comforted by their compliance.

Another pattern prevalent in these wedding reports is that of listing the celebrity guests. The effect is to both certify the celebrity and provide an imaginary sense of the consolidation of wealth and fame by revealing privileged circles of friends and associates. The greater the listing of celebrities, the more spectacular the wedding.

One aspect of celebrity weddings that has become normative is the presence of children. About 45 percent of the couples listed in these issues had been married before, had children from a previous relationship, or had been living together for several years and already had children. Several brides were pregnant at the time of the wedding and some insisted on getting married so that they could have children. In one article in *People,* the writer asserts that the birth of a child becomes the impetus for celebrities to marry and sometimes symbolically replaces the engagement ring. "These days . . . a pregnancy is tantamount to a diamond . . . When couples have children, the child is a sign of commitment."[36] Most notable with regard to this trend is the wedding of Tom Cruise and Katie Holmes. It had all the trappings of a royal wedding complete with castle and featured a who's who of Hollywood couples including Jennifer Lopez and Marc Anthony, Brooke Shields and Chris Henchy, Will and Jada Pinkett Smith, and Jim Carrey and Jenny McCarthy. In the story the reporter from *People* wrote about the presence of Tom and Katie's baby Suri during the ceremony. "At one point during a pause in the ceremony, 'it was quiet, and then Suri cooed loudly,' says a guest. 'It was so sweet.'"[37]

While nationally the social trend is away from thinking of children conceived outside of marriage as "illegitimate," the history of this stigma remains, especially for the poor. For the conservative right and among many politicians, the call for family values is frequently code for "nuclear family," where the children are raised in a two-parent, patriarchal, heterosexual, married household. This ideological position formed the foundation of the marriage campaign embedded within the welfare reform legislation passed by the U.S. Congress. While these groups reject the possibility that children can be raised in a healthy, loving, and growthful environment that does not fit this model, the reality is quite the contrary. The relevance of the nuclear family model is rapidly waning, returning us to a model more similar to the pre-World War II family.[38]

Many people generally believe it is "necessary" to marry when there are children involved. Marriage becomes the way to certify legitimacy, normalcy, and morality. The heterosexual imaginary circulating here prevents people from seeing the role of marriage in preserving heirs and protecting private property. It also conceals from view the various abuses outlined in Chapter 2 and the ways weddings and heterosexuality are used as forms of social control. Instead, the heterosexual imaginary convinces us that what is important is to participate in the legitimizing illusions of the institution. Within some social groupings the arrival of a child is an honored and celebrated event regardless of marital status.

The scale of the celebrity weddings reviewed in *People* and *In Style* is less ostentatious than one might imagine. With a few significant exceptions, most are consistent

"To Have and To Hold: From the wealthy about to wed, the prenuptial agreement is the vow that gets honored first . . .

3. The Precious Bodily Fluid Clauses. Some couples have been using prenuptials to regulate marital behavior . . .

[A] Louisiana man insisted in this prenup that his wife's sexual demands be limited to once a week. He tried to avoid alimony because she violated the prenup by 'seeking coitus thrice daily.' The court ruled in her favor, saying that 'the fault here alleged by the husband is not in law any fault.'"

—Jan Hoffman, "How They Keep It," 1995, p. 104

with national trends, but the wealth and privilege of the families are usually evident in some form of excess, e.g., flowers, other celebrities, cake, special location, or Cinderella coaches. *In Style* places more emphasis on the wedding itself rather than on the celebrity newlyweds. It has a section called "New Tradition: Elements of Style," which highlights the ways music, gowns, and rings say "class act." To accentuate the class standing of celebrities, it lists what kinds of jewelry particular couples give each other. For example, Carolyn Bessette Kennedy (John F. Kennedy, Jr.'s partner) wore an "eternity band of sapphires alternating with white diamonds," and Christie Brinkley's engagement ring was a "hefty sapphire flanked by two diamonds."[39] The recent marriage of Donald Trump to former model Melanie Knauss was referred to as the ceremony of the century, where media called it the "fairy tale wedding with the fairy tale guest list." Of course, no fairy tale would be complete without a guest list featuring a few princes! In this case, the list included Prince Charles, Prince Albert, and Prince Andrew. The bride's jewels included a 15-carat diamond engagement ring, a diamond anklet, and a $132,000 rhinestone encrusted couture gown.[40]

Celebrity is synonymous with spectacle—people wouldn't achieve this status without having already achieved "stardom"—and is the embodiment of spectacle to the consuming public. As a result, celebrity weddings alternate between minimalist—getting away from the spotlight—and mega-extravaganza. Either way, media portrayals of celebrity weddings offer a celebration of style, romance, excess, and expense. Ultimately, they set the evolving standard for what a white wedding should be.

Finally, one section of note is *People*'s "Tying the Not" or *In Style*'s "To Be or Knot to Be?" This is where the editors at *People* and *In Style* try to explain why some celebrity couples haven't married or won't marry. "A romantic world wishes they'd wed, but some celebrity couples believe that happily ever after comes without a hitch."[41] In other words, marriage in the United States is compulsory. This is not the case worldwide, but the heterosexual imaginary convinces us that marriage is both normal and necessary. Rather than seeing the various interests at stake in decisions of this kind and making fully informed decisions, we instead consent to the illusion that you can't have commitment, love, and family without marriage.

Oprah Winfrey has been "engaged" to Stedman Graham for years and told *Redbook Magazine* that she has the "right to not get married." Imagine that! She sees this

Whitewashed Wedding
Another decision that streamlined the day: Everything, from the flowers in Jodi's bouquet to the candles on the reception table, was white. "When you think of weddings, you think white, and in pictures, it looks fantastic against blue water," says Jodi, who consulted with Colin on the planning. Thanks to the whitewashed theme, no time was wasted debating lilac versus lavender tablecloths. Even the tiny wedding party—one best man, one maid of honor, one ring bearer, and two flower girls—was given the monochromatic mandate, as were the guests.

—"Doing It Her Way: An L.A.-based wedding planner takes her party smarts to Mexico" by Paula Rackow, http://www.brides.com/realweddings

as a right, not a requirement. She also said "I'm sorry I ever was such a big-mouth frog about the engagement." And yet, Oprah is well known for her wedding and bridal gown shows, which give out advice to many viewers seeking to enter into matrimony. Alan and Denise Fields, the wedding industry consumer advocates, have appeared on her show.[42]

Goldie Hawn and Kurt Russell have been living together for years. When asked why they hadn't married, Russell commented, "The social prerequisite has no value for me." Hawn, who agrees with Russell, was recently quoted in *Vanity Fair* as saying "I don't believe we own anybody." And, Angelina Jolie and Brad Pitt, now parents of four children, have reported that they will not marry until people of the same sex can. While numerous other famous couples resist marriage, tabloids and magazines like *People* are invested in the wedding. They know that a wedding featuring any one of these couples would yield higher circulation and greater sales. But beyond this, these periodicals are also invested in the institution and play a significant part in the wedding-ideological complex, securing the future of romance and the social controls necessary for maintaining the status quo. As Katherine Hepburn asserted, "It's bloody impractical to love, honor, and obey. If it weren't, you wouldn't have to sign a contract."[43]

"Goin' to the Chapel and We're Gonna Get Married . . ."

The presentation of celebrity weddings by the mass media provides intelligible representations of class for middle-class consumers. Wealth and upper-class status are linked with various forms of conspicuous consumption, which, while excessive, are not unimaginable. For the social elite, the codes of old wealth, while also spectacular, are much more elusive and are frequently concealed behind displays of style and good taste.

The *Sunday New York Times* wedding pages, now called "Weddings/Celebrations," are currently located in the "Sunday Styles" section and are a long-standing institution in American culture. As a site for the wedding announcements of the upper classes, these pages hold particular significance today not just for the upper or owning class but also for the professional-managerial class. With the addition in 1992 of a weekly

"Think of her as Robobride, equal parts Martha Stewart and Arnold Schwarzenegger. In increasing numbers, women in the 20's and 30's are seeking professional help to sculpture a body that's fit to walk the aisle . . . The trend is driven in large part by the evolution in wedding dress styles—from the overblown Cinderella look chosen by the Princess of Wales . . . to the satin slip worn by Carolyn Bessette-Kennedy . . . 'I realized all eyes were going to be on me. He's in a tuxedo . . . but there's 200 of them out there, and this is the memory they're going to keep of you, frozen in time.'"

—Stephen Henderson, "Get Me to the Gym on Time," 1998, p. 9.1

feature story called "Vows," by Lois Smith Brady, the wedding pages have been updated from their role as part of the "Society" pages, announcing the marriages of young women of the upper class, to include announcements of the weddings, commitment ceremonies and civil unions of those who are seemingly more typical *Times* readers. Further, they prefer announcements from both members of a couple and have been updated to reflect both different sex and same sex unions.

No longer just about brides and their wedding party, the mainstay of these announcements is the background information revealed about each couple, their families, and their implied social networks. Readers learn not just who is getting married but where they are from and where they were educated. The format for these announcements includes the listing of preparatory schools, if either the bride or groom attended one, which college they each attended, what jobs they each hold, and where they will live. Beyond this, each parent's occupation, volunteer work or other notable endeavor, where they each were educated, and where they reside are included. The listing concludes by mentioning who officiated at the ceremony and where the wedding and reception were held.

Inserted subtly into each of these passages is whether or not the bride will take her husband's name. In most cases she complies with patriarchal tradition. In those instances where she has elected to keep her name or hyphenate it with her husband's name, it is often explained as necessary for career continuity.

The context for these announcements is the "Sunday Styles" section, where upper-class interests are cloaked in the guise of style. Each issue contains columns called "Pulse," featuring trends in fashion and style, "On the Street," a photographic rendition of emerging grassroots fashion, "Modern Love," about the challenges of love in today's world, as well as a sampling of hip articles on life challenges for the cultured, twenty-somethings. These articles include everything from the emotional language of text-messaging to where the best Cuban-Korean restaurant is. Who's in and who's not is supplemented with the "Evening Hours," the traditional society pages of the older and wealthier crowd only made more user-friendly for the on-the-way-to-old-and-wealthy. This page is comprised of a black-and-white-photo collage of the rich and famous gathering for either celebrity arts, or charity events. These photos give *Times* readers a window into the upper-class social world by revealing who they are, what causes they support, and what their social networks are. Interestingly, however, celebrity weddings are not spotlighted in this section. The reader learns what counts as upper-class style without the spectacle of the photo spread used by magazines such as *People* and *In Style*.

Lead articles in "Sunday Styles" include large color photos and provide magazine-like, glitzy coverage of contemporary trends for the rich and famous. For example, some of the recent topics have included "Love Him or Hate Him (Perez Hilton)," "The Kid Quits the Picture," "How the Glitz Stole Greenwich" (subtitled "In a town where wealth used to whisper, new residents are turning up the volume") or "This Year, the Jet Set is Seeking Nirvana" (subtitled "In an age of cell-phone gurus and E-mail ashrams, trend setters go East to scratch a spiritual itch and play 'Zennis'"). In fact, the only discussion of weddings short of the wedding announcements and "Vows" is an occasional article on upscale wedding trends such as the recent "Get Me to the Gym on Time" (subtitled "Brides are making sure that what they show is shapely").

"Vows," by Lois Smith Brady, is a regular column in the Sunday wedding pages. It features a large and small photo of some moment in a selected newlywed's coupled life or wedding. What's significant about these photos is the elusiveness of their subjects. They provide a glimpse into a wedding or the couple's life together but from what at first seems to be an unusual photo location—e.g., the back of the church, over some spectator's shoulder, the receiving line, the center of clinking glasses, in their kitchen. The photographer never allows the viewer the opportunity to witness or consume the central or iconic wedding image. Instead, by their subjects' elusiveness and the context, these photos seem to preserve the privacy of the featured couple while conveying both style and chic, concealing from view the class interests operating here.

Consistent with the spectacle of accumulation, the narrative that accompanies the photos is primarily about the romance between the bride and the groom. It gives some of the same information provided in the other wedding announcement but fills in with a story about the couple—their childhoods, their dreams and interests, and any significant obstacle they may have overcome to get to this point. Commonplace in this column are stories about couples facing life-threatening diseases or disabling

"Then there was the matter of what name she would use. Years earlier, when it had been suggested that the two should meet, Ms. Jones recalled having been put off by the associations that the surname, Goldfinger, brought to mind. "Think of him as a man with a theme song," Ms. Jones recalled her friend saying.

"I decided it was time to be the real Mrs. Goldfinger and not the make-believe one," she said. "I'll use it when I need it, like, 'This is Mrs. Goldfinger. Where's the car?'"

—*"Vows," by Jane Gordon, New York Times,* December 31, 2006 accidents or momentary lapses in employment in the arts. Central to these stories, however, is how the bride and groom met and how romantic their relationship has been, including, in some cases, a story about the engagement proposal or some humorous anecdote about their lives or their wedding. These accounts usually conclude with a summary of the ceremony, including the location, the music played, and something interesting about the reception, including an occasional quote from a loving parent.

Still, while the "Vows" quarter-page column appears to reveal a story about the experience and romance of wedding, it has the strange effect of leaving the reader with far less than if they had read about the couple in *People* or *In Style*. The difference, of course, is that these are generally not celebrity weddings—though on occasion, a celebrity guest credentials the couple with their presence at the wedding. Additionally, these articles convey an "everyday" kind of quality about the subjects while, at the same time, preserving the class interests of the publication itself and the audience it addresses and serves.

What is significant about the wedding announcements is the inclusion of the education and career of each member of the couple regardless of whether this is a different sex or same sex union. This is a recent trend in *New York Times* wedding announcements, reflecting the historical necessity of work in the lives of the upper classes. Most of the couples represented here are from the professional-managerial class, where all difference is homogenized into a collage of well-educated, career-oriented couples. Each listing begins with their education and occupations, a very different focus from other popular culture representations. What separates this class from the others is the primacy of occupation and career over romance and the rise of women into professional or leadership careers. The only differences evident in the listings are those of race and ethnicity. The vast majority of couples included in these pages are white, with a few obvious—only because of their rarity—exceptions. Between August 1997 and August 2007, for example, only 10.1 percent of the couples whose photographs appeared in these pages qualified as people of color or nonwhite.

Breaking with tradition, the *New York Times* has shifted the focus of these pages from the bride and her pedigree to the couple and their education and careers as well as those of both of their parents. Further, the *Times* has broken with the heteronormative approach to marriage and has embraced both visually and textually the changing landscape of commitment ceremonies of all kinds in the U.S. While to some this seems a superficial change, to others it is a jarring shift from the more formal and heteronormative wedding pages. To see photos of same sex couples smiling lovingly together in such a major world class publication as the *New York Times*, is transformative and challenging and signals a growing paradigm shift in the legitimacy of same sex relationships and commitments. One interesting effect of this mainstream representation of same sex partnerships is the mirroring of heteronormative tradition. In a way, these ceremonies do not disrupt heteronormativity but legitimize the heterosexual imaginary in their ideology and their practice.

Typically, wedding announcements in the *New York Times* represent two groups: couples who are finished with college (some either in or finished with graduate school) and older couples remarrying and settled in their careers. In one example a white heterosexual couple in their forties is photographed in professional attire, their heads together, and smiling into the camera. Below their photo, the announcement focuses on their credentials and social networks. Most of this announcement is devoted to telling the couple's history, occupations, credentials, and family connections. While this might appear nontraditional to the middle-class reader, this narrative fits the norm for their social class.

The social networks in evidence in this announcement are substantial. Links to the federal government, the executive branch, the Senate, the Judiciary and the Department of Justice, and the Department of State, all appear. The couple, one a high-level lawyer and the other a medical specialist, will also have access to the legal profession and to the medical establishment as well as to two different universities. Their ages and their previous marital status indicate that they have had much longer than traditional-age couples to accumulate resources and property. The bride's mother also has connections to the arts. Because of all of these factors the access and privilege afforded this couple by virtue of their class are extensive and powerful. This announcement signals to all of the participants in these networks that this couple's social capital will increase and be available to other members of the same circles.

The second group represented in these announcements is comprised of people in their mid- to late twenties or early thirties who are marrying for the first time. In one typical example, both the bride and the groom are aspiring professionals who have attended prestigious or Ivy League colleges and universities and have completed graduate work in topics and disciplines—art history and classical studies—which are out of the mainstream and not very marketable for the average college graduate. Given their class access, this lack of marketability is not apparent. From the description in the announcement, which leads off with the bride's accomplishments, they have already established connections in the professional-managerial class that will allow them to advance and diversify. With an air of confidence and a sense of direction, the couple reveals their plans to work together in related jobs while the groom completes his doctoral research in classical studies. The bride has chosen to take her husband's name and, though she is credentialed and has a job opportunity in her field, will work in an overseas location compatible with her groom's professional development.[44]

Related to these "credential capsules" are the "Vows" columns, which also appear in each Sunday edition. While the announcements authorize the couple in their own social networks, the narratives in "Vows" provide an ideological tool for the upper classes. Generally, the professional-managerial class bride and groom in these stories are presented as the "everyday" or "just folk" couple. In keeping with the "Style" theme of this section, newlyweds are frequently portrayed as progressive, well-connected, tasteful, "hip," and occasionally multiethnic.

Ideologically, "Vows" works to certify the professional-managerial class as "average" and makes romance and the wedding seem natural, ordinary, and glamorous. The heterosexual imaginary is particularly visible in these stories. Erased from view are the interests of the dominant social order that "needs" to recruit middle-class women into new jobs while preserving patriarchal social arrangements. Rosemary Hennessy, in her book *Materialist Feminism and the Politics of Discourse,* refers to this process as the production of the "New Woman":

> Capitalism in the post-industrial west, increasingly in competition with
> the "third world," has had to revise, readjust, and even abandon
> altogether the ideology of separate spheres in order to draw more
> middle-class women into its labor force. Doing that without risking the
> patriarchal symbolic order has required delicate renegotiations of the . . .

feminine. Throughout the twentieth century these renegotiations have taken the form of various versions of the New Woman. Most recently she is figured as the professional career woman, often juggling work with domestic responsibilities of "home and family."[45]

To do this, the heterosexual imaginary circulating in the "Vows" columns attempts to construct appealing images of this "new woman"—whether heterosexual or not—who is able to accommodate and give priority to domestic life while managing her professional responsibilities as well. The stories presented in these columns mask the contradictions underlying weddings, marriage, and heterosexuality by romanticizing certain images and suppressing others that threaten the legitimacy of these arrangements. Julie Torrant, in her article "For Better or Worse: Marriage in Commodity Culture," explains how this process depends upon the ideological work of sites such as the "Styles" section of the *Times* and the column "Vows" through the "transference of the old order onto new ideas, signs, and activities."[46] Even the entry of same sex unions into this dominant cultural site reifies the operation of these interests by simply mirroring dominant social practices. In this instance, the "updating" that has occurred in the inclusion of all coupled unions manifests as nothing more than a heterosexual shapeshifting with little to no effect on dominant interests.

One of the ideological strategies "Vows" uses to achieve this process is romance. To manage social differences within the couple, a typical pattern in these narratives is to provide an explanation for the potential mismatch of two very different people. The story then resolves this situation by demonstrating how romance and love conquer all. Removing the names of the newlyweds from the actual narratives, the following section provides an in-depth examination of these processes.

In one example, "Vows" feature writer Lois Smith Brady covered the wedding of Clara Binder and Lenny Solar (the names in this story have been changed). The lead photo for this article shows just the hands of wedding guests toasting with champagne glasses. The smaller photo insert shows the bride and groom in wedding regalia looking at themselves in a mirror experiencing the joy of the heterosexual imaginary, examining their own wedding reflection.

The article begins "they were as different as yoga and high-impact aerobics." He is the owner of a home furnishings store in an upscale New York neighborhood and brings with him the knowledge and sensibility associated with "making your home a sanctuary, an ecologically aware oasis full of fresh flowers, favorite scents and couches you can sink into like mud baths." Her apartment is "about as comforting to the soul as junk mail," and Brady characterizes her as a "super-serious career woman" who is employed as a buyer for a clothing catalog and has little time for domestic responsibilities.

Within the first couple of paragraphs we become aware that they have different priorities, different tastes, different values, and may come from different classes. We also observe some reversal of traditional heterogendered behaviors: he's more concerned with the domestic sphere and she is career-driven. But as a column anchoring the wedding pages of a major newspaper, "Vows" must have a happy ending; the reader is invited, therefore, to imagine how this little drama will reach its inevitable conclusion.

When they first meet, they experience an instant attraction, but Lenny is already married and they opt to become close friends. Meanwhile, Clara recognizes she is "falling in love" and distances herself from Lenny. She finds a boyfriend, and Lenny stays with his wife. At this point in the tale, the dominant ideology concerning monogamous marriage is still intact, and "Vows" does its part to reassure us.

A year later, Lenny calls Clara and says he is getting a divorce and would like to have dinner. Clara leaps at the chance by saying, "Great, let's go." They go out to dinner, kiss goodnight, and Clara returns home and tells her boyfriend to move out. As this story unfolds as the tale of a "happily-ever-after" wedding, the heterosexual imaginary suppresses the reasons for "falling in love" as well as the breaking-up-with-boyfriend story. In the interests of "the wedding," "falling in love" is taken for granted and monogamous heterosexuality without marriage is subordinated to the wedding story. A committed and live-in relationship without the wedding ring and the sanction of state and religion doesn't count. The need for the *vow* is secured.

Predictably, Clara's life becomes transformed by Lenny's interest in home furnishings and poetry. "He introduced me to a whole other world I never knew existed," she said. Another difference Brady points out about these two people is their ages—Lenny is 45 and Clara is 31. As the narrative continues, we see Clara become more and more domesticated and mature, leveling not just their gender and class differences but their age differences as well. In the midst of all the style and good taste (read class) Lenny brings to her life, Clara must hide one of her trademarks, a "large jar of dingy pennies"—she no longer thinks it looks very good. She is assimilating into her new class position.

After learning she was pregnant, Clara and Lenny became engaged. Brady assesses the situation: "With a baby due in August, she says she is feeling more domestic and has transformed from a woman obsessed with her resumé to one fascinated with recipes." The transformation is nearly complete. This new woman, this twenty-first-century professional-managerial woman, is about to become an upper-middle-class mother and wife.

The ideology of romantic love permeates the description of the ceremony, and, as Torrant explains, "works to naturalize the hierarchy of romantic relationships over work relationships between men and women, and thus also works to naturalize heterosexuality."[47] The storybook wedding concludes with "a downpour of rose petals thrown by friends," the groom crying and trying to avoid staining his very stylish "platinum Commes de Garçons suit," and the "completely thrilled" bride adorned in a Mary Adams couture gown of "sleeveless silk taffeta," "a wrinkly skirt, a tiered organza overskirt and a furry boa."

In preserving the interests of the wedding industry, Lois Smith Brady ends her piece on Clara and Lenny with quotes from the gown designer and the jewelry designer. The former asserts, "She [the bride] was completely thrilled that everything was happening at once." The latter claims, "There's a tremendous romance in being pregnant and getting married . . . You have a baby, you have marriage, and you have love." Since the author and the two speakers at the end are all female, the alliance of women to carry out the mission of the dominant social order works to secure the consent of women to these arrangements. In the end, the interests of patriarchal heterosexuality and capitalism are both preserved. Clara is both wife and worker without endangering the order of either sphere.

In another example from "Vows" where a same sex couple celebrates their union, Brady employs similar narrative strategies. The commitment ceremony of Carrie Kelly and Emily Slotsky takes place in the Caribbean, a popular destination wedding site. Set against the backdrop of the Caribbean Ocean, the "Vows" photo shows the two white women clad in white wedding dresses looking gleefully out at their guests while the woman officiant presiding over their ceremony stands above them with her arms boldly upraised in a proclamation stance. Breaking from the traditional romantic image of a couple about to be joined in marriage, this photo shows the couple standing far apart from each other and looking out at their guests and not at each other. The smaller photo that accompanies the main image shows a large group of men in matching suits as ushers. The heterosexual imaginary is secure—the two women have men in their ceremony.

As with other "Vows" stories, this one begins by telling the reader about how different these women are from each other. Carrie is a country singer/songwriter who has "little concern for safety, convention, income or comfort." Emily, on the other hand, is a tall, thin "blonde, very elegant, very Town & Country" who is "48, lives near Washington Square Park" and "has an amazing art collection." A public relations executive for the culture industry, Emily clearly displays the style and taste sensibilities of the upper classes.

To illustrate the sameness of this couple to others whose stories are told in these pages, Brady describes Emily's path to finding her one true love: "I had been out and about for a long time . . . It couldn't be worse than being a straight woman in New York." Their first date was at a pub where Carrie was performing. With a clear reference to their class differences, Emily recalls the first date Carrie invited her on. She gave Emily three choices of bars in downtown New York. "I was pretty sure from the names that all the wines came with a screw-off top." Carrie met Emily in faded jeans and Emily wore a designer scarf.

The rest of the narrative details how their time together increased until Carrie moved into Emily's stylish apartment. How did they know it was the kind of love that "needs" vows? As Emily reports, "It is not when you feel like you could live together, it's when you feel you couldn't live without each other."

Carrie "proposed" to Emily on Nantucket the previous summer to which Emily responded with the most popular wedding descriptor: "Perfect." The country singer with her attachment to working-class style is rendered romantic by proposing in one of the vacation spots of the upper class.

The following spring they held a commitment ceremony before 200 guests at a classic wedding destination. They, too, "walked down a rose-petal aisle," each wearing different white designer gowns. The homily proclaimed that "love once found has more staying power than people think. It is not easily destroyed."

The heterosexual imaginary works in a powerful way through this particular narrative. While it breaks from the logic of heterosexuality that requires an "opposite" sex distinction, this narrative naturalizes vows and ceremonies—weddings—as necessary for commitment. Even with centuries of same sex commitment history that provides evidence that scores of relationships have stood the test of time and love without benefit of ceremony or license, these wedding stories and their location in the media work to erase the arbitrariness of these so-called commitment practices.

"Vows" teaches us what counts as a "vow." It is making a commitment to preserve lasting relationships, style, social class, and the assimilation of differences. It is blending a partnership with the dominant social order. In the context of all the social class markers embedded within these ceremonies, the vow becomes the securing of consent to the terms of the dominant class.

The power of the heterosexual imaginary circulating in these stories and in popular culture cannot be overstated. We begin by naturalizing gender as though it is somehow related to our biology and not the result of social processes or organized in the interests of institutionalized heterosexuality. Obscured from view are the powerful ruling interests being served by this institution. Weddings, marriage, romance, and heterosexuality become naturalized to the point where we consent to the belief that marriage is necessary to achieve a sense of well-being, belonging, passion, morality, and love. And we live with the illusion that marriage is somehow linked to the natural order of the universe rather than see it as it is: a social and cultural practice produced to serve particular interests.

These same beliefs also prevent us from imagining childbearing and childrearing as legitimate without state-regulated marriage. Instead we conduct studies of children of divorce and examine the "problems" of "broken homes" and of the loss of "family values" without ever calling into question the very structures that create the conditions that produce these outcomes. By allowing the heterosexual imaginary to circulate freely with our consent and without question, we participate

"This morning . . . the Walt Disney Corporation announced a partnership with Pfizer Corporation in the marketing of the breakthrough sex drug Viagra . . . Disney's theme parks are among the most popular destinations for newlyweds. A marketing partnership promoting the new drug could do the same thing for those people traveling on second honeymoons."

—DND Wirenews (20 May 98)—Lake Buena Vista, Fl.

in the production and perpetuation of racial, class, gender, and sexual hierarchies; legitimize ruling interests; and fail to provide our children with the imaginations and skills they need to become critical citizens of the world. The institution of heterosexuality as it is currently organized serves the interests of capitalist patriarchy, functions as a form of social control, and depends upon the heterosexual imaginary to conceal its regulatory function and effects. Paradoxically, the heterosexual imaginary applies to all relationships, not just those between men and women. Romancing the clone is not about bodies.

Chapter Four

McBride Meets McDreamy

Television Weddings, the Internet, and Popular Film

*I*n the quote above, Howard Brackett's mother has just learned, by way of an Oscar acceptance speech from her son's former student, Cameron Drake, that Howard may be gay. With Howard's wedding just three days away, this revelation comes as a shock to Mr. and Mrs. Brackett, who make it very clear to their son that even if he is gay, he *will* get married whether he wants to or not. At one point, Mrs. Brackett asks, "I can understand that he's gay, but why wouldn't he want a wedding?" Of course, this line is intended to be humorous, but the humor depends upon certain assumptions about the audience. The filmmakers expect the viewer to think this is absurd, laughable. Why would anyone think it's understandable to be gay? At the same time, they expect the audience to find it unimaginable that anyone wouldn't want a wedding. The combination of these two assumptions works to naturalize both institutionalized heterosexuality and its organizing rituals, exemplifying one of the dominant themes in wedding-oriented movies and television shows.

The foundational assumptions in this quote illustrate how some of these ideologies circulate. First, by the string of associations she lays out, Howard's mother asserts her "unconditional" love for her son, indicating that she will love him regardless of how bad or awful he might be. Using the dominant way of thinking about difference, she associates "gay" with color, crime, violence, and murder and places "gay" in a string of descriptors that signify criminal, ugly, unnatural, and deviant. The race theme also surfaces here in her reference to color. While it is somewhat subverted by mentioning red/green as opposed to black/white, the invocation of the color code has the same consequence. According to this passage, to be "of color" is to be "out of the ordinary."

Second, she asserts the primacy of the wedding with her emphasis on the "need" to marry. In her mind, weddings and marriage are natural and compulsory, not optional and certainly not something to take lightly.

Third, she tells us what a wedding means. It is about beauty and order and the desire to escape the real world. The message about heroin is very important here. It is the defining signifier of this passage, making it clear that the wedding is much more than a ritual. It is addictive, compulsory, a "have-to-have." It is the heterosexual imaginary at work, the moment for creating the illusion of happiness, order, well-being, and plenitude. It is the event that allows us to feel comfortable with the dominant social order, conceal any of its contradictions, and anesthetize ourselves against an everyday "state of affairs which needs illusions."[1] Weddings are ritual, drugged, and "feel-good" experiences. Mom needs a fix!

This chapter assesses three cultural sites—wedding movies, television shows, and the internet—for evidence of the power relations organizing both allowed and disallowed meanings. Each of the examples studied makes use of the traditional white wedding theme with a white bride in a white wedding gown—or the "McBride" model. Also, in each instance the actors cast in the film, program, or video are white.

The movies selected for this study include films from the 1990s: *The Birdcage, Father of the Bride II, Four Weddings and a Funeral, In & Out, My Best Friend's Wedding,* and *The Wedding Singer*; and from the 2000s: *American Wedding* and *Wedding Crashers.*

18 Brides for 5 Mothers
Mama mia! Reality television in Italy has taken a new turn, with the introduction of a show that lets mothers choose their son's wives, Reuters reported. Critics responded immediately by saying that the show, "Perfect Bride," insulted women and demonstrated that Italian television . . . had fallen to a new low. In the first episode of "Perfect Bride," carried on RAI, the state broadcaster, the jury of mothers of five single men quizzed 18 bridal candidates about their suitability as wives. Beginning next week the mothers and potential daughters-in-law will live in a "Big Brother"-style house where the candidates' ability to handle household chores can be scrutinized. Viewers will have a chance to take part in voting off the brides they dislike.

—New York Times, April 10, 2007, p. E2, col. 1

These will be considered in relation to a selection of prime-time television weddings from shows telecast in the same decades. From the 1990s: *Ally McBeal, Cheers, Coach, Drew Carey, Ellen, Friends, Heart's Afire, Jag, L.A. Law, Lois & Clark, Mad About You, The Nanny, Northern Exposure, Everybody Loves Raymond, Roseanne, Suddenly Susan, Third Rock from the Sun, Who's the Boss,* and *90210* will be examined. And, since the 2000s ushered in an era where nearly every prime-time situation comedy, soap opera, and most shows on cable television incorporate weddings at some point, a few of the most popular will be examined. These include wedding episodes from *Friends, Frasier,* and *Grey's Anatomy.* Significant to the 2000s is the advent of "reality TV" with shows focused on white weddings. For example, programs such as *A Wedding Story, Bridezilla, Extreme Makeover: Wedding Edition, For Better or For Worse, Platinum Weddings, The Bachelor, The Bachelorette, Who Wants to Marry My Dad?, Whose Wedding is it Anyway?, Wild Weddings,* and the newly minted *The Real Wedding Crashers* have dominated the reality TV landscape. Included in this coverage are a wide variety of daytime television shows that have engaged in interactive weddings, e.g., *Today, Good Morning America, Regis and Kelly.* Finally, the internet is alive with wedding stories, wedding blogs, wedding videos, wedding television, and virtual weddings. In fact, the pervasiveness of wedding material on the internet is so massive it really requires another book-length study. For the purposes of this study, a review of YouTube will be covered in this chapter.

"And We'll Never Be Lonely Any More . . ."

The visual media constitutes the most affective site in the wedding-industrial and ideological complexes. By providing compelling images, popular film, television, and the internet commodify weddings and create the market, the desire, and the demand for the white wedding. Watching our favorite actors achieve happiness or love allows us to live vicariously through the experiences of characters with whom we identify and grow to love and appreciate. The visual simulation of the wedding story is a powerful means for suturing an audience to the interests represented in a film or television show. Even though most of us are able to separate fantasy from reality, we still experience these stories and the emotions they evoke on the level of both the conscious and the unconscious. The romantic illusions created by media weddings construct desire to such an extent that, without realizing it, we place these illusions above reality. With the average bride spending $922 on a wedding gown, $27,852 on a wedding, and incurring a wedding debt far beyond her means, it appears the wedding-ideological complex is succeeding.

Messages from these films make their way into the cultural real—the culturally constructed world—in very powerful ways. Touchstone Pictures' *Father of the Bride* and *Father of the Bride II* were so successful in capturing the imaginations of the American public that Disney, the parent company for Touchstone, developed their own Fairy Tale Wedding Pavilion complete with wedding consultants and spaces modeled on the film. In a commercial advertising the upcoming wedding of *The Nanny*, cast members talked about what a beautiful wedding it was, as though an actual wedding had occurred. These instances are indicative of the influential role popular film and television have on how we think about ourselves, other people, and our values and on how we should behave in the real world. But more than that, they support a wedding-industrial complex that needs the romance fantasy in order to keep weddings and marriage desirable and profitable. Using the heterosexual imaginary, the visual media are highly effective in communicating how to imagine weddings, romance, marriage, and heterosexuality. Consent to the wedding industry, the dominant class, and the capitalist patriarchal social order is assured by the popularity of these images.

Films, television, and internet videos are well liked in part because the tales they present are intelligible to us. The comprehensibility they produce is a product of dominant ideologies about romance, weddings, and marriage. Combined with utopian notions of love and community, a dash of male resistance, and a hint of alternatives, these messages circulate in the culture-at-large as well as in the guise of entertainment and escape. Media tales of all varieties make use of the romance-novel, fairy-tale formula made familiar to many—especially women—since early childhood.

One of the ways these meaning-making processes work is by providing the viewer with stories and visuals that represent our class position, bind us to it,

From Harper's, an actual letter from a bride to her wedding party:

"Dear Bridal Party, . . . I've never wanted a small country-type wedding—Z says this is no wedding but rather a coronation!! Well, not quite. But it sure has been fun so far, and I just cannot wait for everyone to arrive and for all our friends and relatives to have one great, fabulous night . . . Won't each of you come with Z and me to fantasy land— a place where dreams come true and fun abounds for everyone? Where the bride is Cinderella and the groom is the Prince for an evening. You are going to attend a ball at 'Buckingham Palace' (pretend) and the King and Queen have invited only 'royalty'—YOU! This will be a time to remember when you were courting the person to whom you are now married . . . If you have a happy marriage now . . . we expect the Palace to be really electrified with all that LOVE. May your every dream come true! Love, X"

and manage the contradictions we see in the world around us. For example, Oprah Winfrey can provide numerous shows on affordable weddings, wedding gowns, and even wedding consumer advocacy, yet she can claim her "right" not to marry, violating the heterosexual prescription for acceptability—that all eligible women must marry. This contradiction is managed by her service to the middle class through her public celebration of weddings and marriage as well as by her class standing. People can make sense of her as a legitimate exception because of dominant beliefs about fame and wealth that justify her perceived desire to protect her power.

One of the central objectives of the mass media is to provide the images necessary to reproduce the ruling order. As Douglas Kellner points out in his essay "Cultural Studies, Multiculturalism and Media Culture,"

> Media images help shape our view of the world and our deepest values: what we consider good or bad, positive or negative, moral or evil. Media stories provide the symbols, myths and resources through which we constitute a common culture . . . Media spectacles demonstrate who has the power and who is powerless . . . They dramatize and legitimate the power of the forces that be and show the powerless that they must stay in their places or be destroyed . . . Ideologies make inequalities and subordination appear natural and just and thus induce consent to relations of domination.[2]

Consistent with Kellner's argument, weddings in popular culture are powerful sites for the enactment of dominant messages about society-at-large. Film, television, and internet industries know just how to use weddings to reflect and reproduce the kinds of messages necessary to ensure compliance with the dominant social order as they secure their own interests and markets.

In the presentation of wedding stories in popular film and television, the heterosexual imaginary makes the social order appear more manageable and comfortable. Using the power celebrities hold as the embodiment of fantasy to authorize particular social behaviors and beliefs, the visual media demonstrate where the

"'Party of Five' star Jennifer Love Hewitt's next project is a real dream. It's called 'Cupid's love,' a romantic comedy about a wedding planner who falls for the groom. The story came to her in her sleep. 'I had a dream about it, and I woke up and wrote a treatment for it. Then I went to see some producer friends of mine and sort of jokingly pitched them this idea.' . . . Hewitt reportedly got six figures for the pitch alone."

—*Albany Times Union,* "Dream Comes True for Actress's Movie Concept," October 11, 1998, p. A2 margin of acceptability begins and ends. By making visible the consequences of operating outside the norm or the constructed "natural," the film industry legitimizes ruling interests and gains our compliance with practices that keep power in place. For example, the consumption of tales of romance, while profit-making for the producers of soap operas, romance novels, romantic comedies, and media weddings, prevents us from seeing the underlying material consequences (see Chapter 2) these images and practices allow. They promote the "structured invisibility" of whiteness, numb us to excess, and police the boundaries of social acceptability around categories of race, class, sexuality, and even beauty.

In concert with some of the other components of the wedding-ideological complex examined in the previous chapter, weddings in popular film and television contribute to the *creation of many taken-for-granted beliefs, values, and assumptions about weddings*. This wedding-ideological complex works to naturalize romance, weddings, marriage, and heterosexuality rather than present them as the result of meaning-making systems that organize what may or may not be the "natural" world. For example, in *all* of the film and television weddings studied in this chapter, the following references were made by or about the bride:

> "It's my wedding day!"
> "I've been planning for this day all my life (or since I was . . .)"
> "I want a story book wedding."
> "It's the most important day of my life."
> "I've waited my whole life for this day."
> "Everything has to be (is) perfect."
> "This will be the perfect wedding with the perfect guy."
> "This is the happiest day of my life."
> "I have to have the perfect wedding dress."

The pervasiveness of these messages is a sign of the intense socialization effort that the wedding-ideological complex has undertaken in constructing femininity, heterosexuality, and the importance of weddings and wedding consumption to a woman's identity. What does it mean that the most important day of a woman's

"How'd ya like to be in my wedding?
How'd ya like to walk down the aisle?
You could be the center of attention.
Everyone would look at you and smile.
We could send our friends invitations.
You could wear a long black dress.
If you'd like to be in my wedding, darlin'
All ya have to do is say, 'Yes'
Your folks could be seated in the very front row.
And cry when we all turn to look at you.
We could cut the cake
And we could strike a pose
Like the little bitty plastic bride and groom
And then begin our life-long honeymoon."

—"Say Yes" lyrics by Dusty Drake

life is her wedding day? Why go on living after it is over? These messages are so powerful that even when characters in film and television weddings—not to mention women in real life—acknowledge the artificiality of these messages, it is still in the context of "Oh, well, I still want a wedding" or "I guess I'm just old-fashioned." Recently, a friend of mine confessed, "I tried on my old wedding dress, and, I hate to tell you this, but it felt great!"

While many women comply with dominant messages about femininity, heterosexuality, and weddings, some participate in the white wedding mill for other reasons. Weddings can represent a form of resistance among women who must face the social pressures of the workplace and other responsibilities. They can claim the romantic illusion of guarantees, kept promises, and well-being created by the wedding as a way to escape the strain of their real conditions of existence. Regardless of the motivation, the naturalization of the white wedding has been enormously successful.

Cultural theorist Mas'ud Zavarzadeh, in his book *Seeing Films Politically*, argues that this naturalization process is necessary to the reproduction of ruling interest. In using the example of the social production of femininity, Zavarzadeh's argument pertains to the institution it organizes—heterosexuality.

> Capitalist patriarchy . . . requires an idea of femininity that reproduces its relations of production and thus perpetuates itself without any serious challenge to its fundamental **social** norms . . . None of these [feminine] traits are in themselves and "by nature" definitive of femininity and all are in fact political attributes required for maintaining asymmetrical power relations and thus the exploitative gender relations between men and women . . . These traits, however, are not produced in a material vacuum: a society "desires" that which is historically necessary for its reproduction and can be made intelligible to its members.[3]

The examination of white weddings in popular film and television provides some clues concerning the interests society "needs" to serve in this historical moment.

"On Friday, January 17, 1992, Angela, her fiancé, Michael, and three other couples were married in the lobby of an AMC Theater in Hollywood, Florida. The ceremony, which Rick and Suds broadcast live, featured theater ushers acting as, well, ushers and a notary who addressed the brides as Cinderella and the grooms as Prince Charming. It was held to promote Touchstone Pictures' Father of the Bride, a gentle comedy that has about as much to do with reality as Disneyland does—particularly in its depiction of family values, family life, and family finances. But that's why we go to the movies."

—John Clark, "Bride and Joy," 1993, p. 108

Identifying the ideological strategies used in films allows us to unpack the beliefs created about social relations and gives us a critical stance from which to examine our participation in naturalizing them.

"What's Love Got to Do with It?"

With the ratings success of soap opera weddings, these melodramatic ceremonies have also become main fare for prime-time television, capturing the much-coveted consumer market of "18- to 49-year-old women."[4] May "sweeps' week," when television networks compete for the largest share of the viewing audience, has become synonymous with wedding shows (see Table 4.1). Stations usually save their most spectacular production for that week in hopes of eliminating the competition. In an article in *Detroit News,* Michael McWilliams reported that "Weddings are the Icing for the May Sweeps":

> You know it's the May sweeps when everybody on TV gets married. Tonight's Must See TV, for example, turns into Must Say I Do, when three NBC sitcoms . . . crack wise at the altar, or very near it . . . Amid all these wedding bells, marriages figure prominently this month in shows . . . [even those] not exactly known for [their] romantic bliss.[5]

The trend that McWilliams identifies continued into the late 1990s and shows no signs of abating. The 1997–98 season opened with weddings, e.g., *Dharma and Greg,* and closed with them on *Friends, The Nanny, Jag, Spin City, Baywatch, Suddenly Susan, Dr. Quinn, Everybody Loves Raymond, NYPD Blue,* and *For Your*

"Discovery of a Wedding: a Bangalore family was filmed as part of Discovery Channel's series on world weddings which is to be telecast soon."

"We were thrilled when the Discovery people chose my daughter's wedding," said Mrs. Deshpande, a bank employee, and mother of Rashmi, who wed Anand Hunsagi last month. "Now my daughter and son-in-law will be famous throughout the world!"

—Mula Kumar, *The Hindu,* June 4, 2003

Table 4.1 Nielsen 2007 sweeps dates		
May 2007	April 26–May 23, 2007
July 2007	July 5–August 1, 2007
November 2007	November 1–November 28, 2007

Love. The 1998–99 season began with the conclusion of the *Friends* wedding that closed the previous season, carrying the wedding theme through a total of four episodes. *To Have & To Hold* and *Will & Grace* each began their new seasons with weddings. Made-for-TV movies that incorporated weddings during the same time period included *Forever Love, The Marriage Fool, A Marriage of Convenience,* and *I Married a Monster.* (See Appendix for listing of wedding films and television movies.)

Fast forward to the 2000s and you find the same pattern. A sampling of May sweeps weddings for the 2006 and 2007 prime-time programming schedules is shown in Table 4.2.

A similar trend can be seen in the film industry. While the mainstream formula for success used to be "tits and ass" with a dash of violence, contemporary films add weddings to the mix regardless of their relevance to the film. Besides the box office success of *Father of the Bride* and *Father of the Bride II* (1991), subsequent films such as *American Wedding, Four Weddings and a Funeral, My Best Friend's Wedding, The Wedding Singer, In & Out, Muriel's Wedding, License to Wed, My Big Fat Greek Wedding, The Wedding Banquet, The Polish Wedding,* and *Wedding Crashers* have opened the space for the continuing production of wedding films

"Big Day" starts Fall 06 on ABC: Think about how much planning and attention to detail go into arranging a wedding . . . the venue, the dress, the reception, the food, the flowers, the music . . . and on and on and on. Months and months of planning go into a celebration that begins and ends in a single day . . . Everything matters at a wedding, and the tiniest of imperfections can reverberate throughout the event as if lives actually hang in the balance.

—http://abc. go.com/primetime/ schedule/2006–07/ bigday.html

2006	2007
CSI: Miami (ruined)	*ER*: Luka and Abby
7th Heaven	*Bones*
Gilmore Girls	*Desperate Housewives* (2)
One Tree Hill	*Grey's Anatomy*
How I Met Your Mother	*Boston Legal*
New Adventures of Old Christine	
CSI	

Table 4.2 May sweeps wedding episodes of popular television shows, 2006-2007

because of their box office success. Films that target children such as *Shrek*, *Lord of the Rings*, and *Nanny McPhee* also offer wedding ceremonies to seal their happily-ever-after endings. And action films that typically draw a broader audience in terms of race, class, and sex—e.g., *Armaggedon*, *Babel*, *Star Wars: Episode II*—also include a scene with a big white wedding.

The increased prevalence of weddings in popular film and television provides an important opportunity to examine and make visible what the culture "permits" us to believe about romance, weddings, marriage, and heterosexuality. Particular patterns coalesce in the telling of film or television wedding stories to produce a taken-for-granted social order that naturalizes practices that are anything but natural. The creation of social givens, such as weddings and heterosexuality, requires the use of a variety of meaning-making strategies that invite both affirmation and participation in the practices of the dominant class. In the popular films and television shows covered in this chapter, four ideological themes dominate: (1) romantic love and heterogender; (2) marriage and heterosexual supremacy; (3) social difference; and (4) class and accumulation. These meaning-making systems appear in varying combinations in each of the films and television shows examined in this study.

"Here Comes the Bride, All Dressed in White . . ."

The ideology of romantic love and the ideology of heterogender intersect in depictions of weddings in popular culture. Romance, most often expressed as the illusion of well-being, is central to the selling of media weddings. Romance represents the utopian promise of love, joy, happiness, well-being, belonging, and community. Ultimately, romance is ideology at work in the creation of illusion. It is not about the real but is, instead, about the fantasy, fairy-tale, or utopian vision of the real. Applied to weddings and the institution of heterosexuality, romance works in the service of the heterosexual imaginary. Embedded within the film romance are messages about the value of weddings and marriage. In the heterogendered division of labor, romance is primarily the domain of women, or the emotive side of labor. It is the work of women within heterogendered

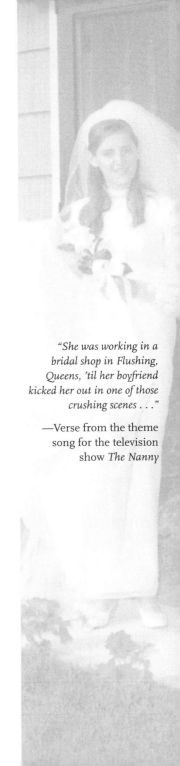

"She was working in a bridal shop in Flushing, Queens, 'til her boyfriend kicked her out in one of those crushing scenes . . ."

—Verse from the theme song for the television show *The Nanny* social arrangements to do the labor of feeling and caring as well as the struggle of providing an affective environment and of eliciting emotion from her partner. It is central to the invisible labor of women whether it be at home or in the workplace, e.g., mother, wife, flight attendant, nurse, therapist.[6] As Marj DeVault explains in her 1991 study *Feeding the Family: The Social Organization of Caring as Gendered Work:*

> Though necessary for maintaining the social world as we have known it, caring has been mostly unpaid work, traditionally undertaken by women, activity whose value is not fully acknowledged even by those who do it . . . Social expectation has made the undefined, unacknowledged activity central to women's identity . . . Both men and women have learned to think of these patterns as "natural."[7]

Popular culture plays a key role in naturalizing these patterns, and weddings are sites for the standardization of this heterogendered division of labor. Women's work is usually both invisible and considered a personal service outside of capital; the bride exemplifies this. The wedding spectacle precedes the subsequent isolation and experience of putting men first.

In many of the movies and in virtually all of the television weddings covered in this book, romance plays a pivotal role in setting up the subordinate position of women in relation to men. Over and over again we get the message that romance and wedding planning are the separate sphere of women or women's work. *Father of the Bride* revolves around the commiseration of Dad, who complains, scowls, and is mystified by how his wife and daughter spend "his" money in the name of a beautiful romantic white wedding. The image created in this movie is of two women sparing no expense to make sure this is the "wedding of a lifetime," one that is befitting the great love the bride-to-be Annie Banks (Kimberly Williams) has found with the groom-to-be Bryan MacKenzie (George Newbern).

The success of this film depends upon the intersection of several ideological frames: prevailing beliefs about romance and the heterogendered division of labor, and their link to class and accumulation interests. For example, in the opening scene of the movie we are greeted by George Banks (Steve Martin), the father of the bride, owner of a successful shoe factory, immediately after the wedding of his daughter Annie Banks-MacKenzie. The father of the bride confides to the audience: "I'll tell you a secret. This wedding cost more than this house when we bought it seventeen years ago. I'm told I'll look back on this day with affection and nostalgia. I hope so." This whole scene lasts for several minutes, as Banks recounts for the audience—and particularly fathers—what they should expect to encounter when their daughters marry. With a mixture of nostalgia for the little girl who once sat on his lap and called him "her hero" combined with complaints about expenses, this opening monologue teaches the audience that weddings are the irrational and expensive domain of women—the irrational and spendthrift sex.

The film makes use of the heterogender stereotype of women as consumers and as hopeless romantics spending excessively to provide something men find both painful and unintelligible unless, of course, they happen to be Franck Eggelhoffer (Martin Short), the effeminate wedding coordinator. The ideological work of this film is to delineate the heterogendered division of labor, portraying Dad as successful factory owner and Mom and daughter as women who spend his money frivolously. What is interesting about this film is how it both trivializes and elevates women's interest in weddings in an effort to secure both a female and male audience and preserve patriarchal heterosexuality and the heterogendered division of labor.

With refrains of "A wedding's a big deal!" and "We have to have a wedding coordinator" and "Welcome to the '90s, George!" from Nina Banks (Diane Keaton), the mother of the bride and George's wife, combined with the father's romance with his daughter, an estimated expenditure of about $45,000 is legitimized, almost twice the cost of the average American wedding. To convey to the viewer a "Father Knows Best" middle-America backdrop to this wedding, the filmmakers use two devices. First, they provide small-town, Main Street images of Dad coming home from work as he narrates how he is not "big on change," "loves this small town," and enjoys every facet of parenting. The first time we see Dad with his daughter is when she returns from a semester in Italy. He hurries home to see her, telling us how much he loves his big white colonial house with the white picket fence and how the best part of this house is the family life it's made possible. He's greeted at the door by his wife and young son and is warned that his daughter, Annie, has changed. Annie greets him by sliding down the banister into his arms, calling up images of what she's probably done since she was a small child, and reassuring him that she hasn't changed that much.

Ideological notions of middle-class, middle-American, traditional family values are securely established in the first ten minutes of this film. This depiction of the white middle-class marriage and family makes use of a number of images already firmly in place in the collective imagination. By calling up themes from *Father Knows Best, Leave it to Beaver,* or *The Donna Reed Show, Father of the Bride* naturalizes notions of the traditional, nuclear, middle-class family and removes from view the reality that such media constructions are historical and serve particular socioeconomic interests.

Later in the movie, we have the opportunity to see "real," big-city wealth when the Banks are invited to visit with the groom's family, the MacKenzies of Los Angeles. They live in a gated community in Bel Air and own "the biggest house on the street." While they present themselves as everyday, nice people, their wealth and privilege are made visible in a variety of ways. As George moves through their house, his thoughts are revealed to the viewer: "All I could think about was the size of this place. I could have parked our whole house in the foyer." When George asks where the bathroom is, Mrs. MacKenzie directs him to the "seventh door on the left" on the second floor, signaling to the audience the enormity of this house and the MacKenzies' wealth. The contrasts between upper-class and middle-class trappings work to suture the viewer to the class "plight" of the Banks. Even though Mr. and Mrs. Banks are both business owners, the audience is invited to sympathize with their "lack," or relative poverty. The film attempts to conceal the class privilege of the Banks by accentuating the excesses of the MacKenzies.

As the story progresses and we watch George's frustration with the excesses of the wedding preparations and the wealthiness of the MacKenzies, the film works to comfort the white middle-class viewer with complaints about consumer rip-offs and feelings of economic inadequacy. The story line of this film depends upon the viewing audience identifying with the Banks and appreciating the contrasts and discomforts between small town and big city, middle-class income and upper-class wealth. Significant in these contrasts is the way they also legitimize the $45,000 wedding for the middle class as well as the interests of the owning class. The expense of this wedding is justified as an expression of the love of the parents for their daughter and as "affordable" for the middle-class family, who may have to give up some things but put the interests of their child's "special day" ahead of any practicality or notion of excess.

Four Weddings and a Funeral, My Best Friend's Wedding, My Big Fat Greek Wedding, The Wedding Planner, and television weddings on the *Sopranos, Suddenly Susan, The Big Day* and *The Nanny* make use of similar ideological devices in that they all provide examples of extraordinarily expensive weddings as reasonable and natural, supporting the interests of the wedding-industrial complex. In each of these examples the weddings represented easily exceed the $45,000 model in *Father of the Bride.* Justifications for these expenditures are virtually invisible and become normalized through the invocation of the "special" romance that requires such class trappings. Of course, all of the examples mentioned thus far are of the traditional white wedding with the white bride in a white wedding gown. *Four Weddings* even goes so far as to provide the viewer with four weddings of varying elegance and opulence, reinforcing the normalization of the upper-class white wedding spectacle.

Beyond the development of the white wedding as a standardizing practice for late-twentieth and twenty-first-century capitalism, these images also convey the illusion that the institution of heterosexuality is stable, made up of promises and dreams fulfilled and invulnerable to crisis or disruption. Considering the various social forces pressuring marriage, these images are both the product of resistance to the realities of contemporary heterosexuality and the construction of propertied interests that depend upon these notions for their survival.

Combined with markers of class and wealth, nearly *all* of the films and television shows considered in this book carry the traditionally heterogendered ideological message about patriarchal heterosexuality. While each of these stories provides an example of the "new woman"—someone who has a career, owns her own business, or has access to the professional-managerial class—subordination to the interests of the husband is romantic, feminine, and normal. In Annie's exchange with her father in *Father of the Bride* when she announces to her family that she is engaged to be married, she argues that she can be both wife and her "own person."

> **Dad:** I thought you didn't believe in marriage. I thought it meant a woman lost her identity. I thought you wanted to get a job before you settled down and earn money and be your own person.

> **Annie:** All right. I didn't think I believed in marriage until I met Bryan. Bryan's not like any other man I've ever known. I want to be married to him. I'm not going to lose my identity with him. He's not some overpowering macho guy . . . He's like you, Dad! Except he's brilliant. (sigh) I'm not going to marry some ape who'll want me to wear go-go boots and an apron.

Reminiscent of stories in the *New York Times* "Vows" column, Annie will pursue her career but will give priority to her marriage *and* to her new husband. The values she espoused about not complying with marriage disappear in the blush of romance. As Annie goes through this explanation with her father, her mother exhibits wistful and loving emotions—indicating that she can identify with her daughter, naturalizing the feminine response to romance. It is in this moment that the heterogendered division of labor becomes visible. The audience learns through these interactions that "falling in love" with the "right" man is what makes marriage desirable and necessary. These instances in popular culture teach us that what counts as "marriage" is compliance with tradition, patriarchy, and the white, middle-class heterogendered social order. It is unimaginable to have feelings of love and desire for commitment without investing in marriage and the expensive white wedding.

"Tell Him That You Care Just for Him, Do the Things He Likes to Do . . ."

In the movie *My Best Friend's Wedding*, Julianne's (Julia Roberts) best friend Michael (Dermot Mulroney) announces he will marry Kimmy (Cameron Diaz). Kimmy is a young, blond, blue-eyed daughter of a very rich man who owns a cable sports network, the ultimate masculine fantasy. Because of her class standing, she has all the opportunities for an education and career befitting someone of her socioeconomic background. Michael is a lower-middle-class sports writer who lives on hot dogs, travels all over the country covering baseball, and sleeps in cheap motels but loves his job. As the story line develops we learn that Julianne, a nationally syndicated food critic, wants to get Michael to marry her instead of Kimmy, and she sets out to win the competition for Michael's love and commitment. The film contrasts the two women, characterizing them as polar opposites, where one, Kimmy, is desirable because she is traditionally feminine, while the other, Julianne, is destined for a life of career without love. At one point in the movie, Kimmy explains to Julianne why she will give up her plans to finish college and law school to travel with Michael and allow him to continue the work he loves so much. "It's his career! I'm supportive. I want to be with the man I love. I can always go to school, but I can't always be with the man I love." After inviting Julianne to be maid of honor, Kimmy takes her to a bridal salon to select a bridesmaid's gown. During the fitting, while Julianne is up on a pedestal being attended to by a seamstress, the following exchange occurs:

> **Kimmy:** You wouldn't be comfortable unless you were distinctive.
>
> **Julianne:** What else did he tell you?
>
> **Kimmy:** You hate weddings, you never go. You're not up for anything conventional or that's assumed to be a female priority, including marriage, romance, or even . . .
>
> **Julianne:** . . . love?! Michael and I were a wrong fit right from the start.

> **Kimmy:** He said that too. Well, I thought I was like you . . . and proud
> to be. But, then I met rumpled, smelly old Michael! And I found out
> I was a sentimental schmuck like all those flighty nitwits I'd always
> pitied. It's funny, huh?

The film sets up a competition between the new woman and the traditional woman, in which the outcome is predictable. The woman who is "sentimental" will join all those "flighty nitwits"—who must not have been so dumb after all— and will become the winner in this feminine competition. The woman who yields to romance and domestic priorities over those of career and profession is the one who will be the bride. The loser, Julianne, will always be just "the bridesmaid." This construction of the bridesmaid parallels depictions in other sites in popular culture, like the black bridesmaids in *Bride's* magazine, signaling to the new woman that she is living on the edge of acceptability if she does not submit to her feminine position in this white, heterogendered, capitalist social order.

The linkage of patriarchal heterosexuality with capitalism is in evidence in this story. Historically, the need to recruit women into the professional-managerial class is increasing, providing women with greater economic independence from men while serving the needs of capitalism. Meanwhile, while the economic need for women to marry a male "breadwinner" is decreasing, the material necessity of marriage is in decline. To maintain a heterogendered division of labor that serves the interests of patriarchal heterosexuality as well as the wedding-industrial complex, the wedding-ideological complex is producing a variety of messages to entice women to continue to marry. By providing images and messages that construct romantic love and the heterogendered division of labor as the "natural order" of things, the continuation of marriage and of patriarchal relations of production that subordinate women's interests to men's power is secured.

The conclusion of this competitive exchange between these two characters takes place in an elevator, where Kimmy tells Julianne she "wins." When Julianne asks what she means, Kimmy responds: "He's got you on a pedestal and me in his arms." For Kimmy, that's the ultimate marker of romantic success. As

Julianne and Kimmy exit the elevator and enter a family gathering, a young woman exclaims: "Look! It's the bride and the woman she'll never live up to!" Ideologically, this film conveys the message that even though "he" finds the professional, ambitious career woman attractive and compelling, his interest in her will succumb to the desire for a woman who adheres to the heterogender codes of femininity, placing his needs above her own.

In addition to the issues of heterogender, class, and accumulation in this film, other dominant ideologies concerning difference are evident. Once again, the all-white cast combined with the linkage of wealth and wedding, much like the images in bridal and celebrity wedding magazines, signals to the viewer that weddings are a code for whiteness. It should be evident by now that weddings in popular culture are sites where the structured invisibility of whiteness and its normative privileges are continually reproduced. If we look at weddings "head-on," we see their true role in our culture.

Another increasingly popular ideological strategy in *My Best Friend's Wedding* is the use of a gay character to secure the heterosexual imaginary. Julianne's closest friend, outside of Michael, is George (Rupert Everett), her editor. As she plots to get Michael back, George plays her confidante, her guy/girlfriend. He does the affective work typically assigned to women, helping her sort through her feelings and comforting and caring for her when she is distraught. George urges her to tell Michael she's still in love with him. When she loses her nerve, she declares that George is her fiancé, in the hope that Michael will discover his jealousy and leave Kimmy. What follows is a charade, in which George pretends to be heterosexual and madly in love with Julianne. At one point, Michael questions this news by saying he thought Julianne had told him George was gay. They all laugh, and George denies that he is and says that sometimes he pretends he is. The personhood of George is erased in this moment, when he is called upon to lie about his very identity—a moment that is a not-so-subtle act of gay bashing. Of course, the taken-for-granted fact here is that if even the gay guy can trivialize and subordinate himself to preserve the interests of the heterosexual imaginary, then so can we the audience. In keeping with the wedding-ideological complex, this makes perfect sense: gay people must be erased in order for heterosexuality to maintain its dominance, a message that holds particular resonance as the recent gay marriage movement escalates.

In a hilarious scene in the movie, George and Julianne must pose as a couple during a lunch with Kimmy's family and Michael. Seated at a large table in a very busy restaurant, George is asked how he and Julianne met and fell in love. To answer their questions, George sings:

> The moment I wake up
> Before I put on my makeup
> I say a little prayer for you . . .
> Forever and ever, I'll stay in your heart
> Oh, how I love you,
> together forever, we never will part.

Everyone is tickled to hear him be so romantic, and they soon join George in singing the entire song, celebrating their romance and engagement. Julianne is less than pleased that George may have foiled her plan by being too demonstrative—that is, too gay—and eventually tells Michael that she is not engaged.

The film ends with Michael and Kimmy's big white wedding complete with white Rolls Royce and firework sprays lining the driveway as Julianne must face the loss of her potential love partner. Once again, George, who apparently has no life of his own, comes to the rescue, appearing at the wedding reception complete with tuxedo and prepared to dance the night away with Julianne.

The use of the gay character as cipher in the service of heterosexuality is a theme prevalent in many films and television shows. As battles over the legitimacy of homosexuality, gay marriage, and human rights for gays, lesbians, and bisexuals are fought out in a wide variety of political arenas today, the contradictory use of gay characters speaks to a state of ambivalence about the institution of heterosexuality, marriage, and the legitimacy of homosexuality. This recent trend in popular film and television weddings is to make use of gays and lesbians to both provide a broader audience appeal—marketing to gays and lesbians—and to target a potential wedding market should legal weddings for same sex couples ever be allowed. The abuse of gay characters serves the interests of heterosexual supremacy and also provides some comfort for those who claim opposition to homosexuality, e.g., factions of the religious right. The question that arises from these patterns is: What are the social consequences of these portrayals of gay men and lesbians?

This theme of the gay male with the heterosexual woman has become enormously popular with the success of this movie, a subsequent film, *Object of My Affection*, and the popular NBC television show *Will & Grace* (1998–2006), where the lead characters are a heterosexual woman and a gay man who are also best friends and roommates.

These examples are successful on two levels. First, they provide the white heterosexual female viewer with the ultimate romantic fantasy of the perfect man. Not only is he handsome and desirable, he is loving, emotional, caring, and sensitive, traits that are hard to find among heterosexual men. The only drawback in these otherwise perfect male/female relationships is the absence of sexual attraction on his part—unimaginable in the heterosexual world. But it is this "lack" that produces the popularity of these shows. The audience, firmly situated in the heterosexual imaginary, is unable to suspend their belief that men are "naturally" attracted to women. Secretly, they hope he will "come to his senses" and consummate a heterosexual union. Interestingly, the use of the gay male as guy/girlfriend resecures the patriarchal order by erasing the heterosexual woman's need for a female friend while creating a space for the possibility of a masculine man as a love interest. In the end, the institution of heterosexuality is preserved as dominant and superior because, by contrast, it appears stable and less confusing.

"They're Writing Songs of Love, but Not for Me . . ."

Similar to the two films discussed thus far, *Four Weddings and a Funeral* makes use of the intersection of the ideology of romantic love, whiteness, and heterogender. This British romantic comedy, which experienced enormous box office success in the U.S., tells the story of Charles (Hugh Grant), a twenty-something white man, and his cohort of friends caught in the flurry of weddings the film portrays as prevalent among people in their twenties.

The movie follows the love story of Charles and Carrie (Andie McDowell), the American woman he falls in love with at the first wedding in the film, in a classic case of poor timing. They meet at the first wedding, are attracted to each other, and spend the night together. The following morning, when he discovers she must leave for the U.S. immediately, they both express their disappointment at a lost opportunity. He encounters her again at the second wedding, only this time she introduces Charles to her wealthy fiancé. Charles is devastated and confesses to his friends that he is in love for the first time in his life. He receives an invitation to Carrie's wedding and, in a serendipitous meeting when Charles checks in on Carrie's bridal registry, confesses to her that he loves her. The third wedding is Carrie's. While momentous to Charles, given his romantic interest in Carrie, it is at this wedding that Gareth, one of Charles's friends, dies of a heart attack. Charles encounters Carrie at the funeral and doesn't see her again until his own wedding day. Rather than risk life without marriage, and with his true love married to someone else, Charles decides to settle and marry someone he believes he loves enough. Carrie appears at the wedding, reveals she is divorced, and the fourth wedding becomes the movie's crisis point. Charles publicly declares his love for Carrie and destroys the wedding. The film concludes with Carrie and Charles reunited and committed to each other but not to marriage.

One of the central themes of this film is what counts as true love. Charles, his friends Thomas, Fiona, Gareth, Matthew, and Charlotte, and his deaf brother David travel from wedding to wedding ruminating about whether they will ever find someone to marry. As we witness Charles experience "love at first sight" with Carrie, as well as subsequent interactions among the other main characters in their quest to find a spouse, we learn that true love and romance are first and foremost about appearances and chemistry. At each wedding, there is reference to someone as "quite attractive," "a dish," or "lovely" when sizing up potential love partners. Interestingly, nowhere in this film is there any reference to what these characters do for a living, if anything, or to what else they care about in life. According to this film, one need only find someone—of the opposite sex—attractive in order to find them suitable for marriage.

The defining moment of the film is when Charles and Thomas go for a walk after Gareth's funeral. At the service, Matthew delivers a very moving eulogy using a poem by gay poet W. H. Auden, revealing how much he and Gareth loved each other.

> He was my north, my south, my east and west,
> my working week and my Sunday's rest,
> my noon, my midnight, my talk, my song.
> I thought that love would last forever.

To the surprise of all of their friends and to the viewers who watched Gareth and Matthew participate as single men in each of the weddings, it is revealed that, in fact, what they've all been searching for was under their noses all the time. As Charles reflects: "It's odd isn't it? All these years we've been single and proud of it, two of us were for all intents and purposes married all this time." In an interesting twist, the heterosexual imaginary in this film depends upon the love shared by two men to illustrate what counts as a "real" marriage. Never is the question posed as to why these two men who were obviously in a committed relationship "passed" for single and heterosexual. Never do any of their "friends" act concerned about why Gareth and Matthew couldn't be open with them. This gay relationship is used throughout the movie to legitimize and justify institutionalized heterosexuality. Gareth and Matthew are always portrayed as celebratory of heterosexual marriage and as key supporters of weddings. It takes the tragedy of Gareth's death and the revelation of their "closeted" love, cloaked in the guise of single heterosexuality, to teach the main characters as well as the viewer what married love is really all about.

> **Charles:** Thomas, one thing I find really . . . uh . . . it's your total confidence that we'll get married. What if you never find the right girl?

Thomas: Sorry?

Charles: Surely if that service shows anything, it shows that there is such a thing as a perfect match. If we can't be like Gareth and Matthew, then, maybe we should just let it go. Some of us are not going to get married.

Thomas: Well, I don't know, Charlie. The truth is, unlike you, I never expected the thunderbolt. I'd always just hoped I'd meet some nice friendly girl, like the look of her, hope that the look of me didn't make her physically sick, and pop the question, and settle down and be happy.

Charles: Yeah, maybe you're right. Maybe all this waiting for one true love stuff gets you nowhere.

The tension of these two positions is evident throughout the film. Should you marry someone you like well enough to share a life with or should you wait for your "one true love"—or as Thomas says, the "thunderbolt?" Throughout the movie Thomas is portrayed as a homely, clumsy, bumbling, boring, but wealthy nerd. Charles, on the other hand, is a glib, attractive, sexy, charming, committed, and not rich bachelor. To embody the "settling for love" position in the character of Thomas creates an association between the character and the position. The film's success depends upon the linkage of "real" romantic love with the handsome and desirable leading man. The "break" the failed wedding represents secures this position, signaling to the viewer the necessity and glory of true heterosexual romantic love while preserving the need for the white wedding.

Another important feature of this film is the way it uses class and the ideology of accumulation to secure the heterosexual imaginary. All of the weddings in the film are extravagant, large, white weddings with brides in white wedding gowns and veils. The ceremonies and vows are all traditionally Anglican, and the churches are all large and ornate. In each instance the viewer is left with the impression that the bride and groom are at least upper-middle-class and more than likely wealthy. Thomas's family is the seventh richest in England, residing in a 137-room castle. Carrie's first marriage is to an extremely wealthy Scot.

The only breaks in the upper-class trappings are at the funeral, which is set in a drab, working-class neighborhood, and at the end, when we get a brief glimpse of Charles's modest middle-class urban flat which he shares with his roommate, Charlotte. Notably, the only two rainy scenes are at the funeral and during the conclusion when Charles and Carrie reunite. In the funeral scene the signifiers attached to gay love and death are of gloom and destitution, while the closing scene transforms the gloom of rain with higher-class surroundings and a symbolic thunderbolt.

During the credits, snapshots of each of the main characters are shown, providing the viewer with the requisite happy ending. Except for Charles and Carrie, each character, including Thomas, is shown wedding their true love. Even Matthew, the remaining gay friend, is shown having some sort of coupling celebration with another man. In the end, while this film allows for an alternative and resistance, neither option is as attractive as the white wedding. The ideology of heterosexual supremacy is secured by rendering same sex love meaningful but dismal.

Similar patterns are used in wedding episodes in *Suddenly Susan* and *Ellen*. In both instances, gay men are used to celebrate the traditional white heterosexual wedding. In *Suddenly Susan*, Vicki wants to marry a rabbi but doesn't have the money for a big white wedding. Two gay male coworkers who are planning a $50,000 wedding for themselves invite Vicki to have a double wedding with them so she won't miss out on all the class trappings of the big white wedding. She accepts. The portrayal of the gay men is flat, with no affection, dancing, or kissing between the two men. Vicki, on the other hand, is at center stage as the white bride with the white wedding gown and the charismatic and handsome rabbi in tow. There is no question that the "real" wedding and the only one of any interest to the viewer is Vicki's.

In an earlier episode of the now-canceled *Ellen* sitcom, Paige is going to wed Matt, a handsome, white police officer. The traditional trappings are in place with one small exception. Ellen as maid of honor is dressed in a pale-blue pants suit. While everyone is waiting for the ceremony to start, Ellen discovers Paige in her wedding dress engaged in a passionate embrace with Spence, Ellen's roommate.

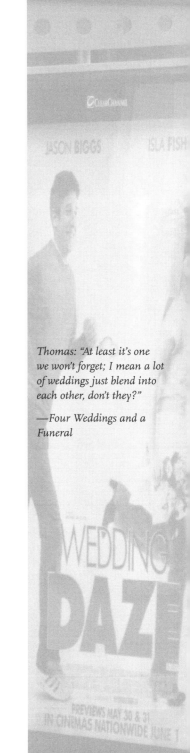

Thomas: "At least it's one we won't forget; I mean a lot of weddings just blend into each other, don't they?"

—*Four Weddings and a Funeral*

After some confrontation Paige reveals that she and Spence have been attracted to each other for a while. Ellen, taking her job as maid of honor very seriously, frantically attempts to pacify the wedding guests while Paige works things out with the groom-to-be. Sitting at a piano in the front of the church Ellen starts to serenade the guests with the song "Heart and Soul." Within a couple of bars, her two gay male friends Peter and Barrett burst into song with Ellen and help her save the wedding from disaster. At one point, Peter exclaims: "Guilty! I love weddings! My father was a wedding coordinator so I guess it's in my blood! Princess Di's was like the moon landing for me." As the audience roars at the absurdity of this, it is clear that gay men can participate in these ceremonies and be acceptable provided they serve as comic relief and both celebrate and appreciate heterosexual weddings. Obscured from view in these displays of heterosexual supremacy is the humanity of gays and lesbians. Historically, heterosexual weddings are frequently painful experiences for gays and lesbians, who are often cast in support/cheerleader roles while their own relationships are trivialized and ignored. As the buffoons or effeminate clowns who "love weddings," gay men are used as a site for ridicule, contributing to the social conditions that legitimize anti-gay discrimination and violence.

"It's a Nice Day for a White Wedding . . ."

The *Wedding Singer* is a campy romantic comedy full of garish colors and unusual-looking people. This film, which ushers in a new era in wedding films, makes use of dominant notions of difference to legitimize romantic love, a heterogendered division of labor, and marriage. Robbie Hart (Adam Sandler) is the wedding singer, performing at working-class to lower-middle-class weddings in a small town where all of the receptions are held at the same banquet hall. Portrayed as a very sweet, considerate guy, Robbie meets Julia (Drew Barrymore), one of the waitresses where he's singing. In their first conversation they tell each other about their engagements and wedding plans. Robbie tells Julia he is getting married next week, and Julia tells Robbie that her boyfriend, Glen, won't set a date.

In the next scene, we watch as Robbie is stood up at the altar, when Linda changes her mind about marrying Robbie and doesn't appear for their formal white wedding. Humiliated in front of half the town, Robbie finds out from Linda that she decided she didn't want to be married to a wedding singer and stay in Ridgefield for the rest of her life. At this point in the film, we learn that Robbie is a nice, small-town guy who cares about kids, old ladies, and being romantic.

Julia, a small, big-eyed blond who dresses sweetly and is kind to everyone, is engaged to Glen (Matthew Glave), a smooth-talking, handsome financial analyst who loves to womanize, talk big, and bully gentle guys like Robbie. In a sense, this film works more like a cartoon than a movie, setting Glen and Linda up as the "bad guys" and Robbie and Julia—a present-day Romeo and Juliet—as the "good guys," who are obviously meant to be together because they have so much in common. Before we reach the predictable romantic happy ending, in which Robbie defeats Glen for Julia's love, we learn through constructions of difference what makes people worthy of marriage.

Robbie's band is made up of three performers. His backup singer is a Boy George lookalike named George. Whenever he is left to fill in for Robbie he sings Boy George's song "Do You Really Want to Hurt Me?" In each instance we watch as the wedding guests get more and more abusive and disgusted by this cross-dressing, gender-bending guy. The humor at this point depends on the audience finding this Boy George "wannabe," coded as stereotypically gay, repulsive and laughable, and the violence of the wedding guests understandable. At several points throughout the movie there are mocking references to gays or homoerotic behaviors. Even Robbie is constructed as having gay behaviors. In several scenes between Robbie and Glen, "the bully," Glen, makes reference to Robbie as "limp-wristed" or effeminate because he's considerate and gentle.

In his first public appearance following his "jilting," Robbie is consumed with emotion and enraged at the prospect that he's not going to marry. It doesn't really matter that he's lost Linda. What's really important is that he believes no one else will want him, that he's not worthy of marriage. To make his point he sings the song "Love Stinks" and invites another marriage reject, a fat man, to sing the song with him. During this sequence Robbie identifies for the audience which people will never marry:

> Some of us will never ever find true love. Take for instance . . . me!
> And take, for instance, that guy right there. And that lady with the
> sideburns and, basically, everybody at table 9. And the interesting
> thing is . . . me, fatty, the lady with the sideburns, and the mutants
> at table 9 will never ever find a way to better our situation, because
> apparently we have absolutely nothing to offer the opposite sex.

In this amazing scene, Robbie identifies all the unfit people in the room and declares that neither he nor any of them are marriageable. No one would want anyone that ugly, useless, and undesirable. This is designed to be one of the most humorous segments in the film, inviting the audience to join Robbie in agreeing that these people are undesirable. In the climax of this scene Robbie moves around the reception inviting each of the "mutants" to join him in singing "Love Stinks." For the first time during the wedding reception, they smile and become excited. The scene ends with the father of the bride punching Robbie.

These constructions of difference act as social control mechanisms, elevating the institution of heterosexuality and weddings by coding those who don't marry as deviant, ugly, unworthy, and resentful. By contrast, those who marry and have the traditional white wedding are constructed as superior. Their joy in singing "Love Stinks" only reinforces the pattern that anyone who doesn't enjoy a wedding or who acknowledges the pain of so-called love relationships is predictably bitter and resentful because they're unfit. The blame for being without a partner or without love is placed firmly on the shoulders of the individual who is not worthy rather than on a culture that sets up these social arrangements and their corresponding social controls. And, finally, the absence of any people of color in this film works to situate whiteness as the prevailing category for marital worthiness.

A similar pattern occurs in the *Lois & Clark* television wedding where Superman marries Lois Lane. A villain called the "wedding destroyer" attempts to murder

Lois at the altar to force Clark to live with the type of pain she's had to endure since her groom-to-be died on his way to their wedding. Ideologically, these messages work to demonstrate that anyone who would dislike weddings is either disfigured or hostile.

The boundaries of acceptability are clearly demarcated in both of these examples, establishing what counts as beautiful, attractive, desirable, and worthy of love and marriage by making visible what typifies the opposite of these things as well as the consequences of occupying these marginalized positions.

In addition to ideologies of difference, *The Wedding Singer* establishes that weddings and wedding preparations are the space of the feminine and the domain of women, that dreams are made of finding true love, and that happiness can be found by a woman surrendering her identity to the right man. As Julia prepares for her wedding, she tries on her white wedding gown and stands in front of the mirror and rehearses what she will say in the receiving line.

> Hi, nice to meet you. I'm Mrs. Glen Gulia. I'm Julia Gulia.
> It's nice to meet you, I'm Mrs. Julia Gulia [she sobs].
> Hi, I'm Mrs. Robbie Hart. Robbie and I are so pleased you could come to our wedding [she beams].

In this moment Julia realizes she loves Robbie but believes she has to go through with the wedding because she thinks Robbie is back with Linda. Robbie finds out Julia and Glen are on their way to Las Vegas to get married and follows her there. Much to his surprise, he realizes they're on the same plane. He finds her while Glen is in the bathroom, sings a romantic song he wrote for her, and they declare their love for each other. Boy meets girl, boy gets girl . . . and the scene ends with a kiss in front of everyone on the plane as they applaud. The conclusion of the film is—you guessed it!—a big white wedding. The ideology of romantic love overcomes all obstacles except those it keeps in place to preserve the interests of patriarchal capitalism and the institution of heterosexuality.

"We Are Family . . . I've Got All My Sisters with Me . . ."

The Birdcage is a remake of the famous French film *La Cage aux Folles*, popular in the 1970s. Armand Goldman (Robin Williams) and Albert (Nathan Lane) are a gay couple who own a gay nightclub in Miami. Their son, Val (Dan Futterman), comes home from college to announce he is getting married to Barbara (Calista Flockhart), the daughter of ultraconservative Senator Keeley (Gene Hackman) and Mrs. Keeley (Dianne Wiest).

After breaking the news of the marriage, Val tells Armand and Albert that the Keeleys will be coming to dinner the next day. He also tells them that the Keeleys think Val's parents are heterosexual and that Armand is a diplomat. What follows is an elaborate charade to provide Val with the trappings of the upstanding—white, upper-middle-class—heterosexual family in order to protect his chance to marry Barbara.

Just as in *In & Out* where the gay character attempts to learn how to be more masculine, a similar scenario is played out in this film. Albert, who is transgendered and a female impersonator of some renown, tries to learn how to be masculine. What's important about these scenes in both films is how they demonstrate the arbitrary and constructed nature of gender while suggesting that it's difficult to overcome nature. Albert fails miserably and, instead, decides to dress as a conservative, middle-aged woman and pretend to be Armand's wife.

Once again, we see a film that makes use of gay characters to portray a heterosexual romantic comedy. There are several scenes in *The Birdcage* that work to erase the identities of the gay men. One in particular is the lie perpetrated by their own son, who asks his parents to deny their sexuality and love for each other. Instead, he wants them to pretend to be both heterosexual and from a different social class. Val adds insult to injury when he asks if Albert can be sent away for the evening and if his real mother (Val is the result of a one-night stand Armand had in his twenties) can come and pretend to be married to Armand. The violence this inflicts upon the two people who've raised Val is translated into humor. The humor in this passage depends upon the audience seeing the ridiculousness of this gay couple, especially in relation to the sanctity of "the wedding." As long as the audience can laugh at these scenes, they don't have to see the humanity of gays or lesbians or take their lives and families seriously.

Senator Keeley has agreed to this wedding to "whitewash" a sex scandal involving his close legislative associate. Of note here, the sex scandal involved an underage African-American woman, only one of two instances where a person of color has any role in this film. By this point in the story, the message to the audience is that both sets of parents live on the margins of acceptability. Val and Barbara, by contrast, appear moderate, stable, rational, and moral, the very model of upstanding heterosexuality and worthy of an elegant white wedding.

The heterosexual imaginary working in this film makes use of the ideology of difference, relegating the gay family to the level of the absurd, constructing the Latino houseboy as silly and stupid, and playing on the racist stereotype of the oversexed black teenager in the depiction of the scandal. All of these examples secure the audience's belief in the stability and superiority of the heterosexual white center of American society. The association of the wealthy diplomat with the values of the ultraconservative senator works to link wealth and accumulation with decency, morality, and "family values."

The story turns when all is revealed. Val claims his love and pride in his parents, and the Keeleys attempt to call off the wedding. The saving moment emerges when the paparazzi surround the building and the senator has to rely on Armand and Albert to help him escape. They dress all of them in "drag" and hurry them out through the crowd in the nightclub. The final scene of the movie is—you guessed it again! A big extravagant white wedding!

"You Were Meant for Me, and I Was Meant for You . . ."

Object of My Affection is not a wedding film in that a wedding is not the central theme, but a wedding is the setting for the turning point in the story. Integral to the new trend in popular culture to pair the heterosexual woman with a gay man, *Object of My Affection* keeps company with *My Best Friend's Wedding* and *Will & Grace,* and in some ways sets the standard for this genre.

Nina saves George from homelessness when his male lover "dumps" him for a new relationship. Even though Nina has a boyfriend and is pregnant, before long she falls in love with George. Their friendship walks the line on closeness, with both loving each other intensely but not sexually. They take ballroom dancing lessons together to varying versions of "You Were Meant for Me." Before long, she realizes she has a better relationship with George and breaks off her relationship with her boyfriend, Vince. She wants to create a family with George who is more than willing to comply. The crisis comes when George falls in love with Paul, bringing home the reality that he is, in fact, gay.

The tension in this movie depends upon the audience believing that a gay man just hasn't met the right woman yet. Throughout the movie, it's clear that George has indeed met the right woman but it doesn't make any difference. He's still gay! Ideologically, this film explores a range of alternatives to the white heterosexual nuclear family but, in the end, upholds the centrality of institutionalized heterosexuality with a twist.

George invites Nina to his brother's wedding. In a scene at another big white wedding, Nina confronts George about his feelings for her. George mistakes her emotions for late-term pregnancy strain:

> **George:** Weddings can be a little much.
> **Nina:** But it works.
> **George:** What do you mean?
> **Nina:** I was watching Frank and Caroline today and I just kept thinking . . . This is real . . . and George and I are not.
> **George:** We're just different.
> **Nina:** But I don't think that I am that different. I want you to be with me. I want you to marry me. I want you to love me the way that I love you. I don't really want to see who you are at all.
> **George:** I think you see me.
> **Nina:** Then tell me the truth. What do you want?
> **George:** I want Paul.
> **Nina:** I know . . . you can't choose who you love.

There are several important things about this passage. In it Nina acknowledges that her romantic feelings keep her from seeing reality—from seeing who George is. It also affirms the white wedding as the standard for what counts as "real" even in the face of the heterosexual imaginary. The song "You Were Meant for Me" plays at significant moments in the film, naturalizing the connection between George and Nina but suggesting that, in the end, if you can't overcome nature there are some alternatives that will uphold the institution of heterosexuality as dominant and superior. Ironically, George and Nina are the same names of the parents in *Father of the Bride*, leading us to wonder if the sequel to this "new family" film will be the wedding of their daughter. The film concludes with Nina partnered with an African-American police officer, George with Paul, and the baby being raised by all of them.

The first time I saw this movie was in a moderately crowded theater. At the point in the above dialogue where George says he "wants" (chooses) Paul, the audience rippled with exclamations of disbelief. Behind me a young man exclaimed, "What?" "Huh?" Even when confronted with the obvious and the real, the heterosexual imaginary is a powerful force.

Following this model in the television sitcom *Will & Grace*, Will and Grace are roommates after Grace leaves her fiancé at the altar. When she realizes that she is closer to Will than to her groom, the wedding no longer makes sense. She and Will call each other best friends and decide to live together. Everything they do together simulates what it means to be an intimate heterosexual couple, except for having sex. This new category—"all-but-married" or ABM—preserves the interests of heterosexuality but confirms the "naturalness" of men and women being together even if they are not sexually involved. Friends and coworkers continually remark that they act like a married couple. Whenever Will seems interested in meeting a man, Grace somehow foils his attempt. Eventually, Will and Grace follow the same path as the pair in *Object of My Affection*, including planning to have a child together. During this sequence in the series, Grace meets and falls in love with Leo, a white Jewish doctor who literally rides in on a white horse to save the damsel in distress. Grace, who is also Jewish, has found the "perfect" partner—same race, same religion, upwardly mobile. The relationship with Will goes through predictable ups and downs as all adjust to the new situation. Leo and Grace have their white wedding and attempt to live happily ever after until Leo decides he needs to fulfill his commitment to provide medical care to poor people in some other part of the world. Will and Grace become close again, Leo has an affair, and the result is the eventual dissolution of his marriage to Grace. Finally, as the series comes to a close, the writers (and the network) "allow" Will to find a love interest and to eventually partner and Grace reconciles with Leo. This modern-day fairy tale ends with the promise that they will all couple successfully.

As a sidebar to the primary relationship in this award-winning television sitcom, two characters—Jack and Karen, gay and straight—start out as a version of Fred and Ethel in the classic 50s comedy, *I Love Lucy*. The charisma of the characters eventually overtakes the script and the comic relief they provide makes their pairing as best friends a parallel story line. But, unlike Will, Jack remains deviant—gay and without a partner—and Karen goes back to her husband.

The presence of gay characters in situation comedies became normalized by this show and its long and popular run made the pattern of casting gay male characters with heterosexual women a potential mainstay in this genre. Significantly, the market the media sought through this period was largely female, young, and consumption oriented. An appeal to their interests and those of potential advertisers generally insured a long run for any show that paired heterosexual women with gay men.

"Wishin' and Hopin' and Thinkin' and Prayin', Plannin' and Dreamin' . . ."

In several television situation comedies the importance of the wedding gown and the dream of a white wedding are dominant themes for female characters. Revealed in these episodes are patterns pertaining to the naturalization of weddings as integral to being a woman. In the sitcom *Third Rock from the Sun*, a series about aliens who inhabit the bodies of humans and must learn the culture of these Earthlings, two of the main characters have a discussion about marriage.

With a style that mixes Joe Cocker with Ray Charles, [Taylor] Hicks was a consistent favorite with viewers [of season 5 of American Idol*] despite some acerbic comments from judge Simon Cowell, who said one of his performances was like "a drunken father singing at a wedding."*

—Reuters, May 25, 2006

Sally says in response to Dick's query about why she agreed to get married, "I'm a woman and he asked me. That's what women are supposed to do." According to this interaction, even an alien from another galaxy can see the significance of the wedding and marriage to women's identity. Sally also realizes what cultural capital weddings provide when, upon agreeing to marry a man in need of a green card, she proclaims, "Finally, I have something I can lord over other women!" It's not simply a matter of feminine duty; it is also a measure of a woman's worth in dominant culture and shows her allegiance to patriarchal priorities.

Everyone Loves Raymond is a situation comedy about the issues a lower-middle-class couple with three young children faces with their family, Ray's parents, and his single brother. In two episodes of *Raymond*, Ray and his wife, Debra, reminisce about their wedding. When Raymond proposed marriage to Debra, several mishaps occurred. To make sure Debra really said yes, Raymond went to her apartment, presented her with a diamond, and asked her all over again if she would marry him. She grabbed the ring, began screaming, and jumped up and down for joy, spinning around the room. Ray still was not convinced that Debra was saying yes to him. He pulled the diamond away from her and asked her again. Finally, she said yes in a way he thought he could believe. When he gave her back the diamond, she began squealing all over again, giving Ray the impression that what she was saying yes to was the ring. Once she calmed down, Debra called Ray to the couch to show him her plans. "I've got to show you all my plans . . . I've been planning this since I was twelve." It turns out Debra has a box full of wedding-planning materials she has been saving for years. Ray remarks that they've only known each other for three months, and wonders how she could have been planning this wedding since she was twelve. At that moment there's a knock on the door, and Debra's parents come in. They've confirmed the country club for the reception. Even though she tells Raymond she wants to have a small wedding, it quickly becomes clear that small for Debra is 200–250 people, affirming the average (natural) expenditure of $27,000 on a white wedding. As Debra and her mother share dream plans for the wedding, Raymond wonders if he even needs to come. Debra exclaims: "It's the happiest day of our lives!"

Once again, the commodification of the wedding and the heterosexual imaginary are secured. How can anyone refuse to participate in the happiest day a woman has been planning since she was a small child? For women, the message is clear. Anything women do or achieve pales in comparison to the moment of the wedding. Happiness, contingent upon such an event in her life, is the ultimate goal, regardless of its cost to the people involved or to the race, class, gender, sexuality, and labor conditions it depends upon and preserves.

This same theme presents itself in the recent *Friends* wedding of Ross and Emily. In one pre-wedding episode, Emily asks Ross's sister, Monica, to pick up her wedding gown at the bridal shop. Monica agrees, goes to the store, and, mistaken for Emily, tries on the wedding gown. In the next scene, we see the saleswoman telling Monica the store is now closing, giving the viewer the impression that Monica has been there most of the day. This dress is so important that Monica has given up an entire day just to try it on. In fact, the feelings she experienced while wearing the gown were so wonderful, she brings it home and wears it while doing the dishes. When Phoebe arrives and appears scandalized that Monica is wearing the gown, Monica explains how good it feels. "You should try it!" she exclaims. In the next scene both Phoebe and Monica are walking around in wedding gowns talking about how good it feels to wear one. When Rachel arrives and is acting sad and depressed, Phoebe and Monica tell her about the "gown thing" saying, "We've got something that will make you feel better!" In the next scene, all three women are sitting on the couch in wedding gowns, eating popcorn and talking about how uplifting it is to wear a wedding gown. These are women whose lives are thus far incomplete. They haven't found a man to marry yet, and the gowns comfort them with the promise of good things to come and the soothing feeling that being feminine and beautiful brings. They can't see each other as valuable and can't talk to each other about anything but men, love, and romance.

In the next episode of *Friends*, the wedding of Ross and Emily takes place in London. When they all arrive there, Ross and Emily go to the church to see how things will be set up, only to find that the wrecking ball has taken away the better part of the building. Emily, in tears, says the wedding is off. Ross sees this as ridiculous given that so many people have flown to England for the wedding. In a scene with his sister, Monica, he angrily exclaims that calling off the wedding is really stupid. Monica responds:

> **Monica:** How long have you been planning this wedding?
>
> **Ross:** A month.
>
> **Monica:** Emily's probably been planning this since she was five, ever since the first time she took a pillowcase and hung it off the back of her head. That's what we did! We dreamed about the perfect wedding and the perfect place with the perfect four-tiered wedding cake with the little people on top. And, we had the perfect guy who understood why this is important to us.

Without question, these scenes from several situation comedies illustrate the pervasiveness of messages naturalizing white weddings as both the woman's domain and as central to her sense of herself.

These themes are pervasive in popular culture, signaling a disturbing trend among the white middle class—the nearly exclusive obsession of young white women with romance and weddings. Without exception, it appears that this is all women think or care about. The consequence to women can be profound, manifesting in a form of anti-intellectualism where women are concerned, reducing their expectations in life to one moment of spectacle, rendering their talents and desires to the domestic sphere, trivializing their interests in the world around them, and situating them as the standard-bearers of traditional femininity and the heterogendered division of labor. This overdetermined emphasis on one event in a woman's life that makes all other moments pale by comparison is the very belief the wedding-industrial complex and the institution of heterosexuality rely upon. Imagine, the birth of a child or winning the Nobel Prize are not only ancillary to this dream but would never equal the significance of one's wedding day.

"That Won't Get You into His Arms . . ."

The twenty-first century posed momentous challenges for the institution of heterosexuality and for the wedding-industrial complex. In addition to changes in the social landscape regarding same sex marriage and civil unions, globalization, terrorism and war, the shifting context for American media was also historic. Consumer behavior, once predictable for print and television marketers, moved dramatically away from long-standing consumption patterns to new media options. The ability to technologically bypass commercials, obtain massive amounts of information via the internet, interact with people all over the world via web logs (blogs), broadcast and market globally via the World Wide Web and *vis-à-vis* satellite communications, all converged to permanently alter consumerism and marketing behavior. Demands from global markets meant more inclusive or multicultural marketing strategies along with those that would not appeal to the broadest consumption base.

To meet these challenges, the print media incorporated online delivery options, and television programming altered their offerings to embed advertising into reality-based shows and movie theaters. Marketers and the media discovered what Henry Jenkins dubs "affective economics":

> By affective economics, I mean a new configuration of marketing
> theory, still somewhat on the fringes but gaining ground with
> the media industry, which seeks to understand the emotional
> underpinnings of consumer decision-making as a driving force behind
> viewing and purchasing decisions.[8]

In other words, the media realized that consumers will attach to buying and viewing behaviors when they "care" about what they are watching. To this end wedding magazines became more racially and culturally integrated and television programming more engaged with weddings and the industry. *Modern Bride,* for instance, signaled to readers that weddings are for all women regardless of race or sexuality. Of course, they still market lavish weddings and excessive expense (and debt) but this magazine became more inclusive. *Brides* also expanded its marketing to a more inclusive audience and Martha Stewart re-emerged from her trials and tribulations stronger than ever and as a central player in the wedding industry. *Martha Stewart Weddings* has become a major competitor for first place in wedding/bridal magazine sales although this magazine is clearly targeting a white, well-resourced clientele. In August 2007, Stewart joined forces with MSNBC's *Today Show* to host "Today Throws a Martha Stewart Wedding," giving Stewart's enterprises high visibility as part of the *Today Show*'s annual interactive wedding event.

The presence of gay men in the media in and in relation to wedding culture became more mainstream. *Queer Eye for the Straight Guy* emerged as a media powerhouse in 2003, building on the ground broken by *Ellen* and *Will & Grace*. The Fab Five, as they call themselves, are five white gay men who set out to bring style and success to fashion-challenged and (sometimes) hygiene-challenged straight men. While the show started by featuring a straight man in search of a girlfriend or a marriage proposal, it eventually expanded to include advice for straight women, a number of wedding anniversary celebrations, and an occasional wedding. The Fab Five brought to Bravo TV (NBC) an applied reality version of *Will & Grace*, complete with product placement and stereotypical portrayals of gay men and heterosexuals.

The early 2000s also marked the beginning years of reality TV. A plethora of reality-based television shows emerged in these years, shifting the focus of networks from the production of situation comedies and dramas to (alleged) real-life programs such as *American Idol, Survivor, The Bachelor,* and *Extreme Makeover.* While many critics viewed this programming initiative as motivated by cost efficiencies for television networks, others became aware that reality TV actually replaced waning old media—TV and commercials—with an interactive model that invited viewers to care about what they were watching, to participate in the outcome, and that included embedded advertising.[9]

Daytime shows such as the *Today Show, Good Morning America,* and *CBS Early Morning* along with *Regis and Kelly,* and *Oprah,* to name a few, all provide wedding advice segments complete with product placement. Advertisers had found a new way to market their wares in the context of the DVR generation that is now able to record their favorite programs and fast forward through commercials. This new advertising approach comes complete with the suggestion of celebrity endorsement in the form of the program's host. This emergent genre provides a large media space for the wedding industry that includes television, cable, and online programming (see Table 4.3)

Type	Title	Network
Series	*A Wedding Story*	TLC
Episode	*Bridal Battles & a Missing Marine*	Style Network
Series	*Bride vs. Bride*	WE/wegobridal.com
Series	*Bridezilla*	WE/wegobridal.com
Series	*For Better or For Worse*	TLC
Series	*Instant Weddings*	Lifetime
Episode	*My Fair Brady: The Wedding Special*	VH1
Series	*Platinum Weddings*	WE: wegobridal.com
Episode	*Rob and Amber Get Married*	CBS
Series	*The "I Do" Diaries*	Lifetime
Series	*The Real Wedding Crashers*	NBC
Online TV	*the Wedding Television Network*	http://www.tvwed.com
Episode	*Trista Rehn and Ryan Sutter's "Bachelorette" Wedding Special*	ABC
Series	*Ultimate Weddings*	Comcast
Online TV	*WeddingTV.com*	Sky channels
Series	*Wild Weddings*	TLC
Series	*Whose Wedding is it Anyway?*	Style Network

Table 4.3 Reality TV Wedding Shows, 2000–2007

Missing from this list is one of the central players in popular culture in this historical moment. YouTube, http://www.youtube.com, an exceedingly popular worldwide online video-sharing website boasts 20 million viewers per month, with 65,000 videos uploaded every 24 hours. Because of its enormous success, YouTube was purchased by Google for $1.65 billion in 2006 and is a key player in the new media arena.

> Nielsen//NetRatings, a global leader in Internet media and market
> research, reported today that weekly U.S. Web traffic to video sharing
> site YouTube grew 75 percent in the week ending July 16th, from 7.3
> million to 12.8 million unique visitors . . . Men are 20 percent more
> likely to visit YouTube than women, with unique audience composition
> indexes of 113 and 88, respectively. Visitors between 12-17 years
> old index the highest among the various age groups, at 142. They
> are nearly 1.5 times more likely than the average Web user to go to
> YouTube.[10]

Considering the audience of this new media site, marketers and media of all varieties are changing the ways they conduct their business. For instance, businesses interested in reaching these potential consumers are using viral marketing strategies. Viral advertisements are essentially small sophisticated videos that capture the attention of a market so much so that viewers forward them to their friends. The contagion associated with the viral is spread by consumers who are doing the marketing for the advertiser. Other options for marketers using YouTube include uploading video information about products. This information is usually in the form of a story of some kind and sets up all sorts of new options for knowledge sharing or the development of knowledge communities.[11] A summary of wedding and bridal usage is provided in Table 4.4.

Type in "wedding" on YouTube and you will find 106,000 online videos of varying lengths. Everything from an actual bridal party performing their choreographed version of Michael Jackson's "Thriller" to Avril Lavigne's wedding song and video to the trailer for *Wedding Crashers*. The power of YouTube is yet to be

Table 4.4 YouTube search entry results for August 5, 2007

WEDDING SEARCH		BRIDE SEARCH		VIRTUAL WEDDINGS	
Wedding(s)	106,000	Bride	29,900	Barbie weddings	48
Wed	116,000	Brides	30,000		
White Wedding	5,030	Bridal	3,740	Virtual Online Worlds	
Wedding reception	4,690	Bridezilla	105	Weddings:	
Wedding ceremony	4,700	Bridal party	1,540	Second Life	202
Wedding crashers	685	Bridal gown	4,330	World of Warcraft	92
Wedding bloopers	336	TV Bride	1,510	There.com	5
Wedding celebrations	827	Bride videos	5,980	Disney's Toontown	3
Wedding flowers	688	Bride toys	2,290	Active Worlds	44
Wedding rings	5,150	Bride doll	584	The Sims	615
Wedding fair	9,620				
Wedding toy	2,290				
Wedding videos	27,600				
TV Wedding	6,630				
Film Wedding	8,360				
Internet Wedding	422				

realized but the potential for influencing consumer trends is substantial. For instance, an average person can achieve star status simply by capturing the interest of viewers on any given day. The result can be seen in the popularity of recent wedding dance performances. Given the success of a couple of videos, people all over the world are producing their own wedding dances and sharing them on this site. For example, one video featuring James and Julia's first dance, replicating the final scene from *Dirty Dancing*, has been viewed by 1,891,869 people.

The role of men in this market has also shifted. While the primary wedding/bridal customer is female, there is a growing trend toward attracting male consumers. To achieve this, a variety of media outlets have changed how they market their products. From the *New York Times* to bridal magazines, images of couples have taken the place of bridal images, including men in the dominant representation of weddings. Magazines targeting the groom are currently available as well. The most dramatic shift, however, is in the classic wedding movie.

Box office hits such as *American Wedding, Groomsmen, Sideways,* and *Wedding Crashers* have altered the wedding film landscape. All the movies have white men playing the lead and the bride playing little or no role in the story line. While her labor is apparent in the backdrop to the wedding, she is rendered invisible. In each instance, the male characters are struggling with having to settle down and commit to a monogamous relationship. Of all of the movies emerging in this shifting genre, none has had a greater impact on the wedding landscape than *Wedding Crashers.* Following its significant box office success, NBC launched a new television series called *The Real Wedding Crashers.*

In those aspects of American culture that continue to be gender segregated or polarized, wedding films have typically been considered "chick flicks." As such, they have been stigmatized as feminine, uninteresting, and trivial to a heterosexual male audience. Breaking this mold and expanding their market share, Hollywood has created "raunchy" wedding films where men act out in every way and where women are constructed as sexual objects and conquests.

The popular film *Wedding Crashers* leads the way in this genre by reunderstanding weddings as sport for straight men. Jeremy Klein (Vince Vaughn) and John Beckwith (Owen Wilson) are two lifelong friends who conduct divorce mediation for a law firm. Their favorite game is to crash local weddings during what they call "wedding season." When the film opens, John and Jeremy are mediating a divorce settlement. The wife is portrayed as shrill and angry and dependent upon tranquilizers. The husband is depicted as victimized and resistant. As the scene opens they are fighting. She refers to his mistress as a whore and a stripper and he makes reference to her as drugged out and undesirable. John and Jeremy rally them into a settlement by reminding them of how wonderful their wedding was, causing them to reminisce and to, eventually, acquiesce to each other's needs. After they rouse the couple's nostalgia regarding their wedding, Jeremy explains to them:

> **Jeremy:** Guys . . . the real enemy here is the institution of marriage. It's not realistic. It's crazy.

In the end, the couple resolve their differences peacefully and sadly.

Later on Jeremy refers to dating as forced and awkward and calls John into his office to go over the plans for the wedding season. At this point he shows John two purple hearts he has acquired to be used as ploys to fool the women they meet into sleeping with them. Nothing is sacred to these two men.

They browse the wedding announcements for opportunities and have a playbook by which they set up their wedding game. They are so practiced at their sport that they have an extensive set of rules passed down to them by Chazz, their wedding crasher coach.

> **Jeremy:** We're going to have tons and tons of opportunities to meet gorgeous ladies that are so aroused by the thought of marriage that they'll throw their inhibitions to the wind.
> **Jeremy [to John]:** Grab that net and catch that beautiful butterfly, pal!

Ideologically, the film reinstalls patriarchal heterosexuality by depicting weddings as sites for sexual conquest, food, and drink and equating weddings with sports. According to this film, weddings, for men, are not meaningful or sacred but are adult playgrounds where they are smarter than women and can exploit women's attachment to tradition for their personal gain. Ultimately, *Wedding Crashers* reassures the male viewer that marriage is a scam and that women are romance junkies looking for their next fix.

In fact, for Jeremy and John nothing is sacred. They are masterful at exploiting a variety of religious ceremonies—Jewish, Hindu, Chinese, Italian, and Irish—as well as a host of heterogender beliefs. For example, they "know" that women are easily taken in by heroes or by stories of bravery or by men who like children or who dance with elderly women. Essentially, the leads in this film have learned the heterogender system so well that they can use it as their sport and can score at will.

Following the mainstream wedding film formula, the central plot line builds around an upper-class white wedding. William Cleary (Christopher Walken), the Secretary of the Treasury and a potential candidate for President of the United States, announces his daughter is to wed. Billed as the social event of the year— "the Kentucky Derby of weddings"—this wedding and reception become the "big game" of the wedding season for Jeremy and John. Sports metaphors are evident throughout the enactment of this wedding scene.

> "It's the first quarter of the big game and you want to toss up a hail mary."
> "Play like a champion!"
> "Use number 10 in the playbook."

These references all serve to suture a heterosexual male audience as subjects of this story.

The film turns into the classic romance when John, who is showing signs that they are getting too old for their sport, falls in love with the Secretary's daughter, Claire (Rachel McAdams). Likewise, Jeremy attracts the attentions of Claire's sister who he falsely believes is stalking him. While his intent is to get as far away from her as he can, it turns out her sexual appetite matches his and they become lovers.

One of the most important scenes in *Wedding Crashers* comes when Jeremy and John return to the Cleary estate for dinner. During the dinner, Jeremy's love interest covertly gives him sexual pleasure while Grandma Mary, Secretary Cleary's elderly mother, offers her commentary on Eleanor Roosevelt and her grandson:

> "Eleanor? Big dyke! Huge dyke! She was real rug-muncher. She looked like a big lesbian mule."

Amused by Grandma's outburst, most of the guests laugh uncomfortably and Claire tells Grandma she can't talk that way. Grandma then turns on Todd, her grandson, and calls him a "homo." In response, Senator Cleary's wife instructs the butler—the only person of color in the entire film—to please put Grandma to bed, to which she responds:

> "I can do it myself, asshole."

This scene is reminiscent of the "mutant" episode in *The Wedding Singer* in that it assaults difference in the interests of securing the heterosexual imaginary. It allows the audience to view the wealthy family as deviant while it naturalizes middle-class love as desirable and real. It is the ideological necessity of Grandma's outburst that provides comic relief at the expense of women, the elderly, lesbians, gay men and blacks. Grandma is the object of ridicule but she is also the site for the enactment of some central value expression in the film. Claire shows her humanity by gently telling Grandma that what she did was wrong. John finds this attractive and the heterosexual imaginary is secured through these interactions.

The wedding-ideological complex circulating throughout these scenes reinforces patriarchal notions that men are "captains" and women are "first mates" and that the women who are not fooled are the ones to change the game plan. The fairy tale ending for the men in this movie is living happily ever after with the party girl who isn't fooled and lets men be who they are in the dominant heterogendered universe.

"Didn't We Almost Have it All . . ."

Grey's Anatomy has taken the television world by storm. Broadcast by ABC—the Disney network—as an adult fairy tale or sexy soap opera, Emmy-nominated *Grey's* has captured the lead in the ratings race. With a multi-ethnic cast that features three black characters in lead roles, a prominent Asian actress, and a sizeable selection of attractive actors of both sexes, *Grey's* has become the favorite of the mostly female 18- to 49-year-old demographic, including the frequently overlooked black viewer. Unlike its predecessor *E.R.,* *Grey's* mixes heterosexual sex, romance, and angst into the mix. With doctors and interns nicknamed McDreamy and McSteamy having sex in stock rooms and lusting after each other over surgery, *Grey's* has an almost cult-like following, made possible by the cultural niche created by shows like *Ally McBeal* and *Sex and the City.*[12]

Concluding their 2007 season, ABC aired a wedding episode of *Grey's Anatomy* called "Didn't We Almost Have it All." The theme plays with the myth that it is possible to have it all and this theme runs through all the story lines for the show's many characters and relationships. The primary story in this episode is the wedding of Preston Burke and Cristina Yang. For several episodes we watch as Burke, an exceptional African-American cardiac surgeon, struggles through hand tremors and other crises. Cristina, who has become a phenomenal surgeon in her own right, covers for Burke in his crisis by scrubbing in with him and performing various procedures in his place. Eventually, the whole arrangement is revealed and Cristina confesses to the Chief. Burke becomes enraged with Cristina and for several episodes they live together but do not speak. Eventually, Burke realizes how much he loves Cristina and proposes marriage. Cristina, who is clearly a brilliant, single-minded, dedicated intern with a bright and promising career ahead, seems dumbfounded by the prospect of participating in something so traditional.

Slowly, through the course of the season, we witness Cristina as she constantly struggles against who she really is to accommodate Burke's desire for normalcy. The heterogender backdrop to this scenario is that for women the more traditional path is that of bride and not that of surgeon. To succeed on this path is to resist many of the messages women receive about what it means to be female in a heterogendered culture. This conflict is complicated by the history of marriage in relation to Asian culture and, for Burke, by African-American history. There is no easy or simple fit when it comes to either career or marriage.

What makes this wedding so compelling is that Burke becomes cast as wedding planner. He brings wedding cake samples to Cristina at the hospital, insisting that she select what she prefers. She, on the other hand, seems genuinely mystified about why this might be important to do. With every decision about the wedding,

Cristina resists or avoids while Burke remains engaged and central to the process. Over and over again, he prods her to comply with the wedding planning and ever so slowly she concedes. On the day of the wedding, where this episode begins, the Chief is informing each of the surgeons about which one of them will succeed him. The opening line is: "Being Chief is about responsibility." This theme resonates through every relationship including the preparation for the wedding.

It is clear that Cristina is being dutiful to Burke but that she doesn't really "get" what all the fuss is about. With comments such as "wedding ridiculous" and how much she's looking forward to "become a piece of chattel," she registers her resistance. As Bailey assigns duties to each of the interns she leaves Yang out. To this Yang proclaims "I'm here! What about me!?" Bailey responds: "It's your wedding day! Which would you rather be doing—prepping a patient for surgery or prepping for your wedding?! Go home!! I'm giving you the day off!" Of course, the assumption Bailey is making is that every woman prefers her wedding day to anything else in her life! Yang is the new woman—who knows she can't have it all if she gives priority to Burke and to being his wife. As she says, "I'm going to like being married. It's the wedding part that's ridiculous." She knows she loves Burke but can't understand the part where she's supposed to like weddings.

In the history of racism, the way in which gender has been used to discriminate against black men has been to feminize them, to construct them as without the masculinity of white men—in charge and patriarchal. In part, it is this history that is working in the manifestation of the new racism where black men are perceived as taking the opposite position to prove that they are real men—aggressive, violent, and without any interest in feminine things. What is fascinating about this episode is the way it participates in the ideology of race and of heterogender. Burke becomes feminized by his investment in the wedding. Yang becomes masculinized by her resistance to all things traditionally feminine.

The climax of this episode comes when Yang is made to wear a choker, a family heirloom. Burke's mother proclaims, "Five generations of Burke women have worn this on their wedding day." Given the African-American history of slavery, the destruction of the African family, the contradiction this represents is dramatic. If there is such an heirloom, how can she refuse to wear it? Once again,

Yang acquiesces. She is the compliant Asian subject and the resistant female. Burke's mother then asks Yang what she plans to do about her eyebrows. Being the non-traditional female that she is, she looks stunned that anyone would think about her eyebrows. In the next scene we find her in the hospital with curlers in her hair, having an emotional meltdown because her eyebrows have been shaved off. She cries out, "I feel like somebody else—someone took my eyebrows and called me a Burke." Once she is in her wedding dress with penciled eyebrows, we no longer recognize her. She has become Burke's wife.

Just as this metamorphosis is about to reach completion, Cristina hesitates about walking down the aisle. Meredith, Cristina's maid of honor, says, "We need you to get your happy ending! Now do this!"

Burke leaves the altar, walks to the back of the church and tells Cristina he can't marry her. He says, "If I loved you . . . I would let you go." He realizes he can't make her be what he wants her to be. He must let her be who she is and to do that means he has to let her go. In the final scene Cristina cries, "He's gone. I'm free. Damn it!" She is totally conflicted—relieved and heartbroken; free and bereft.

The dominant ideologies at work in this episode both comply with and go against messages about gender, race, and class. In the end, however, the audience can make sense of Burke and Cristina as non-white—not McBride and McDreamy—reinforcing the dominant ideological messages that marriage is for white people and any woman who resists her white wedding or who gives her career priority is deviant. As Patricia Hill Collins points out in *Black Sexual Politics,*

> This Black gender ideology constructs this thesis of weak men and strong women by drawing upon heterosexism for meaning. Representations of the Black male "sissy" that mark the boundaries of Black male heterosexuality . . . constitute an outer ring around the heterosexual family drama of weak men and strong women.[13]

As Hill Collins points out, the consequences of these constructions can be nothing less than the reinforcement of all forms of inequality—race, class, sexuality, gender, age, and ability.

The heterogendered division of labor and heterosexual and white supremacy are well preserved in television and popular film, inviting us to laugh and cry while we celebrate the setbacks and triumphs of characters who appear real to us. As we do, we become complicit in the ways of thinking that allow racial, class, gender, and sexual hierarchies, varying kinds of sexual/gender violence, a patriarchal heterogendered division of labor, and subservience to a class/accumulation model for personal relations. The heterosexual imaginary circulating in popular film and television works to obscure these consequences by cloaking them in humor and romance. And it discourages any critical analysis of the consequences of how we've organized and regulated heterosexuality as an institution. In the end, we're left to wonder who it is, exactly, who lives "happily ever after."

"So if you're thinking how great true love is!
All you gotta do is hold him, and kiss him, and squeeze him, and love him.
Yeah, just do it!
And after you do, you will be his.
You will be his.
You will be his!"

Nancy Sinatra

Chapter Five

And They Lived Happily Ever After . . .

Once upon a time, in a land far, far away, a handsome prince met a beautiful maiden, swept her off her feet, married her in a perfect white wedding ceremony, and carried her away to a land of fairy tales and dreams where they raised three gorgeous children and lived happily ever after. This is the dominant romantic fairy tale story line. Following this formula, the last chapter in this story of white weddings is the place where I'm supposed to smooth out rough edges, tie up loose ends, and resolve any conflicts and contradictions from the preceding pages. It is also the point where I'm expected to comfort the reader by offering examples of exceptions to these practices, tales of resistance, and alternatives to the dominant form. I'm supposed to say "I know *your* wedding was (or will be) different" or "I'm sure *your* wedding didn't (or won't) participate in these patterns." In other words, it is time to keep this romance, this securing of the heterosexual imaginary, going by providing the happy ending to this wedding story. Were I to remain critical of the institution of heterosexuality and deny the reader some form of redemption, the social controls that work to suppress wedding resisters would activate. To develop critical consciousness when romance is the prevailing form is to challenge the boundaries of acceptability. To explain my critique the reader could construct me as unfit for marriage, hideously ugly, embittered by love lost, or just not a very happy person. This is the heterosexual imaginary at work, securing the interests of the institution of patriarchal heterosexuality under late capitalism and its wedding-industrial complex.

Examining the social and material conditions upon which white weddings depend does not allow for a happy ending. The consequences of many of the practices associated with white weddings and the wedding-ideological complex are disturbing and unsettling. In a society filled with various types of fairy tales and romance, e.g., love, sports, and religion, it is sometimes difficult to see our real conditions of existence, let alone attend to the hardships and inequities they produce, the ways we are implicated in these problems, and the powerful interests they serve.

Viewing the various sites in popular culture where images and messages concerning white weddings dominate, it becomes clear that the intended audience is women, particularly white women, and that weddings are the domain of the feminine. More importantly, examining all of these sites together reveals the extent to which the dominant social order seeks to produce feminine subjects whose very existence and identity are organized by the ideology of romantic love. In addition to gaining consent to the heterogendered division of labor where women are responsible for and provide unpaid domestic and affective labor, the less obvious outcome is the privileging of romance discourse in women's everyday lives.

As a professor, I learned some time ago that if you want to get the attention of your students you need only mention the word "sex." Considering the findings of this study on weddings, I discovered that the use of the word "romance" among women has much the same effect. In fact, it is a topic about which many young women obsess. "Will I find 'the one,' 'my one true love,' 'the love of my life?'" "Am I attractive or worthy enough?" "Can I make this person happy enough to stay with me?" Or, worse yet, "Will I be alone or lonely?" And why wouldn't women ruminate on these things, when everything from children's toys to adult films to social institutions to various social control mechanisms reinforces these heterogendered messages over and over again?

In recent years, a disturbing trend has emerged. Curious about why young women are not marrying at the same rate as in previous years, I asked students to explain. The primary response was financial but not for the reasons you would imagine. As one student put it so succinctly, "We can't afford a wedding so we plan to live together until we can save up enough money for the wedding." "Why, I asked, couldn't you have a simple less expensive wedding?" "Because," she replied, "this is the most important day of my life and I have to do it right."

Since the publication of the first edition of this study in 1999, I have had a large number of occasions to process the findings of this book with the general public, the media, and with students from a variety of colleges and universities. Most striking in all of these interactions is the degree to which people accept the terms of their social order without ever questioning it. As the new wedding scholarship has made very apparent, what we frequently think of as tradition—or as the way things should be—is by and large the product of a very effective marketing campaign. Nearly every so-called tradition we associate with weddings is not something that has been passed down from generation to generation because it has some familial or community-based meaning, but is part of the taken-for-granted because a marketer did their job well.

On a New York radio talk show a father called in to say that he had three daughters, had spent $40,000 on each of their weddings and would do it again because they are still married and he has beautiful grandchildren. What are the assumptions here? How is the heterosexual imaginary in this story linked up with consumerism? Does this man really believe he "bought" successful marriage for his daughters? Does he really think this is what "guaranteed" grandchildren, beautiful ones at that? When you put these comments up against the sentiments of the students who won't marry because they can't afford it, something important (and disturbing) has occurred in American consumer culture. We have allowed the market to determine the terms for our personal relationships. But, more momentous than that, we have sold our ability to question, to develop a critical consciousness or to function as a critical citizen to the best illusion. When we examine the conditions under which the products we are consuming are made, this real-life fantasy has profound consequences for the quality of life for people around the globe.

Given the role of the heterosexual imaginary in concealing the operation of heterosexuality in structuring gender, race, class, and the division of labor, the promise of romance combined with "the most important day in your life" becomes a powerful means to secure women's consent to capitalist patriarchal social arrangements. It represents the promise of a reward—the white wedding—for compliance with the terms of the dominant social order. But it is, after all, illusory. It is a mechanism that secures whiteness as dominant and patriarchal heterosexuality as superior. The promise of a relationship that will provide unconditional love, shore up self-esteem, meet every affective and physical need, and make one feel worthy and fulfilled is compelling. But it is an ideal, not a reality. In a high-tech, internet-permeated, media-based, and alienated commodity culture where goods replace human interaction and shopping anesthetizes us to the realities of life, romance and its pinnacle, the white wedding, become compulsory and necessary for survival. Under these conditions, the white wedding as packaged and sold by the wedding-industrial complex is both homogeneous—McBride—and the site for the simulation of social relations that we hope will take care of our utopian desires for love, community, belonging, and meaningful labor.[1]

In addition to constructions of women as feminine subjects in wedding culture, this study has examined the use of gay men and lesbians in the service of institutionalized heterosexuality. In 1998, a young man named Matthew Shepard was murdered in Wyoming simply because he was gay. Reports in the media from interviews with friends and family members of the murderers indicated that they "felt humiliated" that a gay man would "make a pass" at them in front of other people. In fact, they were so humiliated that they found it necessary to beat and torture Shepard and leave him strung to a fence for eighteen hours, after which he eventually died in an area hospital. It was hard to ignore the connection between what I was watching in wedding culture and this "hate crime." As a sociologist, I am trained to inquire into the social conditions that produce various forms of social control, violence being one type. The patterns I observed in the use of gay men and lesbians in wedding culture certainly demonstrate one type of anti-gay violence. The erasure of the humanity of gays and lesbians in the interests of promoting and preserving heterosexual supremacy sends the signal to the viewing public that this "erasure" can be either literal or figurative. Combined with messages from a variety of other sites, most notably right-wing political conservatives and the religious right, gays and lesbians are uniformly denied their humanity and their dignity and can be seen as expendable or illegitimate in the culture at large. Violence takes many forms and exists on a continuum. From the violence of the gay joke to the violence that took a young man's life, they all contribute to the conditions that make anti-gay violence and hate crimes possible.

While wedding culture perpetuates notions of heterosexual supremacy, particularly in relation to its use of gay characters, it also secures white supremacy through its use and exclusion of historically underrepresented people. More than that, the implied expectation that people of color assimilate to the cultural practices of white America works to both elevate whiteness and perpetuate racial hierarchies. In both instances, dominant ideologies of difference justify and legitimize these practices. When combined with class power, these messages secure the heterosexual imaginary and the privileging of white middle- to upper-class heterosexual marriage over all other experiences and forms. The effect of this structural advantage on the racial and heterogendered division of labor and on the distribution of economic, political, and social resources is nothing short of life-threatening.

Imagine, if you can, what American culture would be like without romance or the heterosexual imaginary. If we give up the illusions they create or foster, we give up the state of affairs for which we needed illusions.[2] What would take their place? What if we redirected our desires and labor to our real conditions of existence? For example, what if we focused on the creation of a free and democratic society for all, not just for those who represent the dominant interests? The distribution of resources and power would not be based on access to wealth or on who complies with dominant social arrangements but would be based on human rights. Access to health care benefits and hospital visitations would no longer be linked to your marital status, but instead to your status as a person. Your ability to earn a living wage or find work would no longer be based on the success of the wedding-industrial complex but on a community commitment to quality of life. What would it mean if we changed our social priorities to those that would be people-based not marriage-based? Our relationships, our work, and even our celebrations would transform.

Legal marriage for gay men and lesbians has become a powerful and divisive issue. Opening access to the institution of marriage, which has as its primary responsibility the distribution of economic power and resources, is very threatening to those who benefit from that power. In the 1990s, the State of Hawaii passed legislation legalizing marriage for same sex couples. Overturned by the courts, the state instead legalized civil unions for same sex couples. As a result, politicians in the U.S. Congress enacted in 1996 what is now officially called the Defense of Marriage Act. (See Appendix for full text.) According to this new law, no state will be required to honor the legalization of same sex marriage granted in another state. Given the role of the federal government in the distribution of benefits and social services to married couples, this law also defines, for the first time, what is meant by the word "spouse." Since the passage of DOMA, the same sex marriage movement has increased in size and activity as has the opposition. Today, same sex marriage has been legalized in a variety of places and efforts to provide substitutes for marriage rights in the form of civil unions have been on the rise (see Table 5.1).

LEGAL MARRIAGE GRANTED	CIVIL/LEGAL UNIONS GRANTED	RECOGNIZED
US: Massachusetts	Connecticut	Israel
The Netherlands	Vermont	Aruba
Belgium	New Jersey	Netherlands Antilles
Spain	California	
Canada	New Hampshire	
South Africa	Maine	
	Hawaii	
	District of Columbia	
	Washington	

Table 5.1 Status of same sex marriage worldwide, 2007

At the same time as these issues are being played out on the political front, capitalists are discovering a new and potentially lucrative market among same sex couples, a market that is increasing rapidly with the legalization of same sex marriage and the increasing number of commitment ceremonies. Market researchers have targeted this group, and the result has been a proliferation of advertising directed at and making use of same sex couples. IKEA, Banana Republic, Calvin Klein, Absolut Vodka, and AT&T, to name a few, have all contributed to this growing trend. Television programmers have experimented with "the gay kiss" on shows such as ABC's *Roseanne* and *Ellen,* NBC's *Mad About You,* cable television's *Buffy the Vampire Slayer, Dawson's Creek* and *The O.C., Gilmore Girls,* and *OZ* and the acclaimed made-for-TV movie, *Serving in Silence: The Margarethe Cammermeyer Story.* When NBC cut the same-sex kiss in *Will & Grace,* Jack and Will made a surprise appearance on the *Today Show* and they completed the kiss for a live audience. Definitions of heterosexuality have been shifting significantly in areas targeted specifically to teenagers and young adults. MTV has had the most impact in this area, since they frequently present shows, videos, and ads providing alternative views of heterosexuality as well as proactive views of gays and lesbians. And, the by now infamous kiss between Britney Spears and Madonna on the MTV Music Awards contributed to a popular view that women kissing is sexy. HBO and Showtime have both made significant strides in this area with the popularity of *Queer as Folk, Sex and the City, Six Feet Under, Oz,* and The *L Word.* Critically acclaimed and box office hits such as *Kissing Jessica Stein, If These Walls Could Talk 2, The Crying Game, The Wedding Banquet, Love and Death on Long Island,* and *Chasing Amy,* as well as some of those discussed in Chapter 4, have all pressured dominant notions of heterogender and heterosexuality.

Right-wing heterosexual opposition to gay marriage is, in part, grounded in the desire to maintain patriarchal heterosexual supremacy. Those who claim this mantle in the interests of preserving their place of dominance couch their arguments in the rhetoric of morality, as if mere participation in the institution is indicative of moral superiority. Some of the best-kept secrets pertaining to sexuality are held in the name of preserving heterosexuality as the beacon of morality. Obscured from view is the reality that many acts of violence are committed from within the institution of patriarchal heterosexuality: domestic violence, child sexual abuse (over 90 percent of the cases are adult male to female child), marital rape, sexual harassment, and pornography, to name a few. Along with the hysterical fantasies about the consequences of same sex marriages, remarks abound equating legal marriage for gays and lesbians with out-of-control morality and polygamy.

In reality, patriarchal monogamous heterosexuality continues to be in crisis and the petitioning of homosexuals for equal standing under the law is bringing this crisis to light. Claims of extramarital sex or of extramarital affairs are symptoms of real conditions of existence that reveal the sizeable level of non-monogamy in patriarchal cultures. Research suggests that the degree to which men and women experience affective and sexual relations outside the institution of marriage is more normative than deviant.[3]

Within the gay community, the marriage debates have taken on significant momentum as gays and lesbians seek normalization and access to a wide array of rewards and benefits. (See Appendix for listing.) Pro-marriage advocates argue that access to marriage will go a long way toward mainstreaming gay and lesbian relationships. They believe that participation in marriage would open up other possibilities: reduction in hate crimes and employment discrimination and fewer court battles over child custody. The pro side is very compelling as it relates to material resources but it still leaves open the exclusion of these same benefits for people who are not coupled—or not traditionally coupled—regardless of sexuality.

On the anti-marriage side, from within the gay/lesbian community the argument is against assimilation into a culture not of their own making, a culture that has historically served as the gatekeeper for power. To participate in the institution of marriage as it is currently organized is to legitimize the institution of heterosexuality and the heterosexual imaginary, virtually all the practices outlined in this study. This argument is equally compelling given the racial, gender, and class interests preserved and perpetuated through the institution of marriage.

Critical heterosexual studies is not a new idea but is rapidly developing into a legitimate field of study. Nineteenth-century marriage reform activists were very active in challenging church and state control over heterosexual relations, and twentieth-century feminists Adrienne Rich, Charlotte Bunch, Monique Wittig, Rita Mae Brown, and others offered groundbreaking critiques of heterosexuality as compulsory and as an institution. Within the social sciences, research on marriage and family abounds and has had a significant impact on our understandings of these institutions and on policy-making. As sizeable as this body of work is, until recently, few studies have focused critically on the relationship of marriage and family to the institution of heterosexuality. Important critiques have emerged in lesbian/gay/transgendered/ queer studies, cultural studies, psychology, sociology, history, and even business. Among these works, Jonathan Katz's history of heterosexuality, *The Invention of Heterosexuality* (1996, 2007), is an early foundational contribution. *Theorising Heterosexuality* (1996), edited by Diane Richardson, provides important and provocative essays from notable theorists including Stevi Jackson, Jo Van Every, Sheila Jeffreys, Caroline Ramazanoglu, and Carol Smart. *(Hetero)sexual Politics* (1995), edited by Mary Maynard and June Purvis, provides a collection of works by some of the same authors, reflecting contemporary debates on the politics and sociology of heterosexuality. Subsequent contributions to critical heterosexual studies

include *The Trouble with Normal: Postwar Youth and the Making of Heterosexuality* by Mary Louise Adams (1997), *Black Sexual Politics: African Americans, Gender, and the New Racism* by Patricia Hill Collins (2004), *Thinking Straight: The Power, the Promise, and the Paradox of Heterosexuality* edited by Chrys Ingraham (2005), *New Sexuality Studies* edited by Steven Seidman, Nancy Fischer, and Chet Meeks (2006), and *Handbook of Gender and Women's Studies* edited by Kathy Davis, Mary S. Evans, and Judith Lorber (2006).

The first edition of *White Weddings: Romancing Heterosexuality in Popular Culture* (1999) provided one of the first cultural studies of weddings in the United States and contributed to the development of the field of critical heterosexual studies. At the time the first edition was published, it was my hope that this book would provide an impetus for others to take the field of critical heterosexual studies to the next level by researching subjects such as globalization and heterosexuality, heterosexuality and race, heterosexuality and the law, heterosexuality and labor, heterosexuality and medicine, the tyranny of coupling, marriage resistance, and other dominant heterosexual practices and rituals including critiques of the divorce, marriage, and family research and textbooks. Beyond this, it was also my hope that numerous books would be written dealing with the ubiquitous wedding, including interview studies with brides about the meaning-making processes involved in the wedding, the experience of purchasing the bridal gown, and what it means to take someone else's name. Much to my delight, a number of scholars have since made major contributions in these areas. While I'm happy to say they are too numerous to mention here, I want to highlight a few that have created an important foundation on which to build. First and foremost is an historical work that will lead the way in wedding research for years to come. *Cinderella Dreams: The Allure of the Lavish Wedding* (2003), a collaboration between historian Elizabeth Pleck and business scholar Cele Otnes, illustrates quite powerfully the intersection of marketing and tradition in the evolution of the lavish wedding. In addition to this volume there are many new and emerging works that arc also worth listing here:

Brides, Inc.: American Weddings and the Business of Tradition by Vicki Howard

Framing the Bride: Globalizing Beauty and Romance in Taiwan's Bridal Industry by Bonnie Adrian

Here Comes the Bride: Women, Weddings, and the Marriage Mystique by Jaclyn Geller

It's Our Day: America's Love Affair with the White Wedding, 1945–2005 by Katherine Jellison

Marriage, a History: How Love Conquered Marriage by Stephanie Coontz

One Perfect Day: The Selling of the American Wedding by Rebecca Mead

Public Vows: A History of Marriage and the Nation by Nancy F. Cott

The Wedding Complex: Forms of Belonging in Modern American Culture by Elizabeth Freeman

Wedded Bliss, the Art of Marriage and Ceremony, edited by Paula Richter, Peabody Essex Museum, Salem, MA

Here comes the bride!

Epilogue

Writing this book has been a wrenching experience. Without realizing how fully I've been sutured to dominant heterosexual culture, I have frequently found myself engaged in a variety of internal struggles. Watching video after video of wedding stories, there were times when I would feel my emotions and my intellect split apart. Tears would be streaming down my face as I empathized with the characters in a movie while, at the same time, I would be taking notes critiquing the heterosexual imaginary. It was this "splitting apart" that revealed to me the depth and reach of cultural forces in securing our compliance and the strength of conviction needed to counter or resist these forces. What this told me, in ways I hadn't realized to this extent, was how difficult it really is to become antiracist, antihetero sexist, anticlassist, anti-anything oppressive. It requires developing the ability to do the critique, envisioning resistance, enlisting creativity, and making change happen while simultaneously hearing the voices and feeling, the feelings associated with the dominant. It is the experience of splitting the self: the racialized, heterogendered, class-based, sexualized conscious and unconscious. The implications for undertaking critical studies of dominance are profound. They reveal the depth of the indoctrination and the considerable effort required for making social change. Considering the ways the heterosexual imaginary conceals our real conditions of existence, I also did not realize the degree to which this would be true.

Even the lessons I learned in doing this study did not prepare me for what I witnessed in the free trade zones along the U.S./Mexican border. Since the publication of the first edition of this study, I have traveled with several delegations sponsored by the New York State Labor and Religion Coalition and the Earlham College Border Studies Program to Valle Hermosa, Matamoros, and Ciudad Juarez, Mexico, to meet with workers laboring in maquiladoras there. What we witnessed there gave significantly more urgency to what is revealed in these pages. American and other foreign corporations such as Fruit of the Loom, General Motors, Ford, Chrysler, and Wal-Mart, as well as many smaller companies producing electronics and textiles, are making use of NAFTA to cut costs and increase profits at the expense of the people, lands, culture, and children in this region. As witnesses to atrocities being committed in the name of "good business" and free trade, we saw thousands of working people and their families forced to live on top of landfills and toxic waste dumps, in one-room shanties with little or no water. The workers toil more than eight hours every day, with no restrictions on how much mandatory overtime they are forced to work, no child care, little or no protection from workplace hazards and for an average salary of $45 per week, where milk costs $4.50 for a half gallon.

Beth Millett at
Mexican/American
border

Femicide markers in
Ciudad Juarez

Nancy Parker and
Mimosa Lynch working
at a Juarez food coop

We heard stories of women forced to bring used sanitary napkins to work to prove they were not pregnant, of employers who regularly distributed birth control pills, of varying degrees of sexual harassment and abuse. We met families where their children had died of massive birth defects and disease from exposure to toxins in the environment and in the workplace. And we met workers whose health had been so severely compromised that many were unable to work anymore as a result of disabling conditions such as carpal tunnel syndrome and cancers. In Ciudad Juarez, over 400 women—mostly young workers—have been raped and murdered, where their families have little or no recourse in either finding their bodies or getting justice from the authorities.

Sign in domestic violence
shelter, Juarez

Homeless family on
street of Juarez

What was most extraordinary about this trip was the dignity, conviction, and commitment to community and life these people displayed. Under the most severe living conditions imaginable they welcomed us into their homes and their hearts, even in the face of the undeniable realization that our comfort, our privilege, our booming economy in the U.S. depend upon these conditions. Activists such as Martha Ojeda, Manuel Mondragon, and Jaime Salinas of the Coalition for Justice in the Maquiladoras are among the many working to save the lives of their people. American organizations such as New York Labor/Religion Coalition and their International Project led by Maureen Casey and Charles Kernaghan of the National Labor Committee as well the Earlham College Border Studies Program, are all making a difference. And international leaders such as Dame Anita Roddick, Vandana Shiva, and Amnesty International are creating

Casa Amiga domestic violence
shelter in Ciudad Juarez

Russell Sage College students protesting against
sexual/domestic violence in Juarez and in the U.S.

world-class interventions. For all of these people and organizations there is no romance. There is no illusion. There is only the love that comes with fighting against all odds to lift people out of oppression or to help people find the tools to lift themselves out of poverty or to see the health of this earth as a gift to be cherished and cared for.

What allows us to imagine possibilities? To continue to live shrouded in romance is to participate in and benefit from such atrocities. Confronting the reasons for which we need romance is to see what it conceals. It means to be awake to the world and to the ways power secures itself. It means having the courage to live differently so that others can live. Critiquing the heterosexual imaginary is one step in that direction. The most important day in our lives should be the day we make this a better world for all who live here.

Bride and maid of
honor, 1971

Appendix

The Comstock Act: 18 U.S. Code, Section 1461

1461. *Mailing obscene or crime-inciting matter.* Every obscene, lewd, lascivious, indecent, filthy or vile article, matter, thing, device or substance; and—

Every article or thing designed, adapted, or intended for preventing conception or producing abortion, or for any indecent or immoral use; and

Every article, instrument, substance, drug, medicine, or thing which is advertised or described in a manner calculated to lead another to use or apply it for preventing conception or producing abortion, or for any indecent or immoral purpose; and

Every written or printed card, letter, circular, book pamphlet, advertisement, or notice of any kind giving information, directly or indirectly, where, or how, or from whom, or by what means any of such mentioned matters, articles, or things may be obtained or made, or where or by whom any act or operation of any kind for the procuring or producing of abortion will be done or performed, or how or by what means conception may be prevented or abortion produced, whether sealed or unsealed; and

Every paper, writing, advertisement, or representation that any article, instrument, substance, drug, medicine, or thing may, or can, be used or applied for preventing conception or producing abortion, or for any indecent or immoral purpose; and

Every description calculated to induce or incite a person to so use or apply any such article, instrument, substance, drug, medicine, or thing—

Is declared to be nonmailable matter and shall not be conveyed in the mails or delivered from any post office or by any letter carrier.

Whoever knowingly uses the mails for the mailing, carriage in the mails, or delivery of anything declared by this section to be nonmailable, or knowingly causes to be delivered by mail according to the direction thereon, or at the place at which it is directed to be delivered by the person to whom it is addressed, or knowingly takes any such thing from the mails for the purpose of circulating or disposing thereof, or of aiding in the circulation or disposition thereof, shall be fined not more than $5,000 or imprisoned not more than five years, or both, for the first such offense, and shall be fined not more than $10,000 or imprisoned not more than ten years, or both, for each such offense thereafter.

The term "indecent," as used in this section includes matter of a character tending to incite arson, murder, or assassination.

The Defense of Marriage Act (1996)

To define and protect the institution of marriage. <<Note: Sept. 21, 1996–[H.R. 3396]>>

Be it enacted by the Senate and House of Representatives of the United States of America in Congress assembled, <<Note: Defense of Marriage Act.>>

Section 1. <<Note: 1 USC 1 note.>> Short Title.

This Act may be cited as the "Defense of Marriage Act."

Sec. 2. Powers Reserved to the States.

(a.) In General—Chapter 115 of title 28, United States Code, is amended by adding after section 1738B the following:

"Sec. 1738C. Certain acts, records, and proceedings and the effect thereof

"No State, territory, or possession of the United States, or Indian tribe, shall be required to give effect to any public act, record, or judicial proceeding of any other State, territory, possession, or tribe respecting a relationship between persons of the same sex that is treated as a marriage under the laws of such other State, territory, possession, or tribe, or a right or claim arising from such relationship."

(b.) Clerical Amendment.—The table of sections at the beginning of chapter 115 of title 28, United States Code, is amended by inserting after the item relating to section 1738B the following new item:

"1738C. Certain acts, records, and proceedings and the effect thereof."

Sec. 3. Definition of Marriage.

(a.) In General.—Chapter 1 of title 1, United States Code, is amended by adding at the end of the following:

"Sec. 7. Definition of "marriage" and "spouse."

"In determining the meaning of any Act of Congress, or of any ruling, regulation, or interpretation of the various administrative bureaus and agencies of the United States, the word "marriage" means only a legal union between one man and one woman as husband and wife, and the word "spouse" refers only to a person of the opposite sex who is a husband or a wife."

Public Law 104–199

104th Congress

July 11, 12, 1996, considered and passed House.

Sept. 10, considered and passed Senate.

State-Granted Legal Marriage Rights

Assumption of Spouse's Pension

Automatic Inheritance

Automatic Housing Lease Transfer

Bereavement Leave

Burial Determination

Child Custody

Crime Victim's Recovery Benefits

Divorce Protections

Domestic Violence Protection

Exemption from Property Tax on Partner's Death

Immunity from Testifying Against Spouse

Insurance Breaks
Joint Adoption and Foster Care
Joint Automobile Insurance
Joint Bankruptcy
Joint Parenting (Insurance Coverage, School Records)
Medical Decisions on Behalf of Partner
Medical Insurance Family Coverage
Certain Property Rights
Reduced-Rate Memberships
Sick Leave to Care for Partner
Visitation of Partner's Children
Visitation of Partner in Hospital or Prison
Wrongful Death (Loss of Consort) Benefits

Federally Granted Legal Marriage Rights

Access to Military Stores
Assumption of Spouse's Pension
Bereavement Leave
Immigration
Insurance Breaks
Medical Decisions on Behalf of Partner
Sick Leave to Care for Partner
Tax Breaks
Veteran's Discounts
Visitation of Partner in Hospital or Prison

Source: Partners Task Force for Gay & Lesbian Couples, 1998

Federally Granted Legal Marriage Rights Added to the U.S. Code since 1996

Crimes and Family Violence
Education
Employment Benefits and Related Statutory Provision
Federal Civilian and Military Service Benefits
Financial Disclosure and Conflict of Interest Provisions
Foreign Relations Provisions
Immigration, Naturalization, and Aliens
Indians
Social Security and Related Programs, Housing, and Food Stamps
Taxation
Trade, Commerce, and Intellectual Property
Veteran's Benefits

Total number of federal statutory provisions added since 1996: 120
Total number of federal statutory provisions repealed since 1996: 31
Total number of federal statutory provisions granted on the basis of marital status: 1,138
Percentage of increase in federal benefits since 1996: 8 percent

Source: U.S. General Accounting Office, Defense of Marriage Act: Update to Prior Report—GAO-04–353R

Wedding Movies, 1913–2007

American Wedding II (2003)

Barbara's Wedding (1973) (TV)

Baywatch: Hawaiian Wedding (2003) (TV)

Betsy's Wedding (1990)

Big Day, The (2006) (TV)

Christmas Wedding, A (2006) (TV)

Chuppa: The Wedding Canopy (1994)

Circle C Ranch Wedding Present (1910)

Clancy's Kosher Wedding (1927)

Coster's Wedding, The (1910)

Diabolic Wedding (1971), aka *Diabolique Wedding* (1971)

Double Wedding (1933)

Double Wedding (1937)

Double Wedding, A (1913)

Dr. Kildare's Wedding Day (1941), aka *Mary Names the Day* (1941)

Eight Is Enough Wedding, An (1989) (TV)

Emergency Wedding (1950)

Fanny's Wedding Day (1933)

Fatal Wedding, The (1911)

Four Weddings and a Funeral (1994)

Four Weddings and a Honeymoon (1955) (V)

Gasoline Wedding, A (1918)

Gay Weddings (2002)

Golden Wedding, The (1913)

Her Dog-Gone Wedding (1920)

Her Strange Wedding (1917)

Her Wedding Night (1911)

Her Wedding Night (1930)

His Wedding Night (1917)

His Wedding Scare (1943)

His Wooden Wedding (1925)

I Do Diaries: Instant Wedding, The (2004) (TV)

Imagine Me & You (2006)

Invitation to the Wedding (1985)

Joe's Wedding (1996)

Johnson at the Wedding (1911)

Kelly's Wedding Day (1999) (V)

La Cage aux Folles 3: The Wedding (1985)

Last Wedding (2001)

Lili's Wedding Night (1952)

Member of the Wedding, The (1952)

Member of the Wedding, The (1997) (TV)

Midnight Wedding, The (1912)

Monsoon Wedding (2001)

Muriel's Wedding (1994)

My Best Friend's Wedding (1997)

My Big Fat Greek Wedding (2002)

My Brother's Wedding (1984)

My Girlfriend's Wedding (1969)

My X-Girlfriend's Wedding Reception (2001)

On Her Wedding Night (1915)

On His Wedding Day (1913)

Pastry Town Wedding (1934)

Pauline Calf's Wedding Video (1994) (TV), aka *Three Fights, Two Weddings and a Funeral* (1994) (TV)

Plan Your Dream Wedding (2004)

Polish Wedding (1998)

Public Wedding (1937)

Quiet Little Wedding, A (1920)

Quiet Wedding (1940)

Rebecca's Wedding Day (1914)

Royal Wedding (1951), aka *Wedding Bells* (1951)

Ruffa Gutierrez & Yilmaz Bektas Wedding, The (2003) (TV)

Satan's Black Wedding (1975)

Saved by the Bell: Wedding in Las Vegas (1994) (TV)

Shotgun Wedding (1963)

Shotgun Wedding (1993)

Silver Wedding (1974) (TV)

Swing Wedding (1937)

Their Golden Wedding (1915)

Three Thieves and a Wedding (1991)

Tricia's Wedding (1972)

Two Wives at One Wedding (1960)

Undertaker's Wedding, The (1997)

Waikiki Wedding (1937)

Walton Wedding, A (1995) (TV)

Wedded Bliss? (2002)

Wedding (1990)

Wedding, A (1978)

Wedding, The (1986)

Wedding Advice: Speak Now or Forever Hold Your Peace (2002)

Wedding Album, The (2006) (TV)

Wedding Altered (2005)

Wedding and Babies (1958)

Wedding Band (1998)

Wedding Bell Blues (1996)

Wedding Belle (1947)

Wedding Bells (1921)

Wedding Bells (1933)

Wedding Belts (1940)

Wedding Blues (1920)

Wedding Crashers (2005)

Wedding Date, The (2005)

Wedding Dress, The (2001) (TV)

Wedding Gown, The (1913)

Wedding Group (1936)

Wedding in Monaco, The (1956)

Wedding in White (1972)

Wedding Knight, A (1966)

Wedding March, The (1928)

Wedding Night, The (1935)

Wedding Night Blues (1995)

Wedding Nights (1976)

Wedding of Jack and Jill, The (1930)

Wedding of Lilli Marlene, The (1953)

Wedding on Walton's Mountain, A (1982)

Wedding Party, The (1969)

Wedding Planner (2001)

Wedding Present, The (1936)

Wedding Rehearsal (1932)

Wedding Rings (1930)
Wedding Rituals (1995)
Wedding Singer, The (1998)
Wedding Song, The (1925)
Wedding Tape, The (1996)
Wedding That Didn't Come Off, The (1910)
Wedding Toast, The (2003)
Wedding Video, The (2003)
Wedding Vows (1994)
Wedding Wars (2006) (TV)
Wedding Was Beautiful, The (1972)
Wedding Women (1924)
Wedding Worries (1941)
Weddings are Wonderful (1939)
Weddings of a Lifetime's Dream Weddings on a Budget (2002)
White Wedding (1994) (V)
White Wedding (1995) (V)
Wooing and Wedding of a Coon, The (1905)

Some matches were also found among the alternative titles (akas):
Baishey Shravana (1960), aka *Wedding Day, The* (1960/I)
Boadas de Sangre (1981), aka *Blood Wedding* (1981)
Boda secreta (1988), aka *Secret Wedding* (1989)
Brollopsbesvar (1964), aka *Swedish Wedding Night* (1964)

Brollopsdagen (1960), aka *Wedding Day, The* (1960/II)
Bryllupsnatten (1997), aka *Wedding Night, The* (1997)
Catered Affair, The (1956), aka *Wedding Breakfast* (1956)
Don Juan heiratet (1909), aka *Don Juan's Wedding* (1909)
Dugun—Die Heirat (1992), aka *Wedding, The* (1992)
Going to the Chapel (1988) (TV), aka *Wedding Day* (1988) (TV)
Gong zi jiao (1981), aka *Wedding Bells, Wedding Belles* (1981)
Hang choh yan yuen lo (1984), aka *Wrong Wedding Trail* (1984)
He Knows You're Alone (1980), aka *Blood Wedding* (1980)
Hochzaeitsnuecht (1992), aka *Wedding Night—End of the Song* (1992)
Hochzeit im Excentricclub, Die (1917), aka *Wedding in the Eccentric Club* (1917)
Hochzeit von Lanneken, Die (1964), aka *Lanneken Wedding, The* (1964)
Hsi Yen (1993), aka *Wedding Banquet, The* (1993)
Jia qinao fan tian (ND), aka *Undated Wedding* (ND)
Kajak (1933), aka *Wedding of Palo, The* (1937)

Kekkon koshinkyoku (1951), aka *Wedding March* (1951)

Kivenpyorittajan kyla (1995), aka *Last Wedding, The* (1995)

Kogda opazdyvayut v ZAGS (1991), aka *When You're Late For Wedding* (1991)

Kyurun Iyagi (1993), aka *Wedding Story* (1993)

Lebassi Baraye Arossi (1976), aka *Suit for Wedding, A* (1976)

Leprechaun 2 (1994), aka *One Wedding and a Lot of Funerals* (1994)

Mangryongui Wechingturesu (1980), aka *Wedding Dress of the Ghost* (1980)

Medvezh'ya svad'ba (1926), aka *Bear's Wedding, The* (1926)

Million v brachnoy korzine (1986), aka *Million in a Wedding Basket* (1986)

Naszindulo (1943), aka *Wedding March* (1943)

Noce blanche (1989), aka *White Wedding* (1989)

Noces de papier, Les (1989) (TV), aka *Paper Wedding, A* (1989) (TV)

Noces rouges, Les (1973), aka *Wedding in Blood* (1973)

Nozze vagabonde (1936), aka *Beggar's Wedding* (1936)

Nunta de piatra (1972), aka *Stone Wedding* (1972)

Obvinyayetsya svadba (1986), *Wedding Is Accused, The* (1986)

Parvathi Kalyanam (1936), aka *Parvathi's Wedding* (1936)

Plenilunio delle vergini, Il (1973), aka *Devil's Wedding Night, The* (1973) (USA)

Povtornaya svadba (1975), aka *Repeated Wedding* (1975)

Rubezahls Hochzeit (1916), aka *Old Nip's Wedding* (1916)

Sita Kalyanam (1976), aka *Seeta's Wedding* (1976)

Skaz pro to, kak tsar Pyotr arapa zhenil (1976), aka *Tale about Czar Pyotr Arranging Arap's Wedding* (1976)

Svadba (1944), aka *Wedding, The* (1944)

Svadba v Malinovke (1967), aka *Wedding in Malinovka* (1967)

Svadebny podarok (1982), aka *Wedding Gift* (1982)

Turkischen Gurken, Die (1962), aka *Wedding Present* (1962)

Urs al-jalil (1987), aka *Wedding in Galilee* (1987)

Vase de noces (1974), aka *Wedding Trough* (1974)

Vasil Ni Raat (1929), aka *Wedding Night* (1929)

Wesela nie bedzie (1978), aka *Wedding's Off* (1978)

Wesele (1972), aka *Wedding, The* (1972)
Wide-Eyed and Legless (1994) (TV),
   aka *Wedding Gift, The* (1994) (TV)

Gay Weddings, 1997-2007

After Stonewall (1999)
Andrew and Jeremy Get Married
   (2004)
Åpenbaringen (2001)
Chicks in White Satin (1994)
Everyone (2004)
Heren aan de gracht (2004)
Homme que j'aime, L' (1997) (TV)
Jornaleros, Los (2003)
Joys of Smoking, The (1999)
Maris à tout prix (2004)
My Son the Bride (2002)
Not Simply a Wedding Banquet (1997)
Saints and Sinners (2004)
Tim & Patrick (2004)
Wallander – Innan frosten (2005)
Wedding Advice: Speak Now or Forever
   Hold Your Peace (2002)
Wedding Wars (2006) (TV)

Bride Movies, 1912-2007

30 Foot Bride of Candy Rock, The
   (1959), aka *Lou Costello and His 30*
   Foot Bride (1959), aka *Secret Bride*
   of Candy Rock, The (1959)

All for a Bride (1927)
Always a Bride (1940)
Always a Bride (1953)
Always a Bridesmaid (1943)
Arab's Bride, The (1912)
Baby of the Bride (1991) (TV)
Bachelor Brides (1926)
Backdoor Brides 3 (1988) (V)
Backdoor Brides 4 (1993) (V)
Bad Bride, The (1985)
Bartered Bride, The (1913)
Beggar Bride, The (1997) (TV)
Beware of the Bride (1920)
Bingo, Bridesmaids & Braces (1976)
Black Daisies for the Bride (1993) (TV)
Blood Bride (1980), aka *Death of a*
   Nun (1980)
Blushing Bride, The (1921)
Bride, The (1929)
Bride, The (1985/I)
Bride, The (1987)
Bride 13 (1920)
Bride and Gloom (1918)
Bride and Gloom (1921)
Bride and Gloom (1954)
Bride and Prejudice (2005)
Bride and the Beast, The (1958), aka
   Queen of the Gorillas (1958)
Bride by Mistake (1944)
Bride Came C.O.D., The (1941)
Bride Comes Home, The (1935)
Bride for Henry, A (1937)

Bride for a Knight, A (1923)

Bride for Sale (1949)

Bride Goes Wild, The (1948)

Bride in Black, The (1990) (TV)

Bride of Boogedy (1987) (TV)

Bride of Chucky (1998), aka *Child's Play 4* (1998) (working title) . . . aka *Child's Play 4: Bride of Chucky* (1998) (working title)

Bride of Fear, The (1918)

Bride of Frankenstein (1935), . . . aka *Frankenstein Lives Again!* (1935) (USA: working title) . . . aka *Return of Frankenstein, The* (1935) (USA: working title)

Bride of Killer Nerd (1992)

Bride of Lammermoor, The (1909)

Bride of Re-Animator (1990), aka *Re-Animator 2* (1990)

Bride of the Andes (1966)

Bride of the Colorado, The (1928)

Bride of the Desert (1929)

Bride of the Gorilla (1951)

Bride of the Head of the Family (1998)

Bride of the Incredible Hulk (1979) (TV)

Bride of the Lake, The (1934), aka *Lily of Killarney (1934)*

Bride of the Monster (1955), aka *Bride of the Atom* (1955), aka *Monster of the Marshes* (1955) (working title)

Bride of the Regiment (1930), aka *Lady of the Rose* (1930)

Bride of the Storm (1926)

Bride of Vengeance (1949)

Bride Stripped Bare (1994) (V)

Bride Stripped Bare, The (1967)

Bride sur le cou, La (1961), aka *Only For Love* (1961), aka *Please Not Now!* (1963)

Bride To Be (1974)

Bride Walks Out, The (1936)

Bride Wars (2007)

Bride Wore Boots, The (1946)

Bride Wore Crutches, The (1940)

Bride Wore Red, The (1937)

Bride's Awakening, The (1918)

Bride's Bereavement, The (1932), aka *Snake in the Grass* (1932)

Bride's Confession, The (1922)

Bride's Play (1922)

Bride's Relations, The (1929)

Bride's Silence, The (1917)

Bridegrooms Beware (1913)

Brideless Groom (1947)

Brides Are Like That (1936)

Brides of Blood (1968), aka *Brides of Blood Island* (1968), aka *Brides of Death* (1968), aka *Brides of the Beast* (1968), aka *Grave Desires* (1979/I) (reissue title) aka *Island of the Living Horror* (1968), aka *Orgy of Blood* (1968), aka *Terror on Blood Island* (1968)

Brides of Dracula, The (1960)

Brides of Fu Manchu, The (1966)

Brides of Sulu (1934)

Brides Wore Blood, The (1972), aka *Blood Bride* (1972)

Bridesmaids (1989) (TV)

Broadway Bride, The (1921)

Bronze Bride, The (1917)

Bulldog Drummond's Bride (1939), . . . aka *Mr. and Mrs. Bulldog Drummond* (1939) (USA: working title)

Case of the Curious Bride, The (1935)

Cave Man's Bride, The (1919)

Chased Bride, The (1923)

Child Bride (1938), aka *Child Bride of the Ozarks* (1938)

Child Bride of Short Creek (1981) (TV)

Children of the Bride (1990) (TV)

Corpse Bride, The (2005)

Dangers of a Bride (1917)

December Bride (1990)

Delinquent Bridegroom, The (1916)

Demi-Bride, The (1927)

Desert Bride, The (1928)

Desert Bridegroom, The (1922)

Diary of a High School Bride (1959)

Elven Bride, The (1995) (V)

Family Video Diaries: Daughter of the Bride (1997) (TV)

Father of the Bride (1950)

Father of the Bride (1991)

Father of the Bride Part II (1995)

Fire Bride, The (1922)

Fireman's Bride, The (1931)

Fly's Bride, The (1929)

Forged Bride, The (1920)

Frightened Bride, The (1953), aka *Tall Headlines, The* (1953)

G.I. War Brides (1946)

Gay Bride, The (1934), aka *Repeal* (1934) (working title)

Half a Bride (1928)

Happy Is the Bride (1957)

Here Comes the Bride (1919)

Here Comes the Bride (1981)

Here Comes the Bridesmaid (1928)

His Jazz Bride (1926)

Honeymoon: The Bride's Running Behind, The (1990)

I Was a Mail Order Bride (1982) (TV)

I Was a Male War Bride (1949), aka *You Can't Sleep Here* (1949)

Imported Bridegroom, The (1990)

Japanese War Bride (1952)

June Bride (1948)

June Bride (1998)

June Bride, A (1935)

June Bride, The (1926)

Jungle Bride (1933)

King's Quest VII: The Princeless Bride (1994)

Kiss the Bride Goodbye (1944)

Leopard's Bride, The (1916)

Little Bride of Heaven, The (1912)

Lost Bridegroom, The (1916), aka *His Lost Self* (1916)

Lottery Bride, The (1930)

Love That Bride (1950)

Mail Bride, A (1932)

Mail Order Bride (1964), aka *West of Montana* (1964)

Mail Order Bride (1984)

Mail Order Bride, The (1912)

Making of Seven Brides for Seven Brothers, The (1997) (TV)

Masked Bride, The (1925)

Midnight Bride, The (1920)

Missing Bride, A (1914)

Missing Bridegroom, The (1910)

Mother of the Bride (1993) (TV)

Mr. Bride (1932)

Muddy Bride, A (1921)

Night Bride (1927)

Night of the Devil's Bride (1975)

Nobody's Bride (1923)

Old Man's Bride, The (1967), aka *Bride, The* (1967)

One Bride Too Many (ND)

Our Blushing Brides (1930)

Outlaw's Bride, The (1915)

Perfect Bride, The (1991) (TV)

Perplexed Bridegroom, The (1914)

Perry Mason: The Case of the Heartbroken Bride (1992) (TV)

Picture Bride (1995)

Picture Brides (1933)

Price of the Bride, The (1990) (TV)

Princess Bride, The (1987)

Prodigal Bridegroom, A (1926)

Professional Bride (1941)

Pullman Bride, A (1917)

Ranger's Bride, The (1910)

Rebellious Bride, The (1919)

Reluctant Bride (1955)

Ride for a Bride (1913)

Roping a Bride (1915)

Runaway Bride (1999)

Runaway Bride, The (1930)

Rustling a Bride (1919)

Scarlet Bride (1989)

Secret Bride, The (1935), aka *Concealment* (1935)

Seven Brides for Seven Brothers (1954)

Seventeenth Bride, The (1986)

She-Male Bride Exposed (1992) (V)

Sky Bride (1932)

Slave for the Bride, A (1991) (V)

Snow Bride, The (1923)

Some Bride (1919)

Song for a Bride (1958)

Spectre Bridegroom, The (1913)

Stolen Bride, The (1913)

Stolen Bride, The (1927)

Teenage Bride (1970)

There Goes the Bride (1932)

There Goes the Bride (1979)

They All Kissed the Bride (1942)

Too Many Brides (1914), aka *Love Chase, The* (1914)
Troubles of a Bride (1925)
Two Brides (1919)
Two Grooms for a Bride (1957)
Unfortunate Bride, The (1932), aka *Ungluckliche Kale, Die (1932)* (Yiddish title: alternative title)
Unkissed Bride, The (1966), aka *Mother Goose a Go-Go* (1966)
Vendetta: Secrets of a Mafia Bride (1991) (TV), aka *Bride of Violence* (1991) (TV) aka *Donna d'onore* (1991) (TV), aka *Family Matter, A* (1991) (TV)

War Bride (1928)
War Bride's Secret, The (1916)
War Brides (1916)
War Brides (1980) (TV)
Wedding Wars (2006) (A&E TV)
Well-Groomed Bride, The (1946)
World's Oldest Living Bridesmaid, The (1990) (TV)
Young Bride (1932), aka *Love Starved* (1932)
Zandy's Bride (1974), aka *For Better, For Worse* (1974)

Reality TV Wedding Shows

A Wedding Story (TLC)
Bridal Battles & a Missing Marine (Style Network)
Bridezilla (WE)
For Better or For Worse (TLC)
Instant Weddings (Lifetime)
My Fair Brady: The Wedding Special (VH1)
Platinum Weddings (WE: http://wego-bridal.com)
Rob and Amber Get Married (CBS)
The "I Do" Diaries (Lifetime)
The Real Wedding Crasher (NBC)
The Wedding Television Network (http://tvwed.com)
Trista Rehn and Ryan Sutter's "Bachelorette" Wedding Special (ABC)
Ultimate Weddings (Comcast)
WeddingTV.com (Sky channels)
Wild Weddings
Whose Wedding is it Anyway? (Style Network)

Wedding Websites

http://store.fairytaleendeavorsbridals.com/
http://www.101weddingtips.com/
http://www.blissweddings.com
http://www.bridalguide.com
http://www.brides.com
http://www.bridalpeople.com/
http://www.bridesvillage.com/
http://www.destinationbride.com

http://www.ewedding.com

http://www.i-thee-wed.com

http://www.lovepoemsandquotes.com/
WeddingInformationAndEtiquette.
html

http://www.mvsweddinginvitations.
com/

http://www.mywedding.com

http://www.nuptialknickknacks.com/

http://www.TheKnot.com

http://www.theorganizedwedding.com

http://www.theweddingchannel.com

http://www.theweddingparty.com

http://www.theweddingzone.com

http://www.topweddinglinks.com

http://www.vegasweddings.com

http://www.wedalert.com

http://www.weddings-done-right.com

http://www.weddingwindow.com

http://www.weddingzone.net

http://www.weddingdetails.com

http://www.weddingdetails.com/lore/
indcx.cfm

http://www.weddinggoddess.com

http://www.weddingtv.com

http://www.wedlok.com

http://www.wegobridal.com

http://www.yourweddingtv.com

Ethnic and World Wedding Websites: (sampling)

http://www.blissweddings.com/
library/ethnicweddings.asp

http://www.worldweddings.net

http://www.worldweddingtraditions.
com

African-American

http://www.africanbridal.com

http://www.african-weddings.com

http://www.blackbride.com

http://www.blackbrideandgroom.
com

http://www.chocolatebridesmagazine.
com

http://www.nationalbba.com/html/
magazine.html

http://www.vibride.com/

Chinese

http://www.chcp.org/wedding.html

Indian

http://www.mybindi.com

http://www.indianwedding.ca/

Italian

http://www.weddingsinitaly.com
http://www.weddings-in-italy.com

Jewish

http://www.jewishbride.com
http://www.jewishweddingcollection.
com
http://www.mazornet.com/jewishcl/

Latina

http://www.latinabride.com

Gay Wedding Websites

http://www.GayWeddings.com
http://www.RainbowWeddingNetwork.
com
Rainbow Weddings Magazine

Unmarried or Anti-Marriage Websites

http://www.unmarriedamerica.org

Endnotes

Chapter 1

1. Leonard, 1980; Currie, 1993.
2. Jary and Jary 1991, p. 239.
3. Ibid., p. 239.
4. Fairchild Bridal Group 2006.
5. *The Wedding Report* 2005.
6. Rich, 1980.
7. http://www.imdb.com.
8. *TV Guide's Fall Preview, '98,* 1998.
9. Zuber, 1994, p. 70.
10. http://people.aol.com/people/package/ongoing/0,26336,661670,00.html.
11. See Appendix.
12. Katz, 1996.
13. Harman, 1883.
14. This booklet was probably co-authored by his wife, Angela, but her name was kept out of the publication for fear that Comstock would arrest her as well. In addition to having children who needed attending, prison conditions were thought of as particularly deplorable for respectable, middle-class, white women.
15. The official record refers to this as the Markland letter.
16. Bunch, 1975, p. 34.
17. Rich, 1980, p. 631.

18. Wittig, 1992, p. 7.
19. U.S. Bureau of the Census 2005; Federal Domestic Violence Statistics 2005; http:// www.usda.gov/da/shmd/aware.htm#WHO 2006; Stanger, 2006.
20. President's Council, 1992, 1994.
21. http://www.brillig.com/debt_clock/
22. Althusser, 1971, p. 52.
23. Ingraham, 1994, 1999b.
24. Relations of production refers to local and global forms of human and technological interactions involved in the production and reproduction of material life.

Chapter 2

1. Fairchild Bridal Group, 2006; Fields and Fields, 2005.
2. Fairchild Bridal Group, 2006; Fields and Fields, 2005; McMurray, 2006.
3. Dogar, 1997; *Bride's* Magazine Millennium Report, 1999; Fairchild Bridal Group, 2006.
4. Haggarty, 1993; http://www.pbs.org/wnet/moneyshow/cover/061501.html.
5. Spicuzza, 2001.
6. McMurray, 2006; Fairchild Bridal Group, 2006; Fields and Fields, 2005.
7. The language we use for identifying the race and ethnicity of people is frequently very awkward. To identify a group by color helps to perpetuate the social fictions we call race or racialization; to identify in terms of ethnicity erases the experience and effects of racism or of racial hierarchies. Much of the data presented here comes from official sources. Almost without exception those sources use white, black, or hispanic as identifying categories. To be consistent with these sources I have used the racialized categories, though I am not comfortable with this option and generally believe we should rely on cultural signifiers such as African, Latino, or Native American, for example. However, even this type of identification is problematic given that many of us do not belong exclusively to one category. As for hispanic, the debates over identification with Spanish colonialists or with Latino history is a source of great debate. In this case, I have used hispanic instead of Latino primarily because of the earlier explanation. However, I have put it in lower case as a way to diminish its weight in relation to an imperialist history.
8. U.S. Bureau of Census, 2005; *National Vital Statistics Reports,* 2006.
9. College Board, 2004.

10. http://www.auto.consumerguide.com/auto.
11. http://PovertyMap.net, http://World Bank.org, http://worldonfire.org, http://news.bbc.co.uk/2/hi/africa /3189299.stm, http://www.professionaljeweler.com/archives/news/2004/042704story.html, http://www.globalwitness.org/campaigns/diamonds/index.php, http://www.nlc.org.
12. July 13, 2003.
13. Bayot, 2003, p. 1.
14. Orman, 2006; http://Preventingdivorce.com; Poortman, 2005.
15. McMurray, 2006; Fairchild Bridal Group, 2006.
16. With, 1996.
17. Note: it is important to notice that the labor of planning the standard white wedding in the U.S. is the equivalent of a second job for the bride-to-be. This sets up an expectation that she be able to work outside the home full time while working a "second shift" at home. See Hochschild, *The Second Shift*, 1990.
18. With, 1996, 85:1.
19. CDC, *National Vital Statistics Reports*, 2003.
20. *Bride's* 1995/1996; U.S. Bureau of the Census, 1996.
21. Dewitt, 1992.
22. CDC, *National Vital Statistics Reports*, 2003.
23. Bramlett and Mosher, 2001, p. 9.
24. Light, 2006, p. 11.
25. U.S. Bureau of the Census, 2004 Current Population Survey.
26. U.S. Bureau of the Census, 2006.
27. The poverty threshold is the federal guideline that assesses the level of earnings below which one cannot afford to purchase the resources necessary for survival. People who have an income below the federally established poverty line have no discretionary disposable income. For example, for a four-person family unit with two children, the 2004 poverty threshold is $19,157. For more background on poverty thresholds and the problems associated with their calculation see Gordon M. Fisher, "The Development and History of the Poverty Thresholds," *Social Security Bulletin* 55, no. 4 (Winter 1992): 3–14.
28. National Poverty Center, University of Michigan, 2006, U.S. Bureau of the Census, 2005.
29. *The Journal of Blacks in Higher Education*, June 19, 2006.
30. U.S. Bureau of the Census, 2005. New information from the U.S. Bureau of the Census reinforces the value of a college education: workers 18 and over with a

bachelor's degree earn an average of $51,206 a year, while those with a high school diploma earn $27,915. Workers with an advanced degree make an average of $74,602, and those without a high school diploma average $18,734.

31. Francese, August 2, 2000.

32. Besharov and Sullivan, 1996; Steurle, 1995.

33. Cherry and Sawicki, 2000.

34. DeParle, 2005; Ehrenreich, 2002; Hays, 2003; Shipler, 2005.

35. Jones, March 26, 2006, p. B1.

36. Sanders, 2006.

37. On Bush's Healthy Marriage Initiative, see Kirkpatrick and Pear, 2004; Brezosky, 2004.

38. Kibbe, 2006, A1.

39. Sewell, 1998, C2; Humphreys, 2004, p. 3.

40. Fairchild Bridal Group, 2006.

41. Dalin, 2005.

42. Schatz, 2004, D2.

43. Brooke, 2005, A4.

44. *Brandweek*, 8/8/2005, Vol. 46 Issue 29, p. 18.

45. *Deccan Herald*, 2003

46. On the gay wedding market: "The Gay-Marriage Windfall: 16.8 Billion," http://Forbes.com, April 5, 2004. On marriage in Disneyworld: Kingston, 2004.

47. *People*, July 20, 1998.

48. Queen Victoria (1819–1901).

49. Otnes and Pleck, 2003, p. 31; Tomes, 1998, pp. 62–63.

50. Grace Kelly (1929–82).

51. BBC estimates, 1981.

52. *People* 1991, p. 23.

53. Anderson, 1981, p. 1.

54. *Bride's* 1997/1998, 40.

55. *Bride's* August/September 1998 issue.

56. Otnes and Pleck, 2003, p. 54.

57. Fields and Fields, 1998, p. 53.

58. Currie, 1993.

59. Fields, 1998, p. 33.

60. Elson and Pearson, 1981, p. 93.

61. Ross, 1997.

62. Cacas, 1994.

63. U.S. Department of Labor 1996.

64. Cacas, 1994.

65. Sailer, 1997.

66. Fields and Fields, 1997.

67. Ibid.

68. June 1997.

69. See Appendix for listing of organizations addressing sweatshop and labor abuses.

70. National Council of Textile Organizations, "The China Threat," http://www.ncto. org/threat/index.asp, January 2006.

71. *Modern Bride,* 2005; *The Wedding Report,* 2005.

72. Rosen, 1995, p. 100.

73. Hamlin, 1996.

74. *The Wedding Report,* 2005.

75. Hamlin, 1996.

76. Strauss, 1994.

77. http://www.diamondsareforever.com, August 2006.

78. Hart, 2002; Otnes and Pleck, 2005; Epstein, 1982; Kretschmer and Cabral, 1998; *The Economist* 2004.

79. Stein, 2001, p. 23; Oppenheimer, 1998, p. 8.

80. Hart, 2002.

81. *Jewelers'* 1996; http://www.diamondsareforever.com, accessed August 2006.

82. Hart, 2002.

83. *CNN/Money* 2005.

84. American Gem Society, 1998.

85. Fairchild Bridal Group, 2006.

86. American Gem Society, 1998.

87. Reinholz, 1996.

88. Rubin, 1997.

89. Ibid., p. 54.

90. Atkinson, 1998.

91 http://www.debeersgroup.com, accessed November 12, 2006.

92. http://www.dti.gov.uk/about/aboutus/index.html; http://www.un.org.

93. Oppenheimer, 1998.

94. Rubin, 1997, p. 52.

95. Hart, 2002; Campbell, 2004.

96. Sherwin, 1995, p. 30.

97. http://www.pbs.org/wgbh/pages/frontline/shows/cool/giants/ accessed January 16, 2007.

98. http://www.favorideas.com/wedding-themes/fanciful-themes/how-about-a-disney-fairytale-wedding, accessed November 1, 2006.

99. Doger, 1997.

100. Gite, 1992; http://www.ivillage.com, accessed November 2006.

101. Ellen Parlapiano and Pat Cobe, "Hot Home Business: Wedding Planners," http://www.ivillage.com, accessed November 2006.

102. Watts, 1994, p. 1.

103. Fitzgerald, 1994.

104. *People*, 1995a, p. 136.

105. Reynolds, 1992, p. 2.

106. Benner, 2006.

107. *Modern Bride* 1996; http://www.destinationweddingmag.com, 2007.

108. Dogar, 1997.

109. Reynolds, 1992; http://www.cruising.org, 2007.

110. *Travel Weekly* 1996.

111. Salkever, 1995; *Travel Weekly* 1996.

112. Gregory, 1994.

113. Ibid.; http://www.sandals.com, 2006.

114. Kincaid, 1989, p. 4.

115. Bauman, 1998.

116. Hill Collins, 2004, p. 33.

117. Ibid., p. 7.

118. Ibid., p. 19.

119. Hoover's, 1998; PR Newswire 1998.

120. Mattel Annual Report to Shareholders, 2006.

121. http://www.forbes.com/lists/2006/12/6GNF.html.

122. Holstein et al., 1996.

123. Ibid., p. 50.
124. Press, 1996, p. 10.
125. Tousignant, 1995, 8C.
126. Press, 1996, p. 10.
127. Pereira, 1996, p. A1.
128. French, 2007.
129. These terms have become part of the global business lexicon in recent years. *The Wal-Mart Effect* by Charles Fishman (2006) refers to the ways Wal-Mart practices have altered the world's economies. The race to the bottom refers to the global competition for the lowest wages and highest profits.
130. Demian, 1997.
131. The North American Free Trade Agreement (NAFTA), signed into law by President Clinton in 1994, called off the majority of tariffs between products traded among the United States, Canada and Mexico, and gradually phased out other tariffs over a 15-year period.
132. Partners, 1997.
133. Bedrick, 1997.
134. Defense of Marriage Act 1997.
135. Defense of Marriage Act 1997, 6.
136. Toalston, 1998.
137. Associated Press, June 22, 2005.
138. Becker, 1989.
139. Debord, 1995, p. 12.
140. Frankenberg, 1993, p. 6.

Chapter 3

1. Field, 1995, p. 27.
2. Spindler, 1998, p. 9.1.
3. Macionis, 2008, p. 31.
4. Storey, 1993, p. 5.
5. Bourdieu, 1984, p. 5.
6. *Starr Report*, 1998.
7. Field, 1995, p. 29.
8. September 13, 1998.

9. Toussaint, 1997/1998, p. 421.

10. *Guiness Book of World Records*, 2000.

11. Reardon, 2006, p. 1; http://www.brides.com.

12. *Bride's* 1998–2006.

13. U.S. Bureau of the Census, 2006.

14. Ehrenreich, 1989; U.S. Bureau of the Census, 2006.

15. Nibley, 1994, D–7.

16. Navarro, December 14, 2006.

17. http://www.condenastmediakit.com/mod/index.cfm.

18. http://theinsideronline.com/news/2007/05/9771/index.html.

19. Jenkins, 2006, pp. 2–3.

20. Debord, 1995, p. 12.

21. Fields and Fields, 1998.

22. hooks, 1990, p. 24.

23. Ross, 1997, p. 1.

24. Mies, 1986.

25. Schwartz and Scott, 1997, p. 13.

26. hooks, 1981, p. 43.

27. Cole, 1995; hooks, 1981; Stevenson, 1996.

28. Brewer, 1997, p. 27.

29. Stolcke, 1983, p. 163.

30. Niebuhr, 1998, p. 5.

31. http://www.yourgamesworld.com/dream-day-wedding.html.

32. June 14, 2007.

33. *NBC Presents: Diana Revealed*, 2006.

34. Debord, 1995, p. 38.

35. *People* 1995b, p. 125.

36. *People* 1997, p. 169.

37. *People* 2006, p. 59.

38. Coontz, 1997.

39. *In Style* 1997, p. 125.

40. *Vogue*, February 2005.

41. *People* 1997, p. 168.

42. 1996.

43. *People* 1997, p. 168.

44. August 1998, E14.

45. Hennessy, 1993a, p. 106.

46. Torrant, 1998, p. 15.

47. Ibid., p. 17.

Chapter 4

1. The reference to illusion in this analysis comes from a passage by Karl Marx in the introduction to *Contribution to the Critique of Hegel's Philosophy of Law* (1844). With the elegance of a poet, Marx argues that religion is the "sigh of an oppressed people," who need the illusion of well-being rather than confront the source of their oppression and create "real" happiness. "To abolish religion as the illusory happiness of the people is to demand their real happiness. The demand to give up illusions about the existing state of affairs is the demand to give up a state of affairs which needs illusions. The criticism of religion is therefore in embryo the criticism of the vale of tears, the halo of which is religion. Criticism has torn up the imaginary flowers from the chain not so that man shall wear the unadorned, bleak chain but so that he will shake off the chain and pluck the living flower." This metaphor applies to all those sites that we use to numb us to our real conditions of existence. One could substitute the word romance for religion and the meaning of this passage would still hold.

2. Kellner, 1995.

3. Zavarzadeh, 1991, p. 93.

4. Lipton, 1992, p. 1.

5. McWilliams, 1996, p. 7.

6. DeVault, 1991; Hochschild, 1985; Smith, 1987.

7. DeVault, 1991, p. 3.

8. Jenkins, 2006, p. 62.

9. Jenkins, 2006.

10. Nielsen//Net Ratings, July 21, 2006, http://www.nielsen-netratings.com/pr/pr_060721_2.pdf.

11. Tapscott and Williams, 2006.

12. And none of this is surprising given that the creator of *Grey's Anatomy* is the award-winning Shonda Rhimes, one of the few successful African-American screenwriters.

13. Hill Collins, 2004, p. 179.

Chapter 5

1. Twitchell, 1999; Willis, 1991.
2. Paraphrased from Karl Marx, *Contribution to the Critique of Hegel's Philosophy of Law*, 1844.
3. Brand et al., 2007; Whisman and Snyder, 2007.

References

Ackerman, D. 1994. *A natural history of love*. New York: Random House.

Adams, Mary Louise. 1997. *The Trouble with Normal*. Toronto: University of Toronto Press.

Agger, Ben. 1992. *Cultural studies as critical theory*. London: Falmer.

Albany Times Union. 1998. People in the news: Dreams come true for actress's movie concept. (October 11): A2.

Althusser, Louis. 1976. *Essays in self-criticism*. Atlantic Highlands, NJ: Humanities Press.

———. 1971. *Lenin and philosophy and other essays,* trans. Ben Brewster. New York: Monthly Review.

———. 1970. *For Marx,* trans. Ben Brewster. London: NLB.

Althusser, Louis, and Etienne Balibar. 1968. *Reading Capital,* trans. Ben Brewster. London: NLB.

American Gem Society. 1998. *The power of love*. http://www.org/info/lovetour.

Anderson, Susan Heller. 1981. The dress: Silk taffeta with sequins and pearls. *New York Times* (July 30); A2.

Anner, John. 1996. Sweatshop workers organize and win. *The Progressive* (June).

Atkinson, Dan. 1998. Diamonds get facet lift. *Guardian*. PSA–2047.

Auto Consumer Guide. 2006. http://auto.consumerguide.com/auto/new/reviews/full/index.cfm/id/38123/.

Ayers, T. and Brown, P. 1994. *The essential guide to lesbian and gay weddings*. New York: HarperSanFrancisco.

Bauman, Zygmunt. 1998. *Globalization: The human consequences*. New York: Columbia University Press.

Bayot, Jennifer. 2003. Getting married: For richer, for poorer, to our visa credit card limit. *New York Times*. (July 13), p. 1.

Becker, Howard. 1989. Artist and society. *International Encyclopedia of Communications*, 1: 138–142.

Bedrick, Barry. 1997. U.S. General Accounting Office: On the effects of DOMA. Partners Task Force for Gay & Lesbian Couples. (January 31). http://www.buddybuddy.com/marfeda.html.

Benner, Katie. 2006. Have wedding will travel. http://www.thestreet.com. Accessed June 1.

Bennett, Claudette. 1995. *The black population in the US: March 1994 and 1993*. Washington, DC: US Department of Commerce Economics and Statistics Administration and the Census Bureau.

Bernard, Joan Kelly. 1995. Calling it off when pre-wedding jitters are more than that. *Newsday* (June 27): p. B17.

Bernardo, F.M. and H. Vera. 1981. The groomal shower: A variation of the American bridal shower. *Family Relations,* 30: 395–401.

Besharov, Douglas J. and Timothy Sullivan. 1996. Welfare reform and marriage. *The Public Interest* (September 1): 14, 81.

Black, Robert W. 1998. Family of gay man thank public. *Yahoo! News* (October 16); http://dailynews.yahoo.com/headlines/ap.

Blatt, Martin. 1989. *Free love and anarchism*. Chicago: University of Chicago Press.

Boden, Sharon. 2003. *Consumerism, romance and the wedding experience*. New York: Palgrave Macmillan.

Boswell, John. 1994. *Same-sex unions in premodern Europe*. New York: Villard Books.

Bourdieu, Pierre. 1984. *Distinction: A social critique of the judgement of taste*. Trans. Richard Nice. Cambridge, MA: Harvard University Press.

Bramlett, Matthew and William Mosher. 2001. First marriage dissolution, divorce, and remarriage: United States. *Advance data*. Center for Disease Control, Department of Health and Human Services, 323 (May 31).

Brand, R. J., C. M. Markey, A. Mills, and S.D. Hodges. 2007. Sex differences in self-reported infidelity and its correlates. *Sex Roles*. (July) 57(1-2): 360–385.

Brewer, Rose. 1997. Theorizing race, class, and gender: The new scholarship of Black feminist intellectuals and Black women's labor. In C. Ingraham and R. Hennessy, eds., *Materialist feminism: A reader in class, difference and women's lives.* New York: Routledge.

Brezosky, Lynn. 2004. Attorney general hosts summits on helping low-income families. Associated Press. (October 21).

Bride's. 1998–2007. All volumes.

——. 1998. Train of thought. *Bride's* (August/September): p. 6.

——. 1997/1998. Princess bride. *Bride's* (December/January): p. 40.

——. 1997a. *Bride's American marriage today: facts & figures.* New York: Condé Nast.

——. 1997b. *Bride's millennium report: Love & money.* New York: Condé Nast.

——. 1995/1996. *Bridal market acquisition report.* New York: Condé Nast.

Brook, R. 2005. Fake priests in demand in Japan. Tokyo: *New York Times News Service,* (July 9): A4.

Brown, Rita Mae. 1976. *Plain brown rapper.* Baltimore, MD: Diana Press.

Bunch, Charlotte. 1995. *Paying the price: Women and the politics of international economic strategy.* London: Zed.

——. 1994. *Demanding accountability: The global campaign and Vienna tribunal for women's human rights.* New Brunswick, NJ: Rutgers University Press.

——. 1987. *Passionate politics: Feminist theory in action.* New York: St. Martin's Press.

——. 1975. Not for lesbians only. *Quest: A Feminist Quarterly.* (Fall).

Cacas, Samuel. 1994. Clothing designer tries a court order to stifle protests over seamstresses. *Asian Week* (August 5).

Callinicos, Alex. 1993. *Race and class.* London: Bookmarks.

Campbell, Greg. 2004. *Blood diamonds: Tracing the deadly path of the world's most precious stones.* New York: Westview Press.

Center for Disease Control. 2003. Births, marriages, divorces, and deaths: Provisional data for 2003. *National Vital Statistics Reports* 52, 22.

Cherlin, A. J. 1992. *Marriage, divorce, remarriage.* Cambridge, MA: Harvard University Press.

Cherry, Robert and Max Sawicky. 2000. Giving tax credit where it is due. http://www.epinet.org/content.cfm/briefingpapers_eitc.

Chesser, B. J. 1980. Analysis of wedding rituals: An attempt to make weddings more meaningful. *Family Relations* 29: 204–209.

Clark, John. 1993. Bride and joy. *Premiere* (March): 108.

CNC, National Vital Statistics Report. 2006. http://www.cdc.gov/nchs/data/nvsr/nvsr53.

Cole, Harriette. 1995. *Jumping the broom: The African American wedding planner.* New York: Henry Holt.

College Board and Educational Testing Service. 2004. *College board entrance examinations.* Princeton, NJ: College Board and Educational Testing Service.

Condé Nast Publications. 2001. *Bride's 2001 state of the union report.* New York: Condé Nast.

———. 1997. *Bride's wedding planner: The perfect guide to the perfect wedding.* New York: Random House.

Conger, K. J., M. A. Rueter., and R. D. Conger. 2000. The role of economic pressure in the lives of parents and their adolescents: The family stress model. In L. J. Crockett and R. K. Silberiesen, eds., *Negotiating adolescence in times of social change.* Cambridge: Cambridge University Press.

Coontz, Stephanie. 2005. *Marriage, a history: How love conquered marriage.* New York: Penguin Books.

———. 1997. *The way we really are.* New York: Basic Books.

———. 1992. *The way we never were.* New York: Basic Books.

Cott, Nancy. 2000. *Public vows: A history of marriage and the nation.* Cambridge, MA: Harvard University Press.

Currie, D. 1993. "Here comes the bride": The making of a "modern traditional" wedding in western culture. *Journal of Comparative Family Studies* 24(3): 403–421.

Dalin, P. 2005. http://community.theknot.com/cs/ks/blogs.

Davis, Kathy, Mary S. Evans, and Judith Lorber. 2006. *Hardbook of Gender and Women's Studies.* London: Sage.

Debord, Guy. 1995. *The society of the spectacle.* New York: Zone Books.

Deccan Herald. 2003. Living: At the wedding market. *Deccan Herald* (August 30): B1.

Delphy, Christine. 1992. *Familiar exploitation: New analysis of marriage in contemporary western societies.* Cambridge: Polity Press.

———. 1984. *Close to home: A materialist analysis of women's oppression.* London: Hutchinson.

———. 1981. For a materialist feminism. *Feminist Issues* 1.2 (Winter).

———. 1980. *The main enemy.* London: Women's Research and Resource Centre.

Demian. 1997. Partners task force gay and lesbian couples. http://www.buddybuddy.com.

DeParle, Jason. 2005. *American dream: Three women, ten kids, and a nation's drive to end welfare.* New York: Viking Press.

DeVault, Marj. 1993. First comes love . . . : Sociology constructs the family. Paper presented at the Department of Sociology, Boston University, March.

———. 1991. *Feeding the family: The social organization of caring as gendered work.* Chicago: University of Chicago Press.

Dewitt, Paula M. 1992. The second time around. *American Demographics* (November): pp. 60–63.

Diesenhouse, Susan. 1994. Can she take Priscilla's place at the altar? *New York Times* (October 9): p. 7 Section 3.

Discount Bridal Service. 1997. Press release April 25, Baltimore, MD.

Dogar, Rana. 1997. Here comes the billion dollar bride. *Working Woman* (May): 32–35, 69–70.

Economist, The. 1996. Many weddings and a discount. *The Economist* (January 13): 60.

Economist, The 2004. The cartel isn't forever. Retrieved July 26, 2006, from http://www.economist.com/printedition/PrinterFriendly.cfm?Story_ID=2921462.

Ehrenreich, Barbara. 2002. *Nickel and dimed: On not getting by in America.* New York: Henry Holt, Inc.

———. 1989. *Fear of falling: The inner life of the middle class.* New York: Pantheon.

Elson, Diane and Ruth Pearson. 1981. *Women's employment and multinationals in Europe.* London: International Specialized Book Service.

Engels, Frederick. 1942. *The origin of the family, private property, and the state in the light of the researches of Lewis H. Morgan.* New York: International.

Enloe, Cynthia. 1993. *The morning after: Sexual politics and the end of the cold war.* Berkeley, CA: University of California Press.

———. 1989. *Bananas, beaches and bases: Making feminist sense of international politics.* Berkeley, CA: University of California Press.

Epstein, Edward Jay. 1982a. *The rise and fall of diamonds.* New York: Simon & Schuster.

———. 1982b. Have you ever tried to sell a diamond? *Atlantic Monthly.* (February).

Evans, David T. 1993. *Sexual citizenship: The material construction of sexualities.* New York: Routledge.

Fairchild Bridal Group. 2006. The American wedding. http://www.selithebride.com/documents/americanweddingsurvey.pdf.

——— 2002. *The American wedding.* New York: Condé Nast.

Federal Domestic Violence Statistics. 2005.

Field, Nicola. 1995. *Over the rainbow: Money, class and homophobia.* London: Pluto Press.

Fields, Denise and Alan Fields. 2005. *Bridal bargains.* Boulder, CO: Windsor Peak Press.

———. 1998. *Bridal gown guide.* Boulder, CO: Windsor Peak Press.

———. 1997. *Bridal bargains.* Boulder, CO: Windsor Peak Press.

Fisher, Gordon M. 1992. The development and history of the poverty thresholds. *Social Security Bulletin* 55(4): 3–14.

Fishman, Charles. 2006. *The Wal-Mart effect.* New York: Penguin.

Fitzgerald, Kate. 1994. Stewart, Macy's tie knot. *Advertising Age* (May 16): 3, 55.

Foek, Anton. 1997. Sweatshop Barbie. *The Humanitarian.* (January–February): 9–13.

Foley, Barbara and Kathryn London. 1987. Going to the chapel. *American Demographics* (December): 26–31.

Francese, Peter. 2000. People patterns. *Wall Street Journal.* (August 2): B2.

Frankenberg, Ruth. 1997. *Displacing whiteness.* Durham, NC: Duke University Press.

——— 1993. *White women, race matters: The social construction of whiteness.* Minneapolis: University of Minnesota Press.

Freeman, Elizabeth. 2002. *The wedding complex: Forms of belonging in modern American culture.* Durham, NC: Duke University Press.

French, Howard W. 2007. Fast-growing China says little of child slavery's role. *New York Times,* (June 21): A4.

Friedman, Sally. 1997. Designing woman: Michele Piccione of Alfred Angelo bridals. *Jewish Exponent* (January).

GAO/OGC–97–16 Domain. 1996. Defense of Marriage Act. Washington, DC: Government Printing Office.

Geller, Jaclyn. 2001. *Here comes the bride: Women, weddings, and the marriage mystique.* New York: Four Walls Eight Windows Press.

Gerlin, Andrea. 1994. Your wheels need realignment, and you may now kiss the bride. *Wall Street Journal* (May 17): B1.

Gill, Penny. 1988. Here come the brides! *Stores* (April): 10–24.

Gingrich, Newt. 1996. *Meet the press.* NBC News.

Gite, L. 1992. Do you take this business? *Black Enterprise* 22 (July 1): 72.

Gramsci, Antonio. 1971. *Selections from the prison notebooks,* trans. Quentin Hoare and Geoffrey Nowell Smith. Newark: International.

Gregory, Marie. 1994. Sandals resorts number one! *Caribbean News Watch* (August 31): 1.

Hacker, Andrew. 1997. *Money: Who has how much and why.* New York: Touchstone.

Haggerty, Alfred. 1993. Coverage is available if wedding bells don't ring. *National Underwriter* (March 15): 15.

Hamlin, Suzanne. 1996. What to give the newlyweds? Just be practical. *New York Times* (June 12): C1:1.

Harman, Moses. 1901. *Institutional marriage.* Chicago: Lucifer.

——. 1883. *Lucifer the lightbearer.* Valley Falls, KS.

Hart, Matthew. 2002. *Diamond: The history of a cold-blooded love affair.* New York: Penguin.

Hays, Sharon. 2003. *Flat broke with children.* New York: Oxford.

Helms, Jesse. 1996a. The Defense of Marriage Act. Senate. *Congressional Quarterly,* September 9.

——. 1996b. Senate proceedings. *Congressional Record,* September 9.

Hennessy, Rosemary. 2000. *Profit and pleasure: Sexual identities in late capitalism.* New York: Taylor & Francis.

——. 1996a. Lesbians in late capitalism: Queer subjects, class acts. *Das Argument* (Fall).

——. 1996b. Ambivalence as alibi: On the materiality of late capitalist myth in *The Crying Game* and cultural theory. *Genders* 24 (Summer).

——. 1995. Subjects, knowledges . . . And all the rest: Speaking for what? In Judith Roof and Robyn Wiegman, eds., *Who can speak?: Authority and critical identity.* Urbana, IL: University of Illinois Press.

——. 1994–95. Queer visibility in commodity culture. *Cultural Critique* 29 (Winter).

——. 1994. Incorporating queer theory on the left. In, Antonio Callari, Stephen Cullenberg, and Carole Beweiner, eds., *Marxism in the postmodern age.* New York: Guilford.

——. 1993a. *Materialist feminism and the politics of discourse.* New York: Routledge.

——. 1993b. Women's lives/Feminist knowledge: Feminist standpoint as ideology critique. *Hypatia* 8(1): 14–34.

Hennessy, Rosemary and Chrys Ingraham, eds. 1997. *Materialist feminism: A reader in class, difference and women's lives.* New York: Routledge.

——. 1992. Putting the heterosexual order in crisis. *Mediations* 16(2): 17–23.

Hennessy, Rosemary and Rajeswari Mohan. 1989. The construction of woman in three popular texts of empire: Towards a critique of materialist feminism. *Textual Practice* 3(3): 323–359.

Heywood, Ezra. 1876. *Cupid's yokes.* Princeton, NJ: Co-operative Publishing Company.

Hill Collins, Patricia. 2004. *Black sexual politics*. New York: Routledge.

Hochschild, Arlie. 1990. *The second shift*. New York: Viking.

——. 1985. *The managed heart*. Berkeley, CA: University of California Press.

Holloron, Gerry. 1998. People: Gingrich's youngest daughter marries businessman. *Morning News Tribune* (January 25).

Holstein, William J., Brian Palmer, Shahid Ur-Rehman, and Timothy M. Ito. 1996. Santa's sweatshop. *U.S. News & World Report* (December 16).

Hoogasian, Cindy. 1994. Fairy tales do come true. *Florist* 27 (May 1): 40.

hooks, bell. 1992. *Black looks: Race and representation*. Boston: South End Press.

——. 1990. *Yearning: Race, gender and cultural politics*. Boston: South End Press.

——. 1984. *Feminist theory: From margin to center*. Boston: South End Press.

——. 1981. *Ain't I a woman?: Black women and feminism*. Boston: South End Press.

Hoover's. 1998. Business online. http://www.hoovers.com.

Horovitz, Bruce. 2006. Be ready for toy marketers' Christmastime tactics. November 26, 2006. Gannett News Service. http://www.gannett.com.

Howard, Vicki J. 2006. *American weddings and the business of tradition*. Philadelphia, PA: University of Pennsylvania Press.

——. 2003. A "real man's ring": Gender and the invention of a tradition. *Journal of Social History* (Summer): 837–856.

——. 2000. American weddings: Gender, consumption, and the business of brides. Unpublished dissertation, University of Texas at Austin.

Humphreys, Jeffry. 2004. *The multicultural economy: America's minority buying power. Georgia business and economic conditions*. Simon S. Selig, Jr. Center for Economic Growth, Terry College of Business, The University of Georgia.

——. 1998. *African American buying power by place of residence, 1990-1999. Georgia business and economic conditions*. Simon S. Selig, Jr. Center for Economic Growth, Terry College of Business, The University of Georgia.

Illouz, Eva. 1997. *Consuming the romantic utopia: Love and the cultural contradictions of capitalism*. Berkeley, CA: University of California Press.

In Style. 1997. Celebrity weddings. *In Style* (February): 125.

Ingraham, Chrys. 2008a. If it's so natural why do you need to market it?: The wedding-industrial complex. In Steven Seidman, et al. *Heternorm reader*.

——. 2008b. Conformity and resistance in wedding art. In *Wedded bliss: the marriage of art and ceremony*. Peabody Essex Museum, Salem, MA. Exhibit: April–Sept. 2008.

——. 2006a. One is not born a bride: How weddings regulate sexuality. In Steven Seidman, Chet Meeks, and Nancy Fisher, eds., *The new sexuality studies: A reader.* London: Routledge.

——. 2006b. Thinking straight, acting bent: Heteronormativity and homosexuality. In Kathy Davis, Mary S. Evans, and Judith Lorber, eds., *Handbook of gender and women's studies.* London: Sage.

——. 2003. Ritualizing heterosexuality: Weddings as performance. In Robert Heasley and Betsey Crane, eds., *Sexual lives.* New York: McGraw-Hill.

——. 2002. Heterosexuality: It's just not natural! In Diane Richardson and Steven Seidman, eds., *Handbook of lesbian and gay studies.* London: Sage.

——. 2000. Weddings. In Cherie Kramarae and Dale Spender, eds., *Routledge international encyclopedia of women.* London: Routledge.

——. 1999a. Metaphors of silence and voice in feminist thought. With Marj DeVault. In *Liberating method: Feminism and social research.* Temple.

——. 1999b. *White weddings: Romancing heterosexuality in popular culture.* New York: Routledge.

——. 1994. The heterosexual imaginary: Feminist sociology and theories of gender. *Sociological Theory* 12(2): 203–219.

Jackson, Stevi. 1996. Heterosexuality and feminist theory. In Diane Richardson, ed., *Theorising heterosexuality.* Buckingham: Open University Press.

Jary, David and Julia Jary. 1991. *The Harper Collins dictionary of sociology.* New York: Harper Collins.

Jenkins, Henry. 2006. *Convergence culture: Where old and new media collide.* New York: NYU Press.

Jewelers' Circular-Keystone. 1996. Diamond sales hit record. New York: Chilton.

Johnson, Bradley. 1992. Will couples say I do to Disney? *Advertising Age* (March 30): 52.

Jones, R. 2006. Marriage is for white people. *New York Times* (March 21): B1.

Journal of Blacks in Higher Education. 2006. Black student college graduation rates remain low, but modest progress begins to show. http://www.jbhe.com/features/50_black student_gradrates.html (June 16).

Katz, Jonathan. 2007. *The invention of heterosexuality.* Chicago: University of Chicago Press.

——. 1996. *The Invention of Heterosexuality.* New York: Penguin.

Kaufman, Joanne. 1995. Buy, buy love. *Ladies Home Journal* 112 (June 1): 100.

Kellner, Douglas. 1995. Cultural studies, multiculturalism and media culture. In Douglas Kellner, ed., *Media Culture*. New York: Routledge.

Kibbe, David. 2006. Romney: Put gay marriage on ballot. *Cape Cod Times* (June 29): A1.

Kincaid, Jamaica. 1989. *A small place*. New York: Plume Books.

Kingston, Anne. 2004. *The meaning of wife*. New York: Farrar, Straus and Giroux.

Kirkpatrick, David and Robert Pear. 2004. Bush plans $1.5 billion drive for promotion of marriage. *New York Times* (January 14).

Kretschmer, Tobias and Luis Cabral. 1998. *De Beers and beyond: The history of the international diamond cartel*. London: London Business School.

Kuczynski, A. 1998. Arm candy: A sign of the times. *New York Times* (October 3): 9.1.

Lee, Vera. 1994. *Something old, something new*. Naperville, IL.: Sourcebooks.

Lenin, V. I. 1966. *The emancipation of women*. New York: International Publishers.

Leonard, Diana. 1980. *Sex and generation: Courtship and weddings*. London: Tavistock Publications.

Light, Lisa. 2006. *Destination bride*. Cincinnati: North Light Books.

Lind, Amy. 2004. Legislating the family: Heterosexist bias in social welfare policy frameworks. *Journal of Sociology and Social Welfare* 31(4): 21–35.

Linsen, Mary Ann. 1991. Decorated cakes—the icing on bakery sales. *Progressive Grocer* (February): 117–120.

Lipton, Lauren. 1992. TV with a hitch in it: Wedding bells are ringing on at least a dozen series this season. *Los Angeles Times* (April 14): 1.

Los Angeles Times. 1995. Off the cuff: Her job has the ring of romance (January 26): E-4.

Lowry, T. M. and C. Otnes. 1994. Construction of a meaningful wedding: Differences in the priorities of brides and grooms. In J. Arnold Costa, ed., *Gender issues and consumer behavior*. Thousand Oaks, CA: Sage.

Macionis, John. 2008. *Social problems*. New York: Prentice-Hall.

MacDonald, George. 1972. *Fifty years of freethought*. New York: Arno Press.

Marx, Karl. 1977. *Capital*. Trans. Ben Fowkes. New York: Vintage.

——. 1972. *The Grundisse*. Ed. David McLellan. New York: Harper & Row.

——. 1970a. *Capital*, vol. 1. New York: International Publishers.

——. 1970b. *A contribution to the critique of political economy*. New York: International Publishers.

——. 1963. *The eighteenth brumaire of Louis Bonaparte*. New York: International.

——. 1844. *Contribution to the critique of Hegel's philosophy of law*. Moscow: International Publishers.

Marx, Karl and Frederick Engels. 1988. *The Communist manifesto*. New York: Norton.

——. 1976a. *Collected works*. New York: International.

——. 1976b. *The German ideology*. New York: International.

Mattel. 2006. Mattel Annual Report to Shareholders. http://www.mattel.com.

Maynard, Mary and June Purvis, eds. 1995. *(Hetero)sexual politics*. London: Taylor & Francis.

McMurdy, Deirdre. 1993. Banking on bliss. *McLean's* 106 (June 28): 40–41.

McMurray, Shane. 2006. The Wedding Report. http://www.theweddingreport.com (accessed March 18, 2006).

McWilliams, Michael. 1996. Weddings are the icing for the May sweeps. *The Detroit News* (May 16): 7.

Mead, Rebecca. 2007. *One perfect day: The selling of the American wedding*. New York: Penguin Press.

——. 2003. You're getting married: The Wal-Martization of the bridal business. *New Yorker* (April 21): 76.

Mehta, Stephanie. 1996. Bridal superstores woo couples with miles of gowns and tuxes. *Wall Street Journal* (February 14): B1–B2.

Mieher, Stuart. 1993. Great expectations: the stork is a guest at more weddings. *Wall Street Journal* (April 6): A1, A6.

Mies, Maria. 1986. *Patriarchy and accumulation on a world scale: Women in the international division of labor*. London: Zed.

Miller, Cyndee. 1995. 'Til death do they part. *Marketing News* 29. (March 27): 1–5.

Modern Bride. 1996. *The bridal market retail spending study: A $35 billion market for the 90's*. New York: Primedia.

——. 1994. *The bridal market retail spending study: A $35 billion market for the 90's*. New York: Primedia.

Mogelonsky, Marcia. 1994. The world of weird insurance. *American Demographics* (December): 37.

Monsarrat, Ann. 1973. *And the bride wore . . . : the story of the white wedding*. New York: Follett.

Morrison, Toni. 1970. *The bluest eye*. New York: Pocket Books.

Murray, Rebecca. 2005. Interview with Vince Vaughn of *Wedding Crashers*, July, http://www.movies.about.com/Hollywood Movies.

Nagel, Bart and Karen Huff. 1997. Something old, something new. *Might* (March/April): 43–51.

National Center for Health Statistics. 1997. http://www.cdc.gov/nchswww.

National Poverty Center. 2006. Poverty in the U.S. FAQs. Ann Arbor, University of Michigan. http://npc.umich.edu/poverty/.

Navarro, Mireya. 2007. How green was my wedding. *New York Times* (February 11): D1.

———. 2006. Diamonds are for never. *New York Times* (December 14): D1.

Nelton, Sharon. 1990. What she does for love. *Nation's Business* 78 (June): 18–26.

Nibley, MaryBeth. 1994. Editor to divorce herself from long career of helping brides. *Los Angeles Times* (December 7): D–7.

Niebuhr, Gustav. 1998. Just tell us which sin. *New York Times* (September 27): 5.

O'Barr, William M. 1994. *Culture and the ad: Exploring otherness in the world of advertising.* Boulder, CO: Westview Press.

Omvedt, Gail. 1986. Patriarchy: The analysis of women's oppression. *Insurgent Sociologist* 13.3: 30–50.

Oppenheimer, Nicholas. 1998. Chairman's statement. *Annual Report.* De Beers.

Orman, Suze. 2006. http://www.preventingdivorce.com.

Oswald, R. F. 2002. Who am I in relation to them? Gay, lesbian, and queer people leave the city to attend rural family weddings. *Journal of Family Issues* 23: 323-348.

———. 2000. A member of the wedding? Heterosexism and family ritual. *Journal of Social and Personal Relationships,* 17: 349–368.

Otnes, Cele C. and Elizabeth Pleck. 2003. *Cinderella dreams: The allure of the lavish wedding.* Berkeley, CA: University of California Press.

Parker, E. 1995. Federal report finds: Blacks median age younger than whites, women older than men. *Los Angeles Sentinel* (June 7): A–4.

Partners Task Force for Gay & Lesbian Couples. 1997. (January 31). http://www.buddy-buddy.com/mar-feda.html.

Paul, James and Murray Schwartz. 1961. *Federal censorship: Obscenity in the mail.* New York: Free Press.

People. 2006. A wedding to remember: Tom Cruise and Katie Holmes. (November 22): 59.

———. 1998. I finally found someone: Streisand and Bolin wed.

———. 1997. When couples have children. (June 1): 169.

——. 1995a. Cowie as Hollywood's wedding consultant. (June 1): 136.

——. 1995b. Wedding shockers. (June 1): 125.

——. 1991. Once upon a time . . . the world fell in love with a dashing Prince and his enchanting bride. (July 30): 23.

Pereira, A. 1996. Toy business focuses more on marketing and less on new ideas. *Wall Street Journal* (December 10): A1.

Poortman, Anne-Rigt. 2005. http://www.healthymarriageinfo.org/docs/FAQWork.pdf.

Powell, Rachel. 1991. It's one party even the recession can't spoil. *New York Times* (June 23): 10.

PR Newswire. 1998. http://www.prnewswire.com.

President's Council of Economic Advisors. 1992, 1994. *Economic report of the President.* Washington, D.C.: Federal Reserve Archival System.

Press, Eyal. 1996. Sweatshopping. *Z Magazine.*

Purbrick, Louise. 2007. *The wedding present: Domestic life beyond consumption.* London: Ashgate Publishing Ltd.

Rapping, Elayne. 1995. A bad ride at Disney World. *The Progressive* (November): 36–39.

Raub, Deborah Fineblum. 1994. Saying "I do" without going broke. Gannett News Service (February 23).

Reardon, A. 2006. http://www.brides.com.

Redstockings Collective. 1975. *Feminist revolution.* New York: Random House.

Reinholz, Mary. 1996. Spring '96 bridal planner/Jewelry gifts for the wedding party. *Newsday* (February 18): 5.

Reuters. 2006. American idol review. *New York Times* (May 25) http://www.nytimes.com/reuters/arts/entertainment-leisure-idol.html?_r=1&oref=login.

Reynolds, Christopher. 1992. Overseas marriage ceremonies have a certain "ring" for some couples matrimony: Wedding travel specialists help Americans exchange vows in foreign destinations. *Los Angeles Times* (May 17): 2.

Rich, Adrienne. 1980. Compulsory heterosexuality and lesbian existence. *Signs* 5 (Summer): 631–660.

Richardson, Diane, ed. 1996. *Theorising heterosexuality.* Buckingham: Open University Press.

Roberts, Janine. 2003. *Glitter and greed: The secret world of the diamond cartel.* New York: The Disinformation Company.

Robey, Bryant. 1990. Wedding-bell blues chime as marriage markets shift. *Adweek's Marketing Week* (June 25): 10, 12.

Rosen, Margery. 1995. I can't count on him. *Ladies Home Journal* (June): 21–23.

Ross, Andrew. 1997. *No sweat.* New York: Verso.

Rubin, Elizabeth. 1997. An army of one's own: In Africa, nations hire a corporation to wage war. *Harper's* (February): 44–56.

Sailer, David. 1997. *Lifting the veil: A special report.* A white paper published by Union of Needleworkers and Textile Employees, New York.

Salkever, Alex. 1995. Let's get married. *Hawaii Business* (May 1): 45.

Sanders, Lisa. 2006. Advertising: An industry still so white . . . *Advertising Age* (June 19): 16.

Schatz, Elizabeth. 2004. The cranky consumer. Creating a wedding website. *Wall Street Journal* (August 24): D2.

Schifrin, Matthew. 1991. The newlywed game. *Forbes* (September 2): 85–86.

Schoen, Robert. 1988. *Modeling multigroup populations.* New York: Plenum.

Schoolman, Judith. 1997. Love may be free, but it's getting progressively more expensive to tie the knot. *Reuters Business Report* (June 4).

Schwartz, Mary Ann, and Barbara M. Scott. 1997. *Marriages and families: Diversity and change.* New York: Prentice-Hall.

Sears, Hal D. 1977. *The sex radicals: Free love in high Victorian America.* Lawrence: Regents Press of Kansas.

Seidman, Steven, Nancy Fischer, and Chet Meeks, eds. 2006. *New sexuality studies,* London: Routledge.

——. 2003. *The social construction of sexuality.* New York: Norton.

——. 1993. Identity and politics in a postmodern gay culture: Some conceptual and historical notes. In Michael Warner (ed.) *Fear of a queer planet.* Minneapolis: University of Minnesota Press.

——. 1992. *Embattled Eros.* New York: Routledge.

——. 1991. *Romantic longings.* New York: Routledge.

Sewell, Dan. 1998. Blacks' buying power outpaces national trend. *Philadelphia Inquirer* (July 30): C2.

Sherwin, Nina. 1995. Clone this idea: Wedding consultant. *Executive Female* 18 (November 1): 30.

Shipler, David. 2005. *The working poor: Invisible in America.* New York: Vintage.

Smith, Dorothy. 1990a. *The conceptual practices of power: A feminist sociology of knowledge.* Boston: Northeastern Press.

——. 1990b. *Texts, facts, and femininity.* New York: Routledge.

———. 1987. *The everyday world as problematic: Toward a feminist sociology.* Boston: Northeastern University Press.

———. 1975. An analysis of ideological structures and how women are excluded: Considerations for academic women. *Canadian Review of Sociology and Anthropology* 12(4): 131–154.

———. 1974. Women's perspective as a radical critique of sociology. *Sociological Inquiry* 44: 73–90.

Smith, J. 1997. Weddings: A sociology of emotions perspective. Unpublished Master's thesis, University of Calgary, Calgary, Canada.

Smythers, Ruth. 1894. Instruction and advice for the young bride. *The Madison Institute Newsletter* (Fall): 4.

Spears, Dawn. 1995. Till debt do us part. *Kiplinger's Personal Finance Magazine* 49 (May 1): 64–66.

Spicuzza, Mary. 2001. Worryless wedding: For detail-obsessed brides and grooms: wedding insurance. *Metro* (May 24–30): 12–13.

Spindler, Amy. 1998. The bride that ate Hollywood: New movies, TV shows and 5-pound bridal magazines prove how much we love weddings. *New York Times* (September 2): 9.1.

St. Louis Dispatch. 1997. Some targets of Baptist's Disney boycott (June 19): 08A.

Starr, Kenneth. 1998. *Starr Report.* New York: Prima Publishing.

Steurle, C. Eugene. 1995. *Economic effects of health care reform.* New York: AEI Press.

Stevenson, Brenda. 1996. *Life in black and white: Family and community in the slave south.* New York: Oxford University Press.

Stewart, Martha, and Christopher Baker. 1988. *The wedding planner.* New York: Crown Publications.

Stewart, Martha, Elizabeth Hawes, Christopher P. Baker, and Chris Baker. 1987. *Weddings.* New York: Clarkson Potter.

Stoehr, Taylor. 1979. *Free love in America: A documentary history.* New York: AMS Press, Inc.

Stolcke, Verena. 1983. Women's labours: The naturalisation of social inequality and women's subordination. In, Kate Young, Carol Wolkowitz, and Roslyn McCullagh, eds., *Of marriage and the market: Women's subordination internationally and its lessons.* London: Routledge.

Storey, John. 1993. *An introductory guide to cultural theory and popular culture.* Athens, GA: University of Georgia Press.

Strauss, Larry A. 1994. Wedlock has its benefits. Gannett News Service.

Tapscott, Don and Anthony D. Williams. 2006. *Wikinomics: How mass collaboration changes everything.* New York: Penguin.

Thompson, Roger. 1990. Romancing a $30 billion market. *Nation's Business* 78 (June): 18–21.

Toalston, Art. 1998. Boycott may be taking its toll. *The Ethics and Religious Liberty Commission of the Southern Baptist Convention* (April 27): http://www.erlc.com/Culture/Disney.

Tomes, Nancy. 1998. *The gospel of germs: Men, women and microbes in American life.* Cambridge, MA: Harvard University Press.

Torrant, Julie. 1998. For better or worse: Marriage in commodity culture. Unpublished manuscript.

Tousignant, Marylou. 1995. Cycle of love. Pleasantville: *Readers Digest; U.S. edition.* (April) 146(876): 141.

Toussaint, A. 1997/1998. Dangerous liaisons: Rewriting history for Hollywood's classic couples. *Bride's* (Winter): 421.

Travel Weekly. 1996. Romantic places: 1996 Supplement: Honeymoon vacations (November 7): 8–12.

Tucker, B. and C. Kernan. 1995. *The decline in marriage among African Americans.* New York: Russell Sage Foundation.

Twitchell, James B. 1999. *Lead us not into temptation: The triumph of American materialism.* New York: Columbia University Press.

Urban League. 1996. *The state of black America.* New York: Astoria Graphics.

U.S. Bureau of the Census. 2006. *Marital status of the population 15 years old and over, by sex and race: 1950 to present.* Washington, DC: Government Printing Office.

———. 2005. *Income, poverty, and health insurance coverage in the United States: 2004.* Washington, DC: Government Printing Office.

———. 1996. *Statistical abstracts of the U.S.* Washington, DC: Government Printing Office.

U.S. Department of Labor. 1996. Three apparel companies added to labor department's Trendsetters' List. Press release, March 27.

VanEvery, Jo. 1996. Heterosexuality and domestic life. In Diane Richardson, ed., *Theorising heterosexuality.* Buckingham: Open University Press.

Walby, Sylvia. 1989. *Theorizing patriarchy.* London: Blackwell.

———. 1987. *Patriarchy at work.* Minneapolis: University of Minnesota Press.

Watts, Christina. 1994. Here comes the money: Fashioning a bridal consulting business. *Black Enterprise* (July 31): 16.

Whisman, Mark and Douglas Snyder. 2007. Sexual infidelity in a national survey of American women: Differences in prevalence and correlates as a function of method of assessment. *Journal of Family Psychology.* (June) 21(2): 147–154.

Wilkinson, Sue and Celia Kitzinger, eds. 1993. *Heterosexuality; A feminism and psychology reader.* London: Sage Publications.

Williamson, Christine and Mercedes M. Cardona. 1996. Institutions like possible Mattel/Hasbro marriage. *Pensions and investments* (February 5): 1.

Willis, Susan. 1991. *A primer for daily life.* New York: Routledge.

With, Tatiana. 1996. Unveiling wedding hell. *Boston Globe* (March 21): 85:1.

Wittig, Monique. 1992. *The straight mind.* Boston: Beacon Press.

Wright, John W. 1999. *The New York Times almanac 1999 (annual).* New York: Penguin Books.

Zavarzadeh, Mas'ud. 1991. *Seeing films politically.* Albany, NY: SUNY Press.

Zoellner, Tom. 2006. *The heartless stone: A journey through the world of diamonds, deceit, and desire.* New York: St. Martin's Press.

Zuber, Amy. 1994. Time Inc.'s *People* person. *Folio* (December 15): 70, 72.

Web References

http://people.aol.com/people/package/ongoing/0,26336,661670,00.html

http://www.brillig.com/debt_clock/

http://www.forbes.com/lists/2006/12/6GNF.html

http://www.forbes.com/prnewswire/feeds/prnewswire/2007/05/31/prnewswire 200705311350PR_NEWS_B_WES_LA_LATH081.html

http://www.imdb.com

http://news.bbc.co.uk/2/hi/africa/3189299.stm

http://www.PovertyMap.net

http://www.usda.gov/da/shmd/aware.htm#WHO2006

http://www.World Bank.org

http://www.worldonfire.org

http://www.professionaljeweler.com/archives/news/2004/042704story.html

http://www.globalwitness.org/campaigns/diamonds/index.php, http://www.nlc.org

Photo Permissions

Page vi: Author's Parents. Collection of the author.

Page vii: Diamond ring from http://istockphoto.com

Page 1: Bride with Veil. Reprinted with permission of CORBIS.

Page 2: Bosquet–Morra Wedding. Reprinted with permission of subject and collection of the author.

Page 4: Wedding trinkets. Collection of the author.

Page 6: Three women, one with wedding cake hat. Photo provided by and reprinted with permission of *Times Union*/Albany NY. Copyright © 1996.

Page 8: Rose petals at wedding. Collection of the author.

Page 9: Oven mitts. Collection of the author.

Page 15: Backwards wedding photo. Collection of the author.

Page 35: Duck brides. Reprinted with permission of Kristen Constantino.

Page 37: Bride illustration from http://istockphoto.com

Page 38: Bridal gown in window. Collection of the author.

Page 41: Wedding cake display. Collection of the author.

Page 49: Ceramic bride and groom. Collection of the author.

Page 58: *Godey's* Magazine Images. Public domain.

Page 59: 19th century wedding photographs. Collection of the author.

Page 61: Princess Grace of Monaco wedding photo. Reprinted with permission of CORBIS.

Page 62: Princess Diana as a bride. Reprinted with permission of CORBIS/Hulton-Deutsch Collection.

Page 67: Bridal store windows. Collection of the author.

Page 68: Bridal gown store out of business. Collection of the author.

Page 71: Gown tag. Collection of the author.

Page 72: Matamoros maquiladoras housing and NAFTA building photo. Collection of the author.

Page 75: Sweatshop. Reprinted with permission of UNITE, Union of Needletrades, Industrial, and Textile Employees, AFL-CIO, CLC.

Page 75: UNITE workers. Reprinted with permission by UNITE, Union of Needletrades, Industrial, and Textile Employees, AFL-CIO, CLC.

Page 78: Diamond miners in Koidu, Sierra Leone 2007. Reprinted with permission from Tugela Ridley/epa/Corbis.

Page 82: Diamond ring advert. Collection of the author.

Page 86: Diamond producer, Amsterdam, The Netherlands. Collection of the author.

Page 87: Bridal mouse ears. Collection of the author.

Page 90: Deserted beach from http://istockphoto.com

Page 96: Bridal toy photos. Collection of the author.

Page 105: Colgate ad. Reprinted with permission.

Page 113: Straight Path road sign. Collection of the author.

Page 115: Wedding collage. Collection of the author.

Page 129: Bridal magazines in bookstore. Collection of the author.

Page 139: Girl dressed as Barbie bride for Halloween. Collection of the author.

Page 139: Bridal doll in store window. Collection of the author.

Page 143: Gown in window. Collection of the author.

Page 152: Hindu-American wedding. Collection of the author.

Page 169: *Wedding Daze* in kiosk. Collection of the author.

Page 232: Femicide markers in Ciudad Juarez and Beth Millett at Mexican border. Collection of the author.

Page 233: Nancy Parker and Mimosa Lynch working at a food coop. Collection of the author.

Page 234: Sign in domestic violence shelter and homeless family in Juarez. Collection of the author.

Page 235: Casa Amiga domestic violence shelter and Russel Sage College students protesting. Collection of the author.

Page 236: Bride and maid of honor, 1971. Collection of the author.

All other background images from the author's collection.

Index